Financial Risk Management

Financial Risk Management

Brian A Eales

McGRAW-HILL BOOK COMPANY

London · New York · St Louis · San Francisco · Auckland
Bogotá · Caracas · Lisbon · Madrid · Mexico
Milan · Montreal · New Delhi · Panama · Paris · San Juan
Saõ Paulo · Singapore · Sydney · Tokyo · Toronto

Published by
McGRAW-HILL Book Company Europe
Shoppenhangers Road, Maidenhead, Berkshire SL6 2QL, England
Telephone 01628 23432
Fax 01628 770224

British Library Cataloguing in Publication Data
Eales, Brian A.
  Financial Risk Management: Spreadsheet
  Approach
  I. Title
  658.155

  ISBN 0-07-707617-6

Library of Congress Cataloging-in-Publication Data
Eales, Brian Anthony
    Financial risk management : a spreadsheet approach / Brian A.
  Eales.
      p.   cm.
    Includes index.
    ISBN 0-07-707617-6
    1. Risk management—Data processing.   2. Corporations—Finance–
  –Data processing. 3.   Electronic spreadsheets.   I. Title.
  HD61.E15   1994
  658.15'0285'5369—dc20   94-29855
                                        CIP

2345 CUP 98765

Typeset by Mackreth Media Services, Hemel Hempstead
and printed and bound in Great Britain at the University Press, Cambridge.

Printed on permanent paper in compliance with ISO Standard 9706

Contents

Preface

This text provides a practical insight into the main forms of managing the financial risk associated with paper-based securities. It examines how various identified risk exposures, from the differing perspectives of market participants, can be managed using diversified portfolios, exchange-based derivative securities, and over-the-counter derivative securities.

There are a number of audiences who will find this book useful:

- Advanced undergraduates following programmes in business, economic or finance and accounting.
- Graduate students on MBA, MA and MSc programmes where financial markets and instruments receive attention.
- Practitioners who want to develop a deeper understanding of how the instruments work in practice and their limitations.

A suite of Lotus 1–2–3 Release 3.1 semi-automated spreadsheets, to run on an IBM or IBM compatible PC, are available with this book. The spreadsheets, which assume some background computer knowledge on the part of the user, will allow the user to experiment with different types of instruments and run 'what if' simulations based on his or her own projected scenarios, using up-to-date data drawn from the financial pages of the press. In addition many examples using control data are illustrated and discussed in the text.

It must be emphasized that the spreadsheets must be regarded as teaching/learning tools. They provide a vehicle for examining many examples of pricing and hedging that would prove tedious and time consuming using a standard hand calculator — especially where dates or day counts are involved. There are, of course, simplifications that have been made in order to avoid making the spreadsheets overly complex, for example, dividend receipts have been ignored in portfolios of equity, transactions costs are also conveniently omitted as are costs associated with the running of a margin account. The spreadsheets have been constructed to be as transparent and accessible as possible and, in many cases, can be modified easily to allow even more 'real-world' scenarios to be examined by the user.

Each chapter contains descriptions of the instrument being used and, where appropriate, how it is priced together with an outline of the methodology which underpins its derivation. The first eight chapters can also be used in conjunction with spreadsheets which provide an insight into a topic and, in most cases, allow users to simulate the control or their own outcomes. A list of the spreadsheets accompanying each chapter along with a brief description of their function is included as the last section of each of Chapters 1–8. End of chapter questions are also supplied, some of which require the collection of data as input to the spreadsheets. The intention here is that classes will be able to analyse and discuss a variety of outcomes based on different projections of future market movements without the need to undertake manual, tedious computations.

Financial risk management is a subject of growing interest and importance in most spheres of financial and business activity, and for some courses teaching the whole of the book would be a desirable and appropriate course of action. However, in writing a text which gives coverage to each of the major instruments, it is inevitable that parts of it will be of little interest to some readers. With this in mind a structure has been used which provides essential, general background in the early chapters, but allows a good degree of specialization in later chapters.

Chapter 1 introduces and discusses some of the many risk exposures that market participants face on a day-to-day basis. Chapter 2 provides an overview, with examples, of short-, medium- and long-term forecasting techniques that are available to market participants. Chapters 3, 4 and 5 introduce and develop the derivative securities around which the bulk of the text is based: forwards, futures, swaps and options. Chapters 6, 7 and 8 allow for specialization. Those readers interested in managing the risk associated with a portfolio of equity will find a discussion of that area in Chapter 6. Those readers specifically interested in the risk management of portfolios of bonds will find coverage in Chapter 7, while Chapter 8 concentrates on other types of interest rate and currency risk management. Chapter 9 draws conclusions and suggests more complicated financial structures and describes how their associated risk might be analysed and hedged.

Structuring the text into separate, convenient components in this way may engender a belief that the tools for risk management vary from security to security. This, of course, is not the case. For example, caps, collars, floors and range forwards, although usually encountered in the context of currency, and interest rate risk management, could be applied to equity portfolios; duration, used as a major tool in the analysis of bond portfolios, can be applied to swaps; swaps themselves, although thought of in the context of interest rates or currency, could well be applied to portfolios of equity.

While the jargon used by market professionals to describe their instruments varies between markets, the fundamental application of those instruments remains the same. Indeed, the instruments described in this text are also available in commodity markets, which implies that the strategies discussed here in the context of paper-based securities, with some small adjustments, could equally well be applied to those arenas dealing in physical commodities.

Computer background

The text assumes that students will have some familiarity with spreadsheets, and will have some basic knowledge of MS-DOS, for example, how to copy files across disk drives and set up a default directory. University students will normally have completed a one-term introductory computing/information technology course.

All the spreadsheets have been written for Lotus 1–2–3 Release 3 to run on an IBM or an IBM compatible. They can be run on a stand-alone machine or on a PC network. Each spreadsheet has been tested on London Guildhall University's network.

The spreadsheets may be run from either floppy or hard disk drive. Before using the disk containing the spreadsheets for the first time the user is advised to make a back-up copy of the original. The easiest way in which to ensure that the spreadsheets and databases are all readily accessible on the stand-alone PC is to make the directory housing the files accompanying this text the default directory. For networks it is advisable to change the reference directory for databases appearing in macros such as those in TEXT_DAT.WK3 in the following way:

- Original setting for retrieving dates:

      Input_Dates   /fccn date~text_dat.wk3

      Change to   /fccn{?}~{?}~

This allows the user to enter the location of the range and file manually.

- Original setting for retrieving security prices:

      Prices   /fccn{?}~text_dat.wk3

      Change to   /fccn{?}~{?}~

It is advisable to do this for the automatic data input macros on files such as TA_DEMO.WK3, SIM.WK3 and MARKOW.WK3.

Acknowledgements

In writing this book I am indebted to a number of colleagues, students and sources for their support and encouragement: The influence of John Nankervis provided me with the inspiration to write a book on financial risk management; Jerry Coakley, Kostas Giannopoulos and George Hadjimatheou read drafts of chapters and made useful suggestions on content, level, presentational style and construction of some of the spreadsheets; Nick Robinson gave me ideas for portfolios of bonds and swaps, and the dynamics of hedging. Their constructive criticisms have proved invaluable.

Students on the university's MSc Econometrics and Forecasting, Financial Derivative option; MA Economic, Financial Economics option; MBA, Financial Risk Management, and third year BA Financial Economics courses, have all contributed to the development and reliability of the spreadsheets, as well as working through most of the questions at the end of chapters. Without the students' participation the spreadsheets presented in the text would have had no proving ground.

Brendan Lambon at McGraw-Hill proved a valuable source of encouragement and assistance. The anonymous reviewer's comments were also of great help and greatly appreciated.

I am also grateful to London Guildhall University for allowing me one term's sabbatical in which to produce a first draft of the text.

I should also like to thank the following: DATASTREAM International for allowing me to quote and supply data to support the spreadsheets in the text; the London International Financial Futures and Options Exchange (LIFFE) for allowing me to quote its contracts in the text, and use them to illustrate many of the examples of hedging;[1] *The Financial Times* for permitting me to quote from and use its tables of financial data; and *Die Zeit* for permission to use data from an article to support an example of 'Delphi-type' forecasting.

Finally I should like to thank my wife and children for so patiently putting up with the disruption to family life caused by this undertaking.

---

[1] Neither LIFFE, nor its servants and agents, is responsible for any errors or omissions contained in this booklet (material), which is published for information purposes and shall not constitute investment advice. All descriptions, examples and calculations contained in this booklet (material) are for guidance purposes only and should not be treated as definitive. Whilst all reasonable care has been taken to ensure that the details are true and not misleading at the time of publication, no liability is accepted by LIFFE for use of information contained herein in any circumstances connected with actual trading or otherwise. LIFFE reserves the right to alter any of its rules or contract specifications, and such an event may affect the validity of the information contained in this booklet (material).

1 Exposure to risk and diversification

1.1 Specific and market risk

As a means of entry into the topics to be covered by this text, and as a point of reference for the material as it is developed, it is useful to examine what can be understood by the expression 'Financial Risk Management'. The Oxford Dictionary provides definitions of each of the words, or their roots, in the phrase, and gives examples of where the words might be correctly employed. The definition of the word *risk* is given as: '... possibility or chance of meeting danger, suffering loss or injury, etc....'; the definition of the verb *to manage* is given as: 'control'; while that of *finance* is: '(science of) the management of money...'. By putting these definitions to use the expression 'financial risk management' can be interpreted as: the controlling of the possibility or chance of suffering a monetary loss. In financial circles, the activity of controlling such risk is normally referred to as *hedging*. Although this interpretation goes some way towards providing a clearer idea of what financial risk management is about, it does not really provide enlightenment as to the types of risk being faced, why those risks might be perceived to exist, how those risks might be hedged, or why it is even necessary to hedge those risks.

In this text substantial coverage will be given to financial instruments such as forwards, futures, options and swaps which form the building blocks for risk management and whose importance and use have grown considerably in importance over the past two decades. Other types of securities will also be discussed, and as the text progresses many of the risks associated with a particular instrument or security will be looked at in detail. For the moment two main types of risk are identified as being applicable to any instrument. The first of these can be labelled *specific risk* and can be used to describe the risk associated with a particular instrument and that instrument alone. The second type of risk can be labelled *market risk* and can be attributed to the primary market in which that instrument is active. An example will help to clarify this basic idea and will also serve as an indicator of the need for flexibility in using some of the terminology.

Example 1.1

Consider a share (equity) in a company which processes beef into canned stew, vacuum packed roast beef and tins of soup. If government health inspectors discover bacteriological contamination of equipment used at the company's plant, which subsequently necessitates the withdrawal from sale and destruction of all the company's products in that period as well as closure of the plant for a period of time, in order to clear up the contamination, the loss of sales and refunds which will have to be paid to outlets and consumers who have purchased the product will impact on the company's profits and will reduce the company's share price on the stock market. Competitors operating in the same market but given a clean bill of health might well be, *ceteris paribus*, delighted by this event. They will see their own sales rise, as consumers switch to their brands, profits rise and will probably enjoy an increase in their share price.

Clearly in this scenario the negative impact on one particular company is not reflected in the same way throughout the rest of the market in which it operates. Thus buying a share in the company whose plant was subsequently found to constitute a health hazard would have exposed the buyer to specific risk.

Consider now an example where all the firms in the market sector have been affected by some unpredictable event. Suppose that a government report suggests that some cattle have been infected by a virus and that there is a possibility, albeit very small, that this virus could be passed on to humans consuming beef products. In such a case all of the companies operating in this market are, to a greater or lesser extent, likely to be affected in a similar manner. Share prices of all companies in the sector might fall as market players realize the potential impact that this news could have on output and profits. This situation can be described as market risk.

These examples can be extended by introducing interest rates on to the scene. The introduction of this new variable can be used to highlight further the idea of specific and market risk and the interaction between markets, and to demonstrate the need for flexibility in the interpretation of what constitutes specific risk and what constitutes market risk.

To clarify these points take the example used above where one company alone has been hit by an official report. The bad publicity together with the fall in profits could well result in the company becoming regarded as a potential credit risk by the financial community and consequently having to pay a higher rate of interest on any loans that it raises or any paper that it issues in the future. Other companies in that market continue to enjoy untarnished reputations and, as a result of that one company's misfortune, could well be earning increased profits. It is unlikely that financial institutions will treat them in exactly the same way as their unfortunate competitor. Therefore, the price that the unaffected companies pay for money may be changed only minimally or not at all by the adverse report. If, however, attention is now turned to a scenario where an adverse report hits the entire market, risk premiums on loans are likely to be faced by all companies operating in that market: this again constitutes market risk.

It should, however, be recognized that the beef processing market is but one of the many markets which form the entire domestic economy. Thus if discussion of risk is centred on one specific market in the economy is could be referred to as a *sector* risk and, clearly, it could easily be argued that this type of risk could be categorized as a form of specific risk: a risk particular to a sector or one market within the domestic economy. Given a scenario where domestic interest rates are falling or stable. The companies in the beef market that have been affected by an adverse government report will be facing rising interest rates—as risk premiums increase—and falling share prices, while other markets (sectors), *ceteris paribus*, could be enjoying falling or at least stable costs of money and probably rising share prices.

The next logical step is to put the domestic economy into an international framework and recognize that specific country risk can be attached to any individual economy operating in that framework. Taking this broader view implies that the international economy would then constitute the focal point of market risk. Interest rates in individual countries will provide international investors with an indication of a country's riskiness and exchange rates between currencies will make use of interest rates in different countries to adjust future dated exchange rate transactions.

1.1.1 Risk perspectives

From the introductory discussion above it is evident that the word 'risk' can mean different things to different people; risk must always be put into context. Similarly, when identifying exposure to risk, careful examination of the perspective from which a situation is being viewed is needed. For example, although an individual investor may be more immediately concerned with the current performance or expected future performance of a company's equity, the company itself, through its financial director or corporate treasurer, will be more interested in other types of risk. Attention in this case will be focused on the risk associated with the price and availability of the raw materials which it requires for production, the price it pays for credit, and in an open economy the value of the unit of currency in which it performs and records its business against that of other countries. These risks will combine and play a not insignificant role in a company's profitability, competitiveness and ability to survive as a prosperous trading unit into the future.

By way of example consider a company which is operating in a closed economy and further assume that the company faces strong competition for the sale of its products. It was suggested above that the price that a company pays for credit in the form of higher interest rates will, *ceteris paribus*, make that company less competitive compared with its competitors. In the example used earlier it was also suggested that a reduction in sales could ultimately lead to an increase in the price a company pays for credit, which in turn could lead to an increase in costs. This type of situation may tempt a company to raise the prices that it charges its customers in order to recoup some of the increased costs. However, if demand for its products is highly elastic this course of action will only push sales down further and could eventually drive the company out of business. On the other hand, if prices to customers are reduced in an attempt to increase sales, profit margins will be reduced and, should the strategy fail to pay off, the company's ability to maintain investment and its existing market position could well be jeopardized.

In fairness to the company treasurer, apart from taking out some form of operating insurance, there is not a great deal that he or she can do in the bacteriological and viral infection situations described. However, against a background of generally rising (or falling) market interest rates there are actions that could be taken to protect a company once the nature of the exposure and the magnitude of that exposure have been identified. Some possible cases that may arise in practice are described below.

Case 1.1

A company has taken out £1,000,000 bank loan to finance a development project. The rate of interest it pays is reset every three months. The corporate treasurer feels that government action will be needed soon to counteract steadily rising inflation. This could mean that interest rates will be raised as part of government policy.

In this case the treasurer is concerned about the liability side of the company's books. Higher interest rates mean higher costs which in turn, if not passed on in some way, mean lower profits. By way of example assume that the rate of interest that the company is currently paying on the loan—including a risk premium—is 9.6 per cent, this translates to an interest bill of £24,000 each quarter. If the treasurer's fear are realized and at the next reset the interest rate the company pays is raised to 10.6 per cent the new interest payment will be £26,500 each quarter—an increase of £2500 per quarter. This figure could also have been found as follows:

$$£1,000,000 \times (0.106 - 0.096)/4 = £2500$$

Case 1.2

A company is expecting a large tranche of money from the sale of machine tools to be deposited into its bank account in two months' time. The company's financial director feels that interest rates for deposits currently at 7.5 per cent[1] will have fallen, perhaps by as much as 1 per cent, by the time the money is transferred. As a consequence the money will have to be deposited at a rate of interest lower than that currently on offer and the company would not have achieved the greatest benefit from the funds.

In this example the financial director is looking at the problem from the asset side of the company's books. In the case where interest rates fall the company will be worse off, if interest rates rise it will be better off.

In Cases 1.1 and 1.2 the individuals are concerned about exposure of their companies to market interest rate movements—*interest rate risk*. Fig. 1.1 illustrates the identified exposure to interest rate risk faced by the company in Case 1.1 and Fig. 1.2 illustrates the identified risk in Case 1.2. The graphs have been constructed using hypothetical interest rates ranging from 8 to 12 per cent, with annotations highlighting the areas of potential gains and losses in each situation.

Broadening the horizon to allow a company to operate in an open economy environment provides other basic examples of financial risk that might be faced.

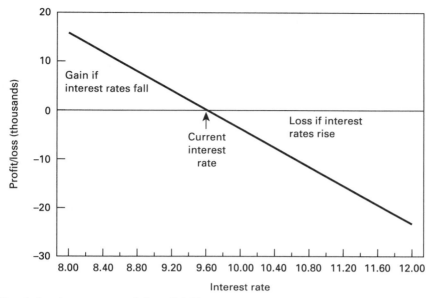

Fig. 1.1. Interest rate risk — liability exposure

Case 1.3

A UK company has just signed a contract with a Japanese company to supply knitwear to a total, current value of ¥1,000,000,000 over the next two years. Payment for goods will be made in yen, in four equal amounts, at intervals over that period with the first receipt due in six months' time. The company's

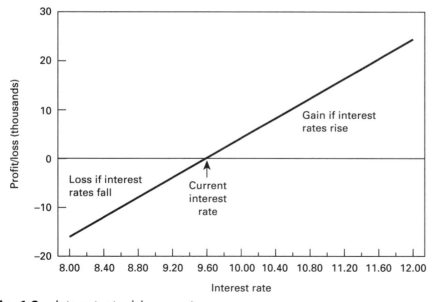

Fig. 1.2. Interest rate risk — asset exposure

managing director, while welcoming the deal, fears that a downturn in world trade and generally falling demand for Japanese products could lead to a worsening of the £/¥ exchange rate over this period.

In this example the managing director is concerned about the amount of money in sterling that the company is to receive as future payments fall due. If the spot rate stands at £1/¥192 and remains fixed at that level until the first payment of ¥250,000,000 is due in six months' time, the amount of sterling received (ignoring all other costs) will be £1,302,083, however, should the exchange rate change to £1/¥215 over the next six-month period the company will only receive £1,162,790.

Figure 1.3 shows the profile of the UK company's long yen (asset position) profit profile for a range of movements in the ¥/£ exchange rate. The horizontal axis is based on the number of yen per £1 and is calculated for hypothetical yen values from ¥170 to ¥220. As the number of yen to sterling increases, the holder (or future receiver) of yen will have to give more to obtain each £1. Conversely, as the number of yen to sterling decreases the holder (or future receiver) of yen will have to give fewer yen to obtain each £1. The annotations on Fig. 1.3 illustrate the currency risk position, from the UK company's perspective, should rates move from the current £1 = ¥192.

Case 1.4

A UK company has just signed a contract with a Japanese company to sell knitwear to the total current value of ¥1,000,000,000. Payment for the goods will be made in four equal amounts at intervals over the next two years. The UK company's managing director, while welcoming the deal, fears that the downturn in world trade and falling demand for Japanese products could lead

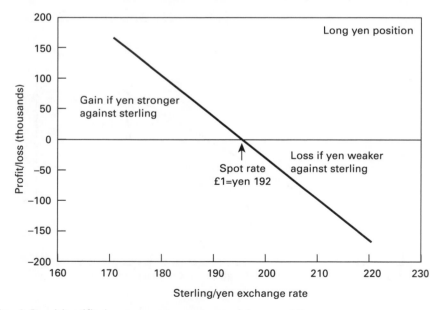

Fig. 1.3.   Identified exposure to currency risk: case 1.3

to a worsening of the £/¥ exchange rate over this period *and insists that all payments be made in sterling as they fall due.*

In this scenario Case 1.3 has been turned on its head. The onus is now on the Japanese enterprise to meet a sterling payment at some future date. Looking at the situation from this perspective it is clear that the Japanese company would be paying more than it originally envisaged should the yen depreciate against sterling. When the first payment falls due (assuming a £1/¥215 exchange rate), the company must pay £1,302,083 as opposed to the £1,162,790 it would have had to have paid had the prevailing rate at the time of signing the contract still been applicable. The Japanese corporate treasurer with an account payable at a future date should be aware of, and concerned about, the possibility of such adverse exchange rate movements.

Figure 1.4, constructed using the same horizontal scale as Fig. 1.3, illustrates the risk exposure from the Japanese company's perspective. In both Cases 1.3 and 1.4 *currency risk* has been identified.

The story does not end here. Many types of companies are concerned with risks directly linked to movements in interest and exchange rates as described above. Other companies, whose activities require the use of raw materials, will also face the risk of adverse price movements in commodity markets.

Case 1.5

A UK-based food chain buys coffee beans as part of its regular business activities. These coffee beans are bought in London, usually on the spot market (almost immediate delivery of the underlying instrument) as they are required. The contract is denominated in US dollars (USD). Civil unrest in

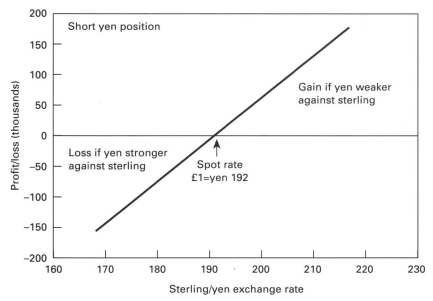

Fig. 1.4.   Identified exposure to currency risk: case 1.4

several coffee growing countries together with poor weather conditions over the previous year's growing period, lead the food chain's purchasing director to believe that coffee beans will be in short supply and that prices will be generally higher the next time the company goes to the market to make a purchase. Moreover, the purchasing director has been advised by the company's financial director that the US economy is showing signs of economic recovery which could mean that the USD ($) will also be stronger against sterling when the next purchase is scheduled to be settled.

Here both the financial and purchasing directors have realized that the company faces a potential commodity price and currency risk when the company next goes to market. It is easy to see that, if bank credit is involved in financing these future purchases, interest rate risk could also enter on to the scene.

The scenario just described in Case 1.5 is exaggeratedly gloomy. Interactions between markets and international developments could, and on occasions probably do, work entirely in favour of a company or at least they might lead to a netting out of gains and losses from different risk exposures. Trying to hedge every identified exposure could in fact lead to loss of competitiveness simply by taking out too much insurance as cover against adverse market movements which do not materialize.

So far nothing has been said about the position of financial institutions in the management of risk. They have, of course, a vital role to play as intermediaries in the marketplace. At one end of the scale they provide loans to individuals and accept deposits from them. At the other end of the scale they issue huge loans to companies at floating and fixed rates of interest in domestic and foreign currencies as well as exchanging foreign into domestic currency and vice versa. From the point of view of a financial institution financial risk exists in all cases identified so far in this section, albeit on a much larger scale and over the complete time spectrum from intra-day to years ahead. As a direct consequence of their market role and activities, the management of their financial risk position becomes imperative if they are to survive in today's volatile markets. Examples of the involvement of financial institutions and how they might manage their own risk positions will be considered in later chapters.

The hypothetical cases developed above are intended to be indicators of the fundamental types of risk that companies may face in their day-to-day trading activities. In the real world the risks described do exist, failure to recognize them or failure to take appropriate hedging action against them could invoke another type of more personal risk: *job risk*. As this text develops the risks described in Cases 1.1–1.4 will be re-examined and appropriate hedging strategies discussed. Commodity market risk (Case 1.5) is not considered in depth in this book.

1.2 Managing risk

Having given some coverage to the idea of the types of risk that an individual investor, a company or a financial institution might face, attention can now be turned to ways in which identified risk might be managed. There are several routes that could be followed:

1   Diversified portfolio of risky assets could be created.
2   Attempts could be made to predict 'accurately' where market prices are going to move.
3   In the absence of the availability of 'accurate' forecasts the effects of adverse market movements might be mitigated by using exchange-based, or specially created financial instruments.

The remainder of this chapter examines how risk can be diversified; Chapter 2 will outline ways in which forecasts can be generated using a variety of techniques and will assess the efficacy of those methods; financial instruments as risk management tools will be examined in detail in Chapters 3 to 8.

1.2.1 Diversification

Creating a diversified portfolio of assets is perhaps the most well-established method of managing risk. A portfolio may comprise one or many risky assets, in this text several types of situation will be used in order to examine how the risk(s) of such a portfolio might be managed. In this section the discussion will be centred around equity and the use of a portfolio consisting of several shares.

In Sec. 1.1 the idea of specific and market risk from an investor's point of view was developed in some detail. Had an investor's original aim been that of achieving the 'best' return for his or her investment but with minimum risk, from a common-sense point of view alone, it would have been more prudent to have created a portfolio made up of shares in a number of companies from a market (sector) rather than limiting a portfolio to the shares of just one company within a market (sector). The loss in the value of one company's share might then have been offset by increases in the share price of other companies in that market (sector) thereby maintaining the overall value of the portfolio.

Following this argument through, if a portfolio has been constructed solely from the shares of companies operating in the food processing sector and a subsequent viral infection cause problems to companies in that market then that market risk might have been reduced by constructing a portfolio of equity where the holdings of shares had been divided among a number of companies operating in different markets. For example, a portfolio could have been constructed with holdings of shares in food manufacturing, general engineering, telecommunications (telephone networks) and banking. Intuitively these sectors of the economy may not all be moving in the same direction at the same time, but even if they are, they will certainly not all be moving at the same pace, so there is a reasonable probability that an underperformance in one sector will be offset by a better performance in one of the other sectors.

Overall market risk will still exist even with a portfolio made up of shares from every available sector in the market. If the overall market is falling then most, if not all, of the constituent sectors of that market will also be falling. Several financial data suppliers produce indexes which permit analysts and portfolio managers to assess the performance of sectors of the economy over selected periods of time. Table 1.1 demonstrates this idea (using fictitious data).

Table 1.1.   Sector indexes

		7 Jan	Year ago	One year % growth
Row	1	897.00	885.00	1.36
Row	2	930.00	870.00	6.90
Row	3	751.00	702.00	6.98
Row	4	318.00	250.00	27.20
Row	5	535.00	450.00	18.89
Row	6	338.00	337.00	0.30
Row	7	400.00	293.00	36.52
Row	8	2100.00	1800.00	16.67
Row	9	1750.00	1622.00	7.88
Row	10	1500.00	1980.00	224.24
Row	11	1203.00	1120.00	7.41
Row	12	2678.00	2331.00	14.85
Row	13	407.00	460.00	211.52
Row	14	185.00	120.00	54.17
Row	15	765.00	730.00	4.79
Row	16	1100.00	1200.00	28.33
Row	17	110.00	115.00	24.35
Row	18	157.00	120.00	30.83
Row	19	203.00	250.00	218.80
Row	20	462.00	390.00	18.46
Row	21	354.00	328.00	7.93
Row	22	728.00	700.00	4.00
Row	23	1494.00	1170.00	27.69
Row	24	687.00	598.00	14.88
Row	25	2988.00	2213.00	35.02
Row	26	2200.00	1795.00	22.56
Row	27	389.00	324.00	20.06
Row	28	2000.00	2143.00	26.67
Row	29	1100.00	850.00	29.41
Row	30	684.00	600.00	14.00
Row	31	583.00	508.00	14.76
Row	32	756.00	890.00	215.06
Row	33	604.00	570.00	5.96
Row	34	843.00	790.00	6.71
Row	35	1540.00	1200.00	28.33
Row	36	1363.00	1215.00	12.18

From Table 1.1 a little arithmetic enables the reader to examine how the four sectors mentioned above fared compared with the other reported sectors over a period of one year. Assuming that food manufacturing sector data is reported on Row 11, it can be seen that it enjoyed growth of 7.41 per cent over the year (calculated as $(1203.00/1120.00)-1 \times 100 = 7.41$ per cent), telephone networks 18.89 per cent (Row 5), general engineering 14.88 per cent (Row 24) and banks 54.17 per cent (Row 14). Food manufacturing was by no means the weakest sector but its relatively poor showing in this specimen portfolio is offset by the better than average performance of the bank sector.

Lotus demo   `INDEX1.WK3`
Digging around in Table 1.1 to find the figures that would have implied the best sector is tedious. It would be far more useful for a busy analyst to be able to pick out the best performing sectors by examining a list where the rankings have already been established. Lotus allows this to be achieved easily by keying in a few instructions.

The information contained in Table 1.1 is stored under the title `INDEX1.WK3`. Retrieve this file into the worksheet using the following steps:

Step 1	Call up menu	/	(Solidus)
Step 2	Type	F	File
Step 3	Type	R	Retrieve
Step 4	Move cursor to highlight `INDEX1.WK3` and press [ENTER]. (It is assumed that the user's spreadsheet is addressing drive a: if this is not the case the appropriate drive must be selected.)		

The screen should now be displaying the columns 1, 2, 3 and 4 of Table 1.1. In order to proceed to sort the data follow the following steps:

Step 1	Call up menu	/	(Solidus)
Step 2	Type	D	Data
Step 3	Type	S	Sort

The user should be faced with a new menu which offers the possibilities:
`Data-Range   Primary-Key   Secondary-Key   Extra-Key`
`Go   Quit`
To define the range to be sorted select `Data-Range`.

Step 4	Type	D	Data-Range
Step 5	Now guide the cursor using the arrow keys to cell A5 (the contents of this cell should be a number 1). Anchor the start of the data range you are going to define to this point by typing a full stop (.). The arrow right should now be pressed until the figure of 19.69 is highlighted. (If the anchor has been correctly attached to cell A5 there should be a trail (usually cyan on a		

coloured monitor) from A5 to E5, if not press escape twice and repeat this step.) Press the keyboard key labelled END followed by the downwards pointing arrow, the whole data range that is to bedefined will now have been defined by this process (A5..E46) and will be highlighted. Press [ENTER].

Step 6   The menu is still active at the top of the screen. Select `Primary-Key:`
Type   P   Primary-Key
A supplementary question is now posed in the menu area: A or D? D.
The user must decide whether, after the sort has been performed, the list will be in ascending (A) lowest number at the top of the list of descending (D) highest number at the top of the list.
Type   D   Descending

Step 7   To sort the defined data range
Type   G   Go
The sorted data is displayed on the screen. The first line will appear as:
Row 14   185   120   54.17
If the original file is to be retained intact (and this is usually advisable: i.e. `INDEX1.WK3`) then the worksheet that has just been created by following the instructions should be saved under a new file name, say `INDEX2.WK3`. The sorted table appears as shown in Table 1.2.

Note that the average of the growth rate over all the reported sectors is displayed in cell F5 (11.33 per cent), this enables the user to see at a glance that although the choice of the bank sector achieved the best results over the year, had the top four sectors in the sorted list been selected for inclusion in the portfolio, as opposed to those discussed above, an even better result would have been obtained.

Returning to the question posed earlier concerning the proportions of shares from each sector that should be included to form a well-diversified portfolio there are two fundamental approaches that can be adopted:

1   Set up an index tracking portfolio.
2   Use some formal methodology to establish the optimal proportions.

1.2.2 Index tracking portfolios

Fund managers over many years have recognized that trying to set up a portfolio which performs better than some benchmark index such as the FT-SE 100 Index in the United Kingdom, the S&P500 in the United States, the Nikkei in Japan, etc., is

Table 1.2. Sector Indexes

		7 Jan	Year ago	One year % growth
Row	14	185.00	120.00	54.17
Row	17	400.00	293.00	36.52
Row	25	2988.00	2213.00	35.02
Row	18	157.00	120.00	30.83
Row	29	1100.00	850.00	29.41
Row	35	1540.00	1200.00	28.33
Row	23	1494.00	1170.00	27.69
Row	4	318.00	250.00	27.20
Row	26	2200.00	1795.00	22.56
Row	27	389.00	324.00	20.06
Row	5	535.00	450.00	18.89
Row	20	462.00	390.00	18.46
Row	8	2100.00	1800.00	16.67
Row	24	687.00	598.00	14.88
Row	12	2678.00	2331.76	14.85
Row	31	583.00	508.00	14.76
Row	30	684.00	600.00	14.00
Row	36	1363.00	1215.00	12.18
Row	21	354.00	328.00	7.93
Row	9	1750.00	1622.20	7.88
Row	11	1203.00	1120.00	7.41
Row	3	751.00	702.00	6.98
Row	2	930.00	870.00	6.90
Row	34	843.00	790.00	6.71
Row	33	604.00	570.00	5.96
Row	15	765.00	730.00	4.79
Row	22	728.00	700.00	4.00
Row	1	897.00	885.00	1.36
Row	6	338.00	337.00	0.30
Row	17	110.00	115.00	24.35
Row	28	2000.00	2143.00	26.67
Row	16	1100.00	1200.00	28.33
Row	13	407.00	460.00	211.52
Row	32	756.00	890.00	215.06
Row	19	203.00	250.00	218.80
Row	10	1500.00	1980.00	224.24

mainly a matter of luck. In the next section of this chapter an introduction will be made to some methodologies that have been developed since the 1950s in an attempt to quantify the optimal holdings of equity in a portfolio. The problem with the methodologies is that, to a great degree, they are based on historic data and will in consequence only continue to generate optimal portfolios if past history repeats itself. To try to overcome this type of problem, portfolios constructed to replicate the movement of a particular index have become quite popular. The composition of any benchmark index, its construction and the way that it is updated (or adjusted as necessary) is readily available. The International Stock Exchange in London publishes a document which provides information on the technical background of the FT-SE 100 Index (see Appendix 1A at the end of this chapter). If the FT-SE 100 is to be *tracked*, shares will be purchased and held in those proportions which best replicate the Index. There are several practical difficulties in constructing this type of index which makes exact replication impossible. The Index is dynamic, the composition of the Index changes over time through company collapses, growth and decline of companies, mergers and acquisitions, etc., in addition the market capitalization of the constituent companies at any given time changes. Rebalancing an index tracking portfolio to reflect a changing index may involve transaction costs that prove to be too high to justify in light of the portfolio's subsequent performance. Moreover, it may not be possible to buy shares at either the prices or quantities used in the construction of a theoretical index. As a result, index tracking portfolios will normally be set up in such a way as to keep their tracking error to a minimum. In the case of the FT-SE 100 Index a tracking portfolio will probably have fewer than the 100 constituent companies in the Index an any one time and rebalancing will be performed at less frequent intervals than the updating of the Index itself.

There are, of course, obvious advantages that an index tracking portfolio enjoys: the portfolio will be well diversified and—depending on the amount of effort and expertise that has gone into its construction—it should perform as the benchmark index performs. Many different types of equity indexes are available over many countries to suit the needs of fund managers. Some are well-known examples that were quoted above and other, UK-based, examples that are worth a mention are the FT-A All-Share, FT-SE Mid 250, FT-SE-A 350, FT-SE Eurotrack 100, FT-SE 200, and a variety of *emerging markets indexes*, for instance the Emerging Market Index launched by Baring Securities in 1992. The FT-SE Eurotrack 100, which was launched by the International Stock Exchange, London in October 1990, is constructed from shares of 100 large companies in Belgium, France, Germany, Italy, The Netherlands, Republic of Ireland, Spain, Sweden and Switzerland. It provides fund managers with the opportunity of setting up internationally diversified portfolios of European stocks which track this index. Moreover, shortly after this index was launched derivatives were introduced by LIFFE and, at the time, the independent LTOM to provide hedge instruments for those portfolios. These instruments took the form of futures and options contracts on the index,[2] about which more will be said in later chapters. For those fund managers wishing to incorporate UK equity into their portfolios, clearly the FT-SE Eurotrack 100 Index is unsatisfactory since UK stocks are excluded. To overcome this problem an index of the weighted average of the FT-SE Eurotrack 100 and the FT-SE 100 is available but insurance in the form of derivative securities on this pan-European index is not offered through the exchanges.

For adventurous fund managers looking outside Europe to the potentially high returns from developing economies of Asia, Latin America and Europe, after a great deal of investigative research Baring Securities launched an Emerging Markets Index in October 1992.[3] The Index currently comprises 214 equities from 12 countries and so offers an index tracking fund manager the opportunity to put together an international, well-diversified portfolio with a key benchmark against which performance can be measured.

1.2.3 The efficient frontier

Apart from the preoccupation in recent years with the construction of index tracking portfolios there are more traditional, well-documented methods of allocating risky assets to portfolios which date back to the 1950s. The two main methodologies which will be developed in this text are strongly related to each other and make use of the idea of returns obtained from holding risky assets and the associated risk of holding those assets. An investor is assumed to be risk-averse and as such will attempt to construct a portfolio that will achieve the highest return for the lowest risk or, looked at from a different angle, the maximum return for a given, acceptable level of risk.

The concept of return can be a contentious issue (Blake, 1990; Levy and Sarnat, 1984). There are geometric average returns, arithmetic average returns, holding period returns, after-tax returns, returns adjusted to take account of dividends, right issues, split issues, etc. However, a concept very frequently employed in financial texts is that of an average figure (expected return) over some specified period of time drawn from the distribution given by:

$$R_t = \ln \left(\frac{S_t}{S_{t-1}} \right) \tag{1.1}$$

where:

R_t represents continuously compounded return at time period, t;

S_t represents a share price at time period, t;

$\ln$ represents natural logarithms ($\log_e$) (see Appendix 1B).

The expected value can then be estimated as:

$$E(R) = \bar{R} = \frac{1}{T} \sum R_t \tag{1.2}$$

Risk is usually measured as the variance (a statistical measure of dispersion about the mean) of the set of data from which the expected return (average) has been estimated. The formula used in the estimation of this value is:

$$Var(R) = \frac{1}{T} \sum [R_t - E(R)]^2 = s^2 \tag{1.3}$$

The sample data used in the process of obtaining R and s^2 is assumed to reflect the population distribution which is assumed to be a lognormal distribution. One justification of adopting the mean–variance approach is that if investors spread their portfolio holdings over many risky assets (shares) the distribution of portfolio returns approximates a normal distribution.

Lotus demo   `RISK_RET.WK3`
To demonstrate how the 'annualized' risk and return figures can be estimated using Lotus load up the `RISK_RET.WK3` spreadsheet. This spreadsheet is illustrated as Table 1.3.

The RTZ Corporation's share price appears in column C of Table 1.3 and represents the share price at the close of business on the last trading day of the month. Calculation of the monthly returns is carried out on the basis of the formulae appearing in column E. The actual figures deriving from these formulae are displayed in column D. To the right of the table the annualized return and risk figures are recorded (6.69 per cent and 10.77 per cent, respectively) with the generating formulae again appearing to their right. The `@AVG` Lotus function calculates the arithmetic average of a defined range (in this example cell D12 to cell D23 inclusive); multiplication by 12 converts the average monthly return to an annualized figure. It is an industry convention to work with annualized values since this gives a standardized time measure which allows direct comparison with other investment opportunities. As mentioned earlier the risk and return figures have been estimated here on a continuously compounding basis following the practice of portfolio managers and the advanced portfolio analysis software that has been developed by companies such as BARRA International, QUANTEC, etc.

Note that a value for annualized volatility has also been estimated (32.81 per cent) which from the calculations that have been performed and the displayed formula is the square root of the annualized variance figure. Although the meaning of this value still needs to be examined in detail, it is useful to note how it has been estimated at this point. Volatility plays a very important part in financial markets' analysis, the pricing of options and indeed the very growth in the types and use of financial instruments emanates directly from the increase in the volatility of share prices, indexes, interest rates, currencies and commodity prices generally.

As stated above the investor is assumed to be risk-averse and will be attempting to minimize risk, as measured by variance (s^2), for any desired level of return. To demonstrate the idea of portfolio construction along the lines outlined above and in a world confined, initially, to two risky assets portfolio return can be defined as:

$$E(R_p) = x_1 E(R_1) + x_2 E(R_2) \qquad (1.4)$$

Equation (1.4) states that the return on the portfolio (R_p) can be found by adding the average returns from risky assets 1 and 2 (R_1, R_2) weighted respectively by

Table 1.3. Risk and return figures (*Source*: Datastream).

	A	B	C	D	E	F	G	H
5								
6			Share					
7			Price					
8			RTZ CORP	Log e		Annualized		
9		Date	(Pence)	Return	Formulae		Return Formulae	
10								
11		30/09/91	578				6.69%@AVG(D12..D23)*12	
12		31/10/91	551	-0.047839	@LN(C12/C11)			
13		29/11/91	514	-0.069512	@LN(C13/C12)	Annualized		
14		31/12/91	472	-0.085244	@LN(C14/C13)	Risk		
15		31/01/92	528	0.112117	@LN(C15/C14)			
16		28/02/92	552	0.044452	@LN(C16/C15)		10.77%@VARD 12..D23)*12	
17		31/03/92	574	0.039081	@LN(C17/C16)			
18		30/04/92	623	0.081917	@LN(C18/C17)	Annualized		
19		29/05/92	618	-0.008058	@LN(C19/C18)	Volatility		
20		30/06/92	625	0.011263	@LN(C20/C19)			
21		31/07/92	571	-0.090362	@LN(C21/C20)		32.81%@SQRT(F16)	
22		31/08/92	500	-0.132781	@LN(C22/C21)			
23		30/09/92	618	0.211880	@LN(C23/C22)			
24								
25								
26								

amount of each asset held in the portfolio (x_1, x_2). In terms of statistical estimates equation (1.4) can be restated as:

$$\bar{R}_p = x_1\bar{R}_1 + x_2\bar{R}_2 \tag{1.5}$$

The risk of the portfolio will be given by:

$$\text{Var}(R_p) = \text{Var}(x_1R_1 + x_2R_2) \tag{1.6}$$

which can be restated in terms of expectations as:

$$\text{Var}(R_p) = E\{x_1(R_1 - E(R_1))^2 + x_2(R_2 - E(R_2))^2\} \tag{1.7}$$

or in terms of estimators of the parameters as:

$$\text{Var}(R_p) = x_1^2 s_1^2 + x_2^2 s_2^2 + 2x_1x_2 s_{12} \tag{1.8}$$

The term s_{12} which appears in Equation (1.8) needs some explanation. It plays a crucial role in the portfolio methodologies being considered here, capturing the very essence of the potential gains from diversification. In statistical terms s_{12} is a measure of the way in which two variables move together: it is called *covariance*. Statistically the covariance term can be represented by:

$$\text{Cov}(R_1R_2) = \{E(R_1 - E(R_1))(R_2 - E(R_2))\} \tag{1.9}$$

To get a better understanding of the role that covariance plays it is useful to introduce another statistical concept, the correlation coefficient (r). This coefficient serves as a useful *dimensionless index* for measuring the relationship between two variables. The value it takes can be anywhere between the limits of -1 and $+1$, more formally:

$$-1 \leq r \leq +1 \tag{1.10}$$

Put in the present context, a negative value for r would indicate a negative relationship (as the return on one risk asset rises the other falls) and the closer that value to -1 the stronger the relationship. A positive value for r would indicate that the return on both assets rise or fall together, again the closer the value of r to $+1$ the stronger the relationship. An r of zero would indicate that no statistical relationship exists between the returns. As might be expected there is a mathematical relationship between covariance and the correlation coefficient. In the case of risky assets 1 and 2 this can be expressed as:

$$r_{12} = \frac{\text{Cov}(R_1R_2)}{\sqrt{(\text{Var}(R_1)\text{Var}(R_2))}} \tag{1.11}$$

In Lotus, estimation of the covariance term can be achieved by using a modified version of Equation (1.11):

$$\text{Cov}(R_1R_2) = r_{12}s_1s_2 = s_{12} \tag{1.12}$$

where

$$s_1 = \sqrt{s_1^2} = \sqrt{(\text{Var } R_1)}$$

and

$$s_2 = \sqrt{s^2} = \sqrt{(\text{Var } R_2)}$$

Summarizing the formulae needed in order to estimate the return and risk associated with a portfolio of two risky assets:

$$\bar{R}_p = x_1\bar{R}_1 + x_2\bar{R}_2 \qquad (1.5)$$

and

$$\text{Var}(R_p) = x_1^2 s_1^2 + x_2^2 s_2^2 + 2x_1 x_2 s_{12} \qquad (1.8)$$

At the moment nothing has been said about the values that x_1 and x_2 should take. If an assumption is now made that a total budget of £1 is available and that this figure may not be exceeded and further that this sum must be completely invested in the two risky assets:

$$x_1 + x_2 = 1 \qquad (1.13)$$

Theoretically there now exists an infinite number of investment possibilities open to the investor, starting with zero investment in x_1 and £1 being invested in x_2 the investor can move through possibilities such as 0.1 in x_1, 0.9 in x_2 to 1 in x_1 and zero in x_2. Each of these allocations satisfies Equation (1.13). These possibilities can be displayed graphically on what is termed the *mean–variance (mean–standard deviation) frontier.*

Lotus demo MVF.WK3
This spreadsheet can be used to demonstrate the gains from diversification. Table 1.4 depicts the Lotus screen initially encountered by the user when this spreadsheet is loaded. The two assets have returns of 10 and 20 units and risk measured as 2 and 8 units respectively, as the control data. These figures can be altered by the user either manually by using the cursor keys or by activating the special menu, Table 1.5, by depressing the Alt and A keys simultaneously. The proportions run from 1 in asset 1 to 0 in asset 1 in steps 0.1. Again these figures can be altered by the user either using the cursor keys or the special menu. Portfolio risks and returns are calculated for coefficients of correlation 1, 0.5, 0, −0.5 and −1. Graphs for each of these cases have been 'named' and can be selected via the special menu.

• Typing R (r) will enable the user to input the returns associated with each of the risky assets. The cursor will highlight the return for asset 1 if no change is required type [ENTER] otherwise type in the new value and press [ENTER]. The cursor will then move through the remaining inputs which may require a new input value: remember to press [ENTER] after each new value has been typed in, do *not* steer the cursor through the cells with the arrow keys if the special menu has been activated!

Table 1.4. Lotus screen to demonstrate gains from diversification

Gains from Diversification: a demonstration
of the two Risky Asset case. Use ALT+A to activate the menu.

ASSET 1   ASSET 2
Return: 10.00   Return: 20.00
Var: 2.00   Var: 8.00

Proportions in Portfolio

Asset 1:	1.00	0.90	0.80	0.70	0.60	0.50	0.40	0.30	0.20	0.10	0.00
Asset 2:	0.00	0.10	0.20	0.30	0.40	0.50	0.60	0.70	0.80	0.90	1.00

Coefficient of
Correlation   Portfolio Risk – measured by standard deviation (X range for graph)

1.00	1.41	1.56	1.70	1.84	1.98	2.12	2.26	2.40	2.55	2.69	2.83
0.50	1.41	1.44	1.50	1.59	1.72	1.87	2.04	2.22	2.42	2.62	2.83
0.00	1.41	1.30	1.26	1.30	1.41	1.58	1.79	2.02	2.28	2.55	2.83
-0.50	1.41	1.16	0.98	0.93	1.02	1.22	1.50	1.81	2.14	2.48	2.83
-1.00	1.41	0.99	0.57	0.14	0.28	0.71	1.13	1.56	1.98	2.40	2.83

Portfolio Returns (Y range for graph)

10.00	11.00	12.00	13.00	14.00	15.00	16.00	17.00	18.00	19.00	20.00

Table 1.5. Special menu

Returns	Returns for Assets 1 and 2
Var_Risk	Variance (Risk) of Assets 1 and 2
Proportions	Proportions of each asset in the portfolio
Graphs	Diagrams of Mean-SD frontiers
Exit	Exits the special menu

- Typing V (v) will enable the user to input the variances associated with each of the risky assets. The cursor will highlight the return for asset 1 if no change is required type [ENTER] otherwise type in the new value and press [ENTER]. The cursor will then move through the remaining inputs which may require a new input value: remember to press [ENTER] after each new value has been typed in. Do *not* steer the cursor through the cells with the arrow keys if the special menu has been activated!
- Typing P (p) will allow the user to change the proportions from their initial control settings. The proportions for this spreadsheet should be in the range $0 \leq p \leq 1$. Again do *not* steer the cursor through the cells with the arrow keys if the special menu has been activated!
- Typing G (g) enables the user to view graphs of the M–SD frontier for various correlation scenarios. Note that standard deviation has been used, rather than the variance discussed above, in order to present return and risk in the same units of measurement. The graph names are:
    NEG_COR_0.5
    NEG_COR_1
    POS_COR_0.5
    POS_COR_1
    ZERO_COR
  A graph is selected by highlighting the name with the arrow cursor keys and pressing [ENTER] when the desired graph has been targeted.
- Typing E (e) exits the macro and returns the spreadsheet to normal Lotus operating mode.

Figure 1.5 shows the gains from diversification very clearly. The curve linking asset 1 and asset 2 displays the mean–standard deviation frontier where perfect negative correlation exists between the two assets. At the other extreme a straight line joining asset 1 and asset 2

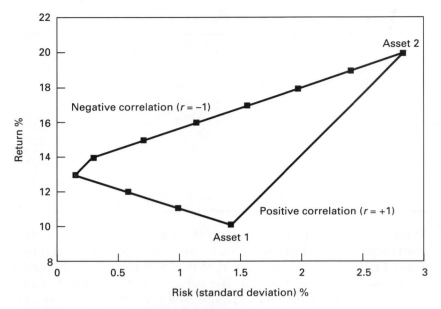

Fig. 1.5.   Efficient frontiers and correlation

demonstrates the case where perfect positive correlation exists. All other possible correlation values will lie inside this boundary.

As Fig. 1.6 suggests, the only case where diversification will not lead to a reduction in risk is the case where $r = +1$. From the figure it also becomes evident that not all points on the frontier (for the cases where

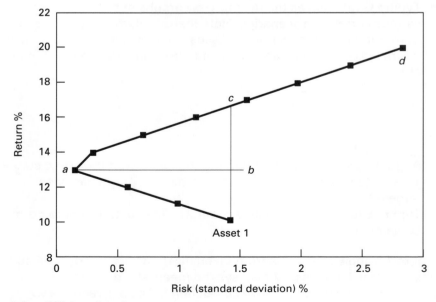

Fig. 1.6.   Efficient frontier

r ≠ + 1) are desirable. To get a clearer idea of this Fig. 1.6 shows the perfect negative correlation case with a line connecting asset 1 to a point labelled *c*. If an investor is acting rationally then he or she will choose the combination of some amount of asset 1 and some amount of asset 2 in the portfolio as defined at point *c* since this will generate a higher return for the same level of risk involved in holding asset 1 in the portfolio. The segment of the frontier which lies below the line *a–b* is in fact redundant. On this section of the frontier the investor will always be worse off, there will always be another combination of the assets which will yield a higher return for the same level of risk lying on the curve connecting points *a* and *c*. The segment of the curve from point *a* to point *d* is kn
own as the *efficient frontier*.

Of course, being able to construct an efficient frontier for two shares tells us nothing about where an individual investor (portfolio manager) is going to be on a frontier where many risky assets are available to choose from; nor does it tell us what the optimum holding of each one of those risky assets should be. In Chapter 6 ways will be explored in which optimal (in the sense of minimizing the 'historically' estimated risk deriving from a portfolio of shares) portfolio weights can be estimated for portfolios of shares.

1.3 Spreadsheets

There are three demonstration spreadsheets used in this chapter:

1 INDEX.WK3 which is described in Sec. 1.2 and illustrated in Table 1.1.
2 RISK_RET.WK3 which is described in Sec. 1.2.3 and appears as Table 1.3.
3 MVF.WK3 which examines the mean–variance efficient frontier and can be operated using a special menu. The technical aspects of this particular spreadsheet will be explained in this section.

1.3.1 MVF.WK3

The special menu, which appears as Table 1.5, offers five automated macros, three of the macros guide the input of data by the user:

(Returns, Var_Risk, Proportions);

one provides output in the form of graphs:

(Graphs);

and one exits the special menu returning the spreadsheet back to normal Lotus operating mode:

```
(Exit).
```

Questions

1.1   A pension fund concentrates its entire investment portfolio in UK shares. What financial risk might be associated with this strategy over a time horizon of:

(a)   less than one year?

(b)   greater than 10 years?

1.2   Mrs Sterling, a UK resident, is planning a holiday in the United States and intends to take travellers cheques with her. Which strategy would be sounder:

(a)   buying sterling denominated travellers cheques?

(b)   buying US dollar denominated travellers cheques?

1.3   Examine the financial risks faced by a US dollar-based financial institution agreeing to buy a substantial amount of Italian lire from a corporate customer two months from today.

1.4   A large company is planning to raise a large amount of capital in order to finance an investment project. From the financial risk point of view explain the role that interest rates will play in the company's analysis of the project.

1.5   Using the following month-end share prices calculate the annualized return, annualized risk and annualized volatility:

Date	Share price
30/04/92	430
31/05/92	435
30/06/92	425
31/07/92	432
31/08/92	435
30/09/92	440
31/10/92	450
30/11/92	470
31/12/92	485
31/01/93	490
28/02/93	510
31/03/93	525
30/04/93	540

Critically appraise the statistics that you have calculated.

1.6   The following estimates of return and risk have been calculated:

Asset 1: return 18 per cent, risk 42 per cent

Asset 2: return 11 per cent, risk 24 per cent

Use the demonstration spreadsheet `MVF.WK3` to obtain graphs of the mean–standard deviation.

Appendix 1A

The FT-SE 100 Index has a base date of 30 December 1983 at which time the Index of 100 selected constituent companies has a value of 1000. The value of the index has since been calculated using the formula:

$$\frac{\Sigma I_{it} P_{it}}{\Sigma I_{i0} P_{i0}} \times 1000 \qquad\qquad\qquad (1A.1)$$

where:

I_{it} represents company i's issued share capital at time, t;
I_{i0} represents company i's issued share capital at the base date, 0;
P_{it} represents company i's share price at time, t;
P_{i0} represents company i's share price at the base date, 0;
and the summation (Σ) is performed over $i = 1$ to 100.

Some notes on the calculation:

- The base is adjusted whenever a constituent company's issued share capital changes; for example rights issues, issue of additional shares under an employee's equity scheme, issues of new shares on the execution of equity warrants.
- For the purposes of calculating a company's market capitalization partly paid new issues will be adjusted to be equivalent to a fully paid price.
- The Stock Exchange Automatic Quotation (SEAQ) system is used to provide exact mid-prices for the calculation of the Index.
- In calculating the Index the number of shares in issue for each constituent company will be rounded to the nearest million.

(*Source: Quality of Markets FT-SE 100 Share Index*, 3rd edn, The International Stock Exchange, London).

Appendix 1B

Natural logarithms provide a convenient way of measuring returns. Consider an investment of £100 which will return £115 over a period of one year. The *continuously compounded rate (r)* on the investment can be found by equating the r to the starting and finishing principals in the following way:

$$e^r = \frac{\text{Finishing principal}}{\text{Starting principal}} = \frac{£115}{£100}$$

where e represents the exponential (2.7182...).

Taking $\log_e$ of both sides of the expression yields:

$$r = \log_e \frac{\pounds 115}{\pounds 100}$$

So that the continuously compounding rate is 0.1398 or 13.98 per cent.

This idea can be readily extended to cover interest rate, currency and share returns. In Table 1.3 $\log_e$ has been used to generate monthly returns which have then been averaged and annualized. The same method could be adopted to find the continuously compounded return for a holding period of less than one year. In general the following formula can be used to calculate continuously compounded returns:

$$r = \frac{\log_e (\text{Principal}_{t+T}/\text{Principal}_t)}{T}$$

where T represents time in years.

Example 1A.1

Suppose that an investor buys one share today at a price of 500 pence and sells that share in 160 days' time for 535 pence. The continuously compounded return on the investment, assuming a 365 day year, can be calculated as:

$$r = \frac{\log_e (535/500)}{160/365}$$

which yields a return of 15.43 per cent.

Notes

1 The different interest rates quoted for Cases 1.1 and 1.2 indicate the financial institutions' bid–offer margin. The institution will lend money as 9.6 per cent (offer rate including a risk premium) but will only pay 7.5 per cent on deposits (bid rate).
2 Trading in the futures contract on this index was suspended on 17 June 1992. The options on the index are still quoted.
3 An index tracker fund on the Emerging Markets Index was launched by the State Street Bank of the United States in May 1993.

References and further reading

Blake, D (1990) *Financial Market Analysis*, McGraw-Hill, London.
Elton, E.J. and Gruber, M.J. (1991) *Modern Portfolio Theory and Investment Analysis* (4th edn), Wiley, New York.
Levy, H. and Sarnat, M. (1984) *Portfolio and Investment Selection: Theory and Practice*, Prentice-Hall International, Englewood Cliffs, NJ.

2   Forecasting market movements

2.1 Forecasting background

In attempting to make any forecast concerning the likely whereabouts of the future price of the risky asset that is currently being held, or may be held in the future, it is necessary to specify a time scale over which the forecast is required: is it over a period of minutes, hours, days, weeks, months or even years? What must also be ascertained is whether an actual figure of a variable needs to be forecast or whether it will be sufficient to predict the direction of any change that is expected to occur in that variable. It is worth noting that in being able to forecast accurately where the price of any financial instrument—or commodity price—will move could prove to be as frustrating as it is useful. Take Case 1.5 in Chapter 1 as an example, the financial director and the purchasing director both recognized that risks were operating against them, both in terms of the commodity's price and exchange rates. If their suspicions were to be confirmed by some forecasting methodology which provided them with exact values for the future price of coffee beans as well as the £/$ exchange rate, the information they possess will be of no use to them if finance is not available to effect a purchase today or if they have the finance but do not have access to storage space which would allow them to accept delivery. Even worse, if both the necessary finance and storage space are available but the holding period will be so long that coffee beans will deteriorate before they can be processed, what use is the 100 per cent accurate forecast?

The example just used is extreme and assumes that there is no alternative to outright purchase of the financial and physical risky instruments. In most instances an estimate of the approximate future values of instruments, or the direction in which those instruments might move, is what market participants are seeking to establish in order to assist them in their planning activities and manage any perceived risk by taking the appropriate action in derivative instruments. That being the case the question then arises: how can forecasts be obtained?

Although somewhat artificial for practical purposes, it is helpful to divide the need for forecasts into time scales and to examine which market participants are likely to be interested in which forecasting methods, and for what reasons.

At one end of the time scale market makers, traders and sales staff, employed by banks, commodity dealers and investment houses, will be taking an extremely short-term view about prices in the markets in which they are working: short term in this arena can be interpreted as intra-day price movements. The buying and selling of an instrument by these players will be transacted in seconds many times a day. Such hectic actions can be driven by several motives; one might be the belief that there is mis-pricing of an instrument, such an apparent anomaly would be seized upon by buying (or selling) at that instant in time and reversing the transaction moments later when the market price moves back to its perceived 'fair' level. A second motive, and probably more realistic given the lack of real arbitrage (risk-free profit) opportunities that exist in today's rapid-access technology markets, might be the taking of a particular position in an instrument prior to the release of government statistics or some official statement in anticipation of a price rise or fall in that instrument and unwinding the position immediately after the impact of the statistics have been felt.

Other participants in that same market may be more interested in developments taking place over months or several years—Cases 1.1–1.5 could well fall into this category as could equity and bond portfolio managers, too. The question that these participants will be concerned with is: where is the price of a security or instrument likely to be in, say, three months' time? This does not mean that between now and the dateline three months hence that those participants have no interest in the development of market prices, they may have a very real interest and may be watching the markets very closely. However, unless something totally unexpected happens they will, in the main, be prepared to leave their underlying position untouched until the time arrives for a strategic review of the portfolio performance. Nevertheless, they would be prepared to put on a hedge should a forecast suggest that it would be prudent to do so.

Other participants may well take an even longer time period as their frame of reference. The need to finance a large, expensive investment project at the best possible rate of interest and with a stable exchange rate over several years would fall into this category. Forecasts in this theatre could well involve financial analysts, economists and corporate decision makers in projecting the development of the domestic and international economy over a period of years in order to devise an appropriate financing plan and strategy.

It is worth stressing again that the separation suggested in the preceding paragraphs is, to an extent, artificial. At one extreme traders working in or close to a market and dependent on minute-by-minute market movements in the prices of instruments to make their living will always be taking a short-term point of view. At times fund managers, companies engaging in international trade and investment project managers may have to take very serious account of short-term market movements, too, and put on short-term hedges to provide cover for their medium-long-term portfolios whatever their composition.

Having categorized participants roughly into three compartments—short, medium and long term—attention can now be focused on the types of forecasting tools that each group might be likely to take note of and use.

2.2 Technical analysis

At one extreme there are analysts who concentrate in looking at the way in which the price of a security has developed over a period of time. Little or no attempt is made to establish what factors might have led to that manifestation of the series they are examining and the future development of prices is projected in some way by the past values in that series of observations. In the short term, traders and portfolio managers—although often reluctant to admit it—tend to place a great deal of emphasis on the use of forecasts derived from *technical analysis*. A complete coverage of the methods that can be classified as technical analysis is beyond the scope of this text. However, some knowledge of the approaches used can be gained by considering the examples introduced below.

Case 2.1

Assume that it is 2/1/1993 and that a fund manager is looking to restructure a client's portfolio of equities as part of a standard quarterly review. The Abbey National plc share price data over the period 31/12/1991–31/12/1992 (*Source:* DATASTREAM) has risen from 295p to 389.5p and the company has attracted some good press comments throughout that period. To help reach a decision the portfolio manager has decided to look at some 'technicals'.

Lotus demo   `TA_DEMO.WK3`
This spreadsheet enables the user to undertake some simple technical analysis initially applied to the Abbey National plc share price, but please note that some data on other share prices, exchange rates and interest rates is also available for analysis. This sample data, which has been obtained from DATASTREAM, is saved on file: `TEXT_DAT.WK3`. It is not necessary to access the `TEXT_DAT.WK3` file directly unless the user wishes to update and/or add to the data set.

2.2.1 Momentum indicators

The first method that will be considered is the *momentum indicator*. This method is a member of a family of indicators which can be aligned under the title of *oscillators*. These 'technicals' are intended to provide a clear picture of the direction in which markets are trending, they also have the advantage that they tend to be useful even if markets are drifting sideways. The simple momentum indicator is easy to construct:

$$\text{Momentum indicator} = P_t - P_{t-i} \tag{2.1}$$

where i can take any value but normally, if days are the time period being used, a number between 9 and 30 should be selected. `TA_DEMO` uses 10 so that Equation

(2.1) becomes:

$$\text{Momentum indicator} = P_t - P_{t-10} \tag{2.2}$$

The indicator takes both positive and negative values. A movement from a positive value can be interpreted as a sell signal and if the price moves from negative to positive, it can be interpreted as a buy signal.

A slightly more involved indicator within this family is the *relative strength index* (RSI). This momentum indicator oscillates between an upper bound of 100 and lower bound of 0 or +1 and −1, depending on the convention used in its calculation. The oscillator values move between the defined upper and lower bounds and are, just like the momentum indicator introduced above, easy to interpret. The formula presented here was developed in the United States by J. Welles Wilder. The value it calculates is based on the ratio between the sum of the daily price rises over a given time period and the sum of the daily price falls over that same period and adopts the 100 upper bound and 0 lower bound convention.

$$\text{Current RSI} = 100 - \frac{100}{\Sigma(+\text{ changes}/-\text{ changes}) + 1} \tag{2.3}$$

In calculating this ratio two assumptions are usually made:

1   If the sum of the positive changes over the time period selected is zero then the sum of the negative changes is also assumed to be zero.
2   If the sum of the negative changes is zero over the selected time period then to avoid the problem of division by infinity in the main formula the sum of the negative changes is put equal to one.

Note: TA_DEMO.WK3 is for demonstration purposes and over the time period used the sums are seldom likely to be zero, thus these assumptions have not been programmed into the spreadsheet. A further functional assumption has been made in the construction of the spreadsheet and that is that the absolute value of the sum of the negative values is used in order to fix the operating bounds for the RSI to between 0 and 100.

Example 2.1
To clarify this point and to help interpret the RSI graph assume that the following sums have been calculated over the previous 30 days:

1   $\Sigma + \text{changes} = 500$; $\Sigma - \text{changes} = -500$. Using Equation (2.3) to calculate the RSI yields:

$$\text{RSI} = 100 - \frac{100}{(500/500) + 1} = 50 \tag{2.4}$$

The interpretation of which is that the buying and selling activities are balanced. The security is neither over-bought nor over-sold.

2   $\Sigma + \text{changes} = 1000$; $\Sigma - \text{changes} = -250$. Using Equation (2.3) to calculate the RSI yields:

$$RSI = 100 - \frac{100}{(1000/250) + 1} = 80 \tag{2.5}$$

In this example an interpretation would be that demand is outstripping supply and up to a point could be regarded as normal trading activity. Users of the RSI, however, impose a rule-of-thumb upper warning limit at an index value of between 75 and 80 depending on the analyst's convention. When the calculated RSI exceeds this value the market is viewed as over-bought and pressure may be on for the price of the instrument to move downwards as profits are taken.

3   Σ + changes = 250; Σ − changes = −1000. Using Equation (2.3) to calculate the RSI yields:

$$RSI = 100 - \frac{100}{(250/1000) + 1} = 20 \tag{2.6}$$

This is the opposite to 2 and again up to a point a drift in the RSI to below 50 may be regarded as normal but beyond a certain level the market would tend to be regarded as being over-sold. This lower warning limit may be imposed at a value of between 25 and 20, again depending on the analyst's convention, below that boundary the analyst's expectation would be that the price would begin to rise as those participants who had sold short were forced to buy to cover their commitments.

Thus in connection with Case 2.1 the fund manager might well consider the 10-day momentum indicator and/or the 30-day RSI as tools to help him or her to reach a

Table 2.1.   Abbey National share price in the period 2 January until 31 December 1992

	A	J	K	L	M	N
1		ABBEY NATIONAL (P) £				
2		23-Feb-93	Latest	Latest		
3			RSI	10-day	Annualized	Annualized
4			Relative	Momentum	Volatility	Return
5			Strength	Indicator	%	%
6			Indicator			
7				21.50	29.99	
8			67.40			27.90
9						
10						
11		Maximum			Minimum	
12		Value:	392		Value:	251
13						
14	over the period: 02/01/92		31/12/92			
15						
16						
17						

decision as to whether to buy the Abbey National plc share now or wait in the expectation of an easing of the share's price. Table 2.1 has been extracted from TA_DEMO.WK3 and provides information about the Abbey National plc share price in the period 2 January 1992–31 December 1992. The RSI on 31/12/1992 stood at 67.40 and the 10-day momentum indicator at 21.5. On the basis of the RSI at a warning limit of 75 the index appears to be close to the over-bought region. Figures 2.1 and 2.2 give a clearer indication of the track of the securities price.

Figure 2.1 shows that although the momentum indicator is in the region of strength it is declining towards the zero—strength/weakness—dividing line. This conclusion is confirmed by Fig. 2.2 showing the 30 day RSI which shows that although on the high side the index does seem to be easing back. On the basis of this type of technical analysis the portfolio manager could well decide to postpone the purchase of the security until the price trend reverses.

2.2.2 Charts

Another popular method used in attempting to predict where the price of a security could be heading is looking for patterns in the movement of the security's price. Analysts who undertake this type of activity are often referred to as *chartists*. These analysts obtain graphical plots of the price history of the security or instrument, e.g. bond, options, futures contract, index, etc., in which they are interested and then proceed to draw lines on the graph; the lines are given labels such as: head and shoulders, bullish or bearish rectangles, rising or falling wedges, pennants, fans, channels, support and resistance levels (Meyers, 1989). TA_DEMO.WK3 allows the user to plot the daily price of the share over a period.

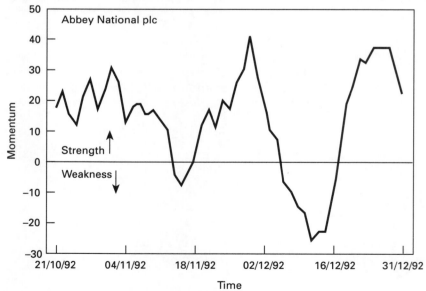

Fig. 2.1.   Ten day momentum indicator

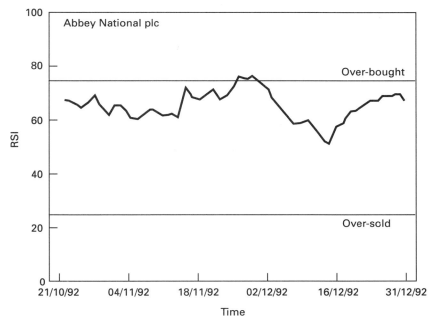

Fig. 2.2.   Thirty day relative strength index (RSI)

The user can then test his or her chartist skills to predict where the share price might move and then compare with where the share price actually moved once that future data becomes available. Figure 2.3 demonstrates the idea of an

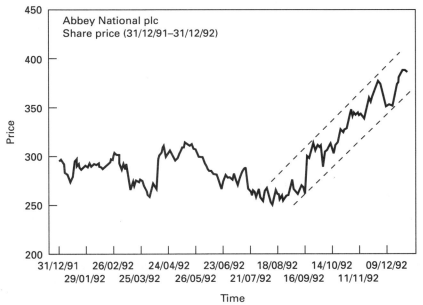

Fig. 2.3.   Instrument's price — closing prices (up-trend channel)

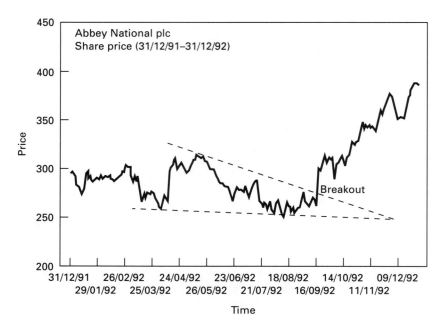

Fig. 2.4.   Instrument's price — closing prices (falling wedge)

'*up-trend channel*' while Fig. 2.4 demonstrates the idea of a falling wedge.

If the portfolio manager is basing his or her analysis of the Abbey National plc share price on the trend channel in Fig. 2.3 the decision to buy may again be postponed. If the share price continues to track in the same way as it has, roughly, over the previous four months the price may drift down to around 375p before recommencing its climb. The method is seductive but it is fraught with difficulties, for example, where does the line drawing process start? Different analysts will have genuine differences of opinion about where any lines should be drawn on a data plot. Another problem is that *breakouts* occur—i.e. the term used to describe the case when a line confining the share price movements is breached—and it is really just such reversals of trend that need to be spotted in order to decide if risk management is required and to determine what hedges need to be put in place.

2.2.3 Moving averages

Yet another method that have proved very popular is that of moving averages. This involves the calculation of a smooth long run moving average of the underlying data and a shorter run, less smooth moving average. The two calculated series are then plotted together on a graph to gain an idea of the trend in the security price. Figure 2.5 has been obtained from TA_DEMO.WK3 and depicts a 15-day versus 100-day moving average scenario. A crude interpretation is that when the shorter moving average line cuts the long run moving average line from above the security price is trending down. If the short run moving average cuts the long run from below the trend in the securities price is up. Considering this figure it

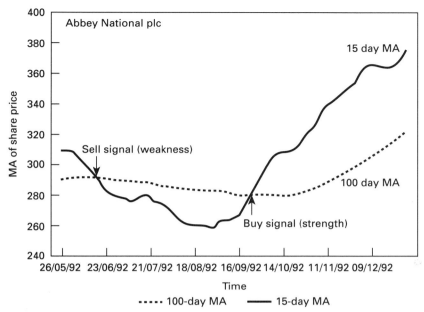

Fig. 2.5. Moving average of share price: 100 day versus 15 day

appears that the weakness in the Abbey National plc share price discovered using the previously discussed technical analysis methods has, perhaps, already been reversed. The 100-day moving average and the 15-day moving average both appear to be trending upwards so it may be advisable for the fund manager contemplating the purchase of the shares to act now rather than be faced with paying a higher price in the future.

Lotus demo   `TA_DEMO.WK3`
Used in conjunction with `TEXT_DAT.WK3` this spreadsheet enables the user to undertake technical analysis as described above on the data sets shown in Table 2.2.

The spreadsheet offers several automated routines which can be accessed via the special menu activated via the Alt + A keys. The choices shown in Table 2.3 are available.

- Typing I (i) enables the user to input dates from a previously constructed file (initially this is the `TEXT_DAT.WK3` file, but the user may create his or her own data files for use in this spreadsheet). The control date used here is fixed at 31/12/1991–31/12/1992.
- Selecting P (p) enables the user to input a new set of data on prices or exchange rates. The graphs and technical calculations will all be updated when the new data is copied into this file. The process for copying the data into the file is semi-automated. The user is prompted to type in the name of the data required and press

Table 2.2.   Data sets

```
Names of data ranges available for this spreadsheet

Control Data on File: TEXT_DAT.WK3

Name of
Range:                    Closing Share Prices for:
FTSE100                   The FTSE 100 Index
ABNAT                     Abbey National plc
BARCLAYS                  Barclays Bank plc
BT                        British Telecom plc
HANSON                    Hanson plc
SAINSBRY                  Sainsbury plc
WELSHWAT                  Welsh Water plc


                          Exchange rates:
YEN_STER                  Yen to £1 Sterling
DM_USD                    DM to $1 US
```

[ENTER], a name from Table 2.2 must be input unless the user has created a new data file and altered the spreadsheet macro accordingly.

- Selecting G (g) allows the user to select a graph from the named set: MA (Long run versus short run moving average), Momentum (the 10-day momentum indicator), Price (the securities price over the previous year recorded on a daily basis), and the 30-day RSI (Relative Strength Indicator). At the prompt highlight the desired graph by moving the cursor with the left or right arrows and press [ENTER]. Typing [ENTER] (or pressing any key) when the graph has been viewed will bring back the special menu.

- Selecting T (t) will display a table of information on the security as described earlier (refer to Table 2.1). This information will be updated automatically when new price data is input via P (p).

- The available names of data ranges that can be copied into this file can be viewed by typing R (r) (refer to Table 2.2).

- To exit the special menu and return to normal operating mode type Q (q).

2.2.4 Technical analysis—conclusions

Technical analysis can provide some useful information to market players interested in the very short or longer term development of prices. It is, though,

Table 2.3.   Special menu for `TA_DEMO.WK3`

Input_Dates	Import dates from a named data range
Prices	Import share prices from a named data range
Graph	RSI, MA, Momentum Graphs
Table	Information on: RSI, Momentum, Annualized Volatility and Return
Ranges	Names of data ranges available for copying to this spreadsheet
Quit	Exit Macro

only one way of trying to forecast where prices might move and if the theories concerning capital markets efficiency are accepted then no amount of studying of past prices will reveal anything about their possible future movements. In its strongest form the efficient market hypothesis maintains that *all* available information is captured by and reflected in the current price of a security. In its weak form the hypothesis maintains that the current price of a security fully reflects the information contained in the historical sequence of its prices. (The debate on the concepts, of market efficiency and the efficient market hypothesis has generated a vast amount of literature. A detailed consideration of the topic is outside the scope of this text but interested readers are referred to Blake (1990, Ch. 11)).

2.3 Fundamental analysis

Another group of forecasters can be categorized as those who seek to understand reasons that might justify the current price of a security. These forecasters are fundamentalists; they base their projections on their interpretation of the underlying factors that they have identified. Obviously not all securities are affected by the same variables if the example of Chapter 1 is used again—the food processing company which suffers the misfortune of a bacteriological contamination of some equipment. The implicit assumption throughout the development of that example was that the share prices of other companies operating in that same sector would not be negatively affected. Such operational differences generate a need for company analysts to research market sectors with the aim of establishing what makes one company, sector or market, more profitable than another and, having discovered those reasons, whether they will persist into the future. The way in which they attempt to achieve this is by researching and reporting on such questions as:

1   What are the strengths and weaknesses of the object of their research?
2   How is it likely to be affected by domestic economic developments?
3   How is it likely to be affected by international events?

As source material for research they focus on data published in company accounts, comments in chairmen's reports, press comments, published economic and financial statistics, in fact analysts make use of any source that might be useful in the investigative process. The goal is to keep their traders and portfolio managers as fully informed as possible and, potentially, provide an edge in the market.

There are numerous ways in which these types of forecasts can be obtained; some methods are based on quantitative analysis while others use qualitative appraisal techniques. As with technical analysis a thorough examination of these methods and a discussion of their limitations is beyond the scope of this text. The following examples are intended to provide the reader with an appreciation of some of the main techniques.

2.3.1 Accounting ratios and scenario writing

Ratio analysis is one way in which analysts attempt to glean information from data reported in company accounts. Roughly speaking basic ratios can be divided into four categories:

1   Profitability and return
2   Solvency (long and short term)
3   Working capital
4   Shareholders' investment ratios.

The following examples are provided in order to give the reader an idea of how some of these ratios work in practice, how they are calculated and how they may be interpreted.

One ratio that would be categorized under the first heading would be the *return on capital employed* (ROCE). The figure obtained from the ratio will allow an analyst: (i) to see how, on an intra-company basis, the ROCE has changed from one year to the next; (ii) to compare ROCEs on an inter-company basis; and (iii) to compare a company's ROCE with its current cost of borrowing money. The formula used to calculate this ratio is given by:

$$ROCE = \frac{PBIT}{CE}$$

where:

PBIT represents profit on ordinary activities before interest and taxation;
CE represents capital employed.

Clearly the higher the ROCE relative to other ROCEs or borrowing rates with which it is being compared the better. One danger with this ratio is that some components of a company's fixed assets may appear as undervalued items on its balance sheet, if this is the case then the ROCE might be higher than justified and be presenting a misleading signal. When carrying out an analysis it would be sensible to take this figure in conjunction with other ratios, such as gross profit as percentage of sales and asset turnover ratio.

In category 2 the *debt ratio* would provide a useful measure of a company's debt burden. The greater the debt burden the greater the possibility that the company may become regarded as a risky prospect when it comes to raising further finance for whatever purpose. The higher risk rating may manifest itself in the form of higher interest rates being charged by banks and other institutions, or further loans only being advanced under the provision that the institution advancing the money has a voice on the company's board, or no further advances being made. The debt ratio is calculated using:

$$\text{Debt ratio} = \frac{\text{Total debts}}{\text{Total assets}}$$

Just as in the warning limits used in the RSI, above, there is no established level that can be taken as a safe upper limit to the debt ratio but a rule-of-thumb guide is usually set at 50 per cent. If the calculated debt ratio is over this figure, and rising, an analyst should consider looking more deeply into the company's debt position. Other ratios in this category would be: gearing ratios, interest cover and the cash flow ratio. As a measure of a company's riskiness, gearing ratios in the form of debt/equity are often quoted. The higher this ratio the greater the amount of interest that must be paid to creditors. If the debt/equity ratio is very high then at some point not only will shareholders no longer receive dividends, there may not be enough funds in the company to service the interest rate on outstanding loans. In recent years there have been several examples of this situation arising: Trafalgar House being but one recent example.

In the final category there are some very well-known ratios: the price/earnings (P/E), earnings per share, divided cover, dividend yield and earnings yield. The P/E ratio is one that has received wide coverage and is simply the ratio of a company's share price to the earnings per share. A high P/E ratio suggests that shareholders are confident about a company's future prospects. What constitutes a high P/E depends on comparisons of P/Es of similar companies operating in the same sector, but once again it would be advisable to look at more than one ratio in assessing a company's potential outlook and the impact that outlook might have on the future share price of the company.

The ratios described above are all tools that can be used to assist analysts to prepare forecasts about the prospects of a single company or a sector. The numbers generated via the use of ratios may then be incorporated into an overall *scenario* as justifications for the arguments used in the analysis concerning that company or sector. Scenario writing, though, often goes far deeper, digging into the fundamentals that underpin the economy and impinge on all types of business, commercial and financial activities. In the case of interest rates, for example, an increase in money supply figures could be interpreted as potentially increasing the risk of inflation thus putting pressure on interest rates and causing a fall in the price of bonds and other interest rate related instruments as well as their linked derivative securities such as futures or options, a rise in the consumer price index could be taken in the same way. On the other hand a fall in gross national product (GNP) might be taken as an indication of a slow down in economic activity which could lead to an easing of money supply and exert downward pressure on interest rates. A very brief indicative example of how this type of forecasting might be presented appears below.

Example 2.2

Against a background of rising unemployment, now over 3 million, falling house prices and a general lack of consumer and business confidence in the United Kingdom, the government has announced a package of interest rate cuts and increases in public spending in an attempt to stimulate economic recovery. This package, however, is unlikely to have any great or lasting impact. Consumers, sucked into the speculative carnival of seemingly ever increasing house prices in the second half of the 1980s, are finding now that their debt is greater than the value of the asset they purchased. Although the cost of servicing interest rate payments on mortgages has fallen significantly over the past few months, as a direct result of interest rate cuts that have been announced by the Chancellor, the ever growing, and very real, fear that redundancy is stalking around the corner is enough to deter the purchase of the more expensive consumer durables in all but a few cases. In addition manufacturers are being further squeezed by the higher cost of imported raw materials following the recent depreciation in the value of sterling resulting from the interest rate cut.

The outlook for the consumer durable sector on this basis is bleak. Registration of new vehicles is expected to fall by a further xx per cent in the next quarter, while the demand for 'white' domestic products is expected to drop by yy per cent. The home-based electronic products will also take a knock. The Japanese electronics giant, Maixyyska Inc., has announced that it will not be going ahead with plans to open a new assembly plant in the north of England as it expects demand to plummet by millions of units overall this year. The only sector which holds some promise for this year is the food retail sector; Asburys, Sainsco, Rosetes and Tesda all report buoyant demand and before tax profits are expected to rise by an average of zz per cent across all outlets. Such is the optimism that both Sainsco and Tesda have announced plans to open two new hypermarkets in the south-east. All expect profit margins to be squeezed later this year as increases in food prices on imported foods filter through the system but are not passed on to consumers in full.

This year will possibly see a fall in the price of shares in the automobile and electronics sectors. The food-chain groups are likely to experience some growth with profits showing an increase over last year.

From this type of scenario an equity portfolio manager might well decide to sell, or at least reduce holdings, in the negatively reviewed sectors/shares and increase holdings in more positively regarded sectors/shares. A bond portfolio manager might consider the scenario presented as one where pressure might be applied to introduce more interest rate cuts in order to stimulate economic activity. In that case he or she would be looking to increases in bond prices and may well be tempted to increase holdings of certain types of bonds in a portfolio and pick up capital gains or lock into the higher yields that bonds are offering at the present time.

2.3.2 Econometrics and time-series analysis

Clearly in the above example percentages have been used as a numerical indicator of the potential size of the impact of the economic influences, and it is easy to imagine how the ratios discussed above could have been incorporated into the scenario report, but otherwise very little has been used in the way of quantitative assessment. In an attempt for forecast more exactly what the future holds for prices, economists and other researchers have developed the science of *econometrics* to quantify the relationships that are believed to exist between economic variables. Using economic theory as a base many types of models have been constructed. Some models comprise but a single equation, perhaps, trying to establish the relationship between the price of a share and the price of oil, the relationship between the oil price and long-run interest rates, or the relationship between a share price and an index.

Example 2.3

Using two sets of data provided on `TEXT_DAT.WK3` the relationship can be found between, say, the price of the Sainsbury plc share and the FT-SE 100 Index. Clear any existing spreadsheet currently being displayed—do not forget to save any current files, if they are intended for future use:

`/WEY`

Then copy the following ranges to the empty spreadsheet:

`/FCCNsainsbry` [press ENTER] `TEXT_DAT` [press ENTER] the Sainsbury plc share price data will now be displayed on screen. The title of the data set will appear in cell A1 and the numerical observations will start in cell A4. The Lotus menu at the top of the screen will have disappeared, To continue, move the cursor to cell B1 and reactive the Lotus menu. Repeat the steps described above for the FT-SE 100 data:
`FCCNftse100` [press ENTER] `TEXT_DAT` [press ENTER] the FT-SE 100 data will now appear alongside the Sainsbury plc data. *Note:* although no dates have been copied into the file the data spans the period 31/12/91–31/12/92 as with the examples used in `TA_DEMO` above.

   With both data sets in place a regression can be performed. First, however, place the cursor on cell A4—the first observation in the Sainsbury data set.

Call up the Lotus menu by typing / followed by:
DRY. [press END] ↓ [press ENTER] X →. [press END] ↓ [press ENTER] O →
→ [press ENTER] G
The regression will be performed and the output in Table 2.4 will be displayed.
This output requires a little explanation for those unfamiliar with the method.
   The statistical technique just employed estimates an equation of the form:

$$Y = a + bX + e \tag{2.7}$$

where:

   Y represents the dependent variable;
   X represents an independent variable.

Since the relationship between Y and X will not generally speaking be exact, a
variable e is incorporated into the equation as an error term. This error term
takes up the slack between the observed Y and the predicted Y which will be
obtained from the equation $a + bX$.
   Unknown values which the technique is attempting to estimate are
represented by a and b.
   The printout of the regression results in Table 2.4 reports a constant term =
-123.16, this value corresponds to a in Equation (2.7). Towards the foot of the
table the value of 0.22146 is reported against the legend X coefficient(s), this
value relates to b in Equation (2.7). Another of the reported statistics, which
was mentioned in the context of diversification in Chapter 1, is the value R
squared, 0.31355. This value provides an indication of the degree of
relationship that exists between Y and X over the sample period. In this
example approximately 31 per cent of the variation in Y is being explained by
Equation (2.7). A figure much closer to 100 per cent would, of course, have
been more desirable. The square root of this value is known as the coefficient
of correlation, which was also encountered in Chapter 1 in the discussion of
the gains from diversification. The single equation that has been estimated
here could thus be reported as:

Sainsbury plc share price = $-123.16 + 0.22$FT-SE 100 Index   (2.8)

Table 2.4.   Regression results

	Regression Output:
Constant	−123.163
Std Err of Y Est	43.62064
R Squared	0.313554
No. of Observations	256
Degrees of Freedom	254
X Coefficient(s)	0.221464
Std Err of Coef.	0.02056

Example 2.3 is intended only as an illustration of the method of regression as a model building tool, the methodology will be used in more advanced portfolio applications later. *The reader should not interpret the results from the regression above as a way of forecasting share prices!*

At the other end of the spectrum sets of interacting equations are constructed in which the whole economic framework is seen as a series of variables, somehow related, feeding into each other and are estimated to provide forecasts of the value(s) that a variable or set of variables could take under different policy assumptions. Examples of this type of approach in the United Kingdom would be the Treasury model, the National Institute model, and the London Business School model. The connecting feature between these models is that they seek to explain how the value of an economic variable is reached by explaining the relationship that that variable has with other variables in a simultaneous equation framework.

Example 2.4

$$EMG = f\,(WPMG,DP,WP) \tag{2.9}$$

$$IMP = g\,(EMG,WPMG,DP,WP) \tag{2.10}$$

Equation (2.9) represents an equation for export of manufactured goods (EMG) while Equation (2.10) represents an import equation (IMP). The other variable mnemonics are:

WPMG, world production of manufactured goods;
DP, domestic prices;
WP, world prices.

To illustrate the notion of interacting variables and equations notice in the equations above that the variable EMG appears on the right-hand side of the import equation and is thus regarded as an explanatory variable but as the left-hand side dependent variable in the export equation. Also note that the variables DP and WP are assumed to play a role in the determination of both imports and exports.

The type of approach discussed above has enjoyed much publicity in the United Kingdom particularly. However, the recent forecasting performance record of *econometric models* is not convincing, indeed the major UK models have all failed to predict the depth of the current recession and did not perform too well in predicting the strength of the boom which preceded the recession. Explanations for this are usually along the lines that some of the basic relationships used in the original construction of the model have changed and the models will need to be modified in order to capture these new relationships. Some forecasters recognized earlier than others that the fundamental economic relationships used in the large econometric models were undergoing a dramatic change and decided to develop their own *ad hoc* equations or to abandon the economic approach and rely more on intuition and their own judgement of events.

In the United States less emphasis has been placed on constructing models that are based on mathematical relationships which attempt to explain how variables interact with each other, considerably more attention has been paid to the development of a rival system using vector autoregressive models (VAR). This approach returns to the notion of modelling a variable on its own past values—*time-series analysis*. The method appears to be a promising new avenue for exploration and is currently attracting attention in the United Kingdom (Davies and Shah, 1992). But whether this method will achieve good results under all types of economic states remains to be seen.

2.3.3 Delphi-type forecasting

In concluding this section it is worth considering some projections published in the German newspaper, *Die Zeit* in February 1991. Fourteen participants (refer to Appendix 2A) contributed to the construction of forecasts which spanned the period from the end of January 1991 until the end of July 1991. In total eight graphs were published depicting forecast ranges for the variables in Table 2.5.

An initial reaction to these figures is that the bands all appear to be very wide. They reflect the range of different forecasters' interpretations of the implications that international and domestic developments would have on the variables they were asked to forecast. Based on the participants' forecasts a point forecast was estimated for each of the variables and these summarized in Table 2.6.

Table 2.5.   Variables for the period January–July 1991

Variable	Current	Low	High
Deutsche Akteinindex (DAX)	1,475	1,250	1,800
Dow Jones Industrial Average (DJIA)	2,600	2,100	2,900
Nikkei Index	24,000	22,000	28,000
German Interest Rates	9.00	8.00	9.40
US Interest Rates	8.00	7.50	9.00
US Dollar/DM (exchange rate)	1.49	1.40	1.57
100 Yen/DM (exchange rate)	1.14	1.08	1.20
1 ounce gold/USD	380	350	415

How accurate were the forecasts in retrospect?

The results were not overwhelmingly good (Table 2.7). In fairness is must be stated that:

1   The asterisks indicate that exact weightings given to interest-bearing paper of different maturities in the construction of the German and US interest rate are not known, so that any comparison would be misleading.
2   The reported start-up, six-month period forecasts were to be backed up by shorter term forecasts which would be reviewed monthly and those forecasters achieving the best results would have their updated forecasts more highly weighted in the production of revised forecasts.

Table 2.6.   Point forecast for variables in Table 2.5

Variable	Overall forecast
Deutsche Akteinindex (DAX)	1,488
Dow Jones Industrial Average (DJIA)	2,573
Nikkei Index	24,626
German Interest Rates	8.89
US Interest Rates	7.85
US Dollar/DM (exchange rate)	1.4609
100 Yen/DM (exchange rate)	1.1449
1 ounce gold/USD	372.63

Table 2.7.   Accuracy of forecasts

Variable	Forecast	Actual	Error
Deutsche Akteinindex (DAX)	1488	1662	+11.7%
Dow Jones Industrial Average (DJIA)	2573	3025	−452 +17.6%
Nikkei Index	24626	24121	−2.05%
German Interest Rates	8.89	*	*
US Interest Rates	7.85	*	*
DM/US Dollar (exchange rate)	1.4609	1.7431	−19.32%
100 Yen/DM (exchange rate)	1.1449	1.2700	−10.93%
1 ounce gold/USD	372.63	363	+2.58%

Forecasts by any team of experts, however, that are so wide of their mark in as short a period as six months cannot give much confidence to the individuals and institutions wishing to use these forecasts in making decisions about how to invest vast sums over even longer time horizons.

This said, however, it must be pointed out that forecasting, by whatever means, is an essential feature of the sensible use of financial instruments in the process of hedging positions. Hedging every eventuality simply to establish a stable price would be a costly, regular exercise and would ultimately lead to the company adopting this strategy becoming uncompetitive. By way of example consider a company with a long position in an underlying security. It will be seen in later chapters that such a position could be hedged using a short forward contract which would effectively *lock-in* a price today that would hold at some future date. This strategy is fine if, as time advances, the price of the underlying security falls. On the other hand if the price of the security rises any gain that would have accrued to the holder of the long position, will have been sacrificed by having taken out a short forward hedge. If in this case competitors exist with equivalent unhedged. long positions they will enjoy a profit and, *ceteris paribus*, will be better off.

Thus taking a view about the direction in which a market is likely to move will often be founded on a forecasting technique or mixture of forecasting techniques whose generated outcome will almost certainly be adjusted to reflect judgemental expertise on the part of the forecaster.

2.4 Spreadsheets

There are two demonstration spreadsheets used in this chapter:

1   `TEXT_DAT.WK3` which is described in Sec. 2.2 and illustrated in Table 2.2.
2   `TA_DEMO.WK3` which enables the examination of some of the methods used in technical analysis. The operation of this spreadsheet is described in Sec. 2.2 and appears in Table 2.3.

2.4.1 `TA_DEMO.WK3`

The special menu, which appears as Table 2.3, offers six automated macros, two of the macros guide the input of data:

`(Input_Dates, Prices);`

to provide output:

`(Graph, Table);`

one enables the user to view the names of the data housed on

`TEXT_DAT.WK3:`
`(Ranges);`

and one exits the special menu returning the spreadsheet back to normal Lotus operating mode:

`(Quit).`

Questions

2.1 Explain what is meant by a momentum indicator. In what sense may it be useful as a forecasting instrument?

2.2 Using `TA_DEMO.WK3` and the special menu copy the Sainsbury plc share price data into the spreadsheet.
 (a) On the basis of the RSI does the share appear to be over- or under-sold?
 (b) Call up the moving average graphs and comment on the position of the long- and short-run lines.
 (c) Obtain hardcopy of the track of the share price over the period and using charting methods argue a case for where the share price might be in one month's time.

2.3 Obtain the actual share prices for Sainsbury plc from 02/01/93 until 31/03/93 (Use *The Financial Times* or *Guardian* financial pages or, if available, DATASTREAM) and assess how good your analysis of Question 2.2 was.

2.4 Why might technical analysis prove to be an unreliable guide to the future movement of security/financial instrument prices?

2.5 Explain how 'fundamental' analysis differs from technical analysis.

2.6 Why might hedging every conceivable financial risk, just to obtain an element of price stability, prove to be a poor strategy for a company in the long run?

Appendix 2A

The participants in the study were:

- Banque Paribas Capital Markets
- Bayerische Hypotheken- und Wechselbank
- Bayerische Vereinsbank
- BfB:Bank
- BHF-Bank
- Citibank
- Commerzbank
- Deutschebank
- Dresdner Bank
- Industriekredit Bank/Deutsche Industriebank
- Schröder Münchmeyer Hengst Investment

- Schweizerische Bankgesellschaft
- Schweizerische Kreditanstalt
- Westdeutsche Landesbank Girozentrale.

References and further reading

Blake, D. (1990) *Financial Market Analysis*, McGraw-Hill, London.

Bookstaber, R. (1985), *The Complete Investment Book*, Scott, Foresman and Company, New York.

Davies, G. and Shah, M. (1992) New methods for forecasting GDP growth in the United Kingdom. Research Paper. Goldman Sachs, London.

Gujarati, D.N. (1988), *Basic Econometrics* (2nd edn), McGraw-Hill, Singapore.

Maddala, G.S. (1992), *Introduction to Econometrics* (2nd edn), Macmillan, London.

Meyers, T.A. (1989), *The Technical Analysis Course*, Probus Publishing, New York.

3 Forwards and futures

3.1 Market volatility

In the previous chapter methods were suggested that would enable an individual investor or portfolio manager to reduce the risk associated with holdings of shares in a portfolio. However, those traditional risk-reduction, diversification or, more recent, index tracking approaches only hedge for part of the risk involved in holding assets. In effect those approaches are designed to manage that part of risk that was described in Chapter 1 as specific risk. The portfolio approach alone does not enable the management of the market risk of a portfolio. Moreover, the risk diversification analysis in Chapter 1 was conducted in a share-based framework, it does not really help a company or individual when the problem arises of how to manage the types of risk that were identified in Cases 1.1 to 1.5.

To help manage risk—in the sense of protecting the value of a more generally constructed portfolio—arising from adverse market movements, recent years have seen rapid growth in the creation and use of a variety of financial instruments. The building blocks for risk management in a broader framework can be narrowed down to four basic instruments. The flexibility of these instruments facilitates the engineering of portfolios of financial positions that would otherwise, in many cases, be impossible. The instruments that form the real shell for this type of risk management are:

1 Forwards
2 Futures
3 Swaps
4 Options.

The operational characteristics together with the advantages and disadvantages of forwards, futures and swaps will receive attention in this chapter, options will be considered in Chapters 4 and 5.

With the exception of swaps these instruments are not new. Forwards, futures and options have enjoyed usage in a variety of markets, in some cases in one form or another dating back to the Middle Ages. However, it is since the 1970s that their use and importance in financial markets has grown significantly. The main reason for this has been the increase in volatility of markets that has come about as a direct result of changes that the world economy has undergone since the end of the Second World War.

A classical example of this is the oft quoted breakdown of the Bretton Woods agreement. In 1944 the International Monetary Fund (IMF) was established; its role was envisaged as being part of a institutional framework that would help manage the world's economic system. One of several principles on which it was established was that of fixed (pegged) exchange rates. The system allowed for changes in exchange rates to take place only when a country's balance of payments was deemed to be in fundamental disequilibrium and then only after consultation with the Fund. It was thought that the establishment of an IMF would overcome the disruptive currency experiences of the 1930s which had seen huge speculative movements of capital and competitive exchange rate depreciations. Exchange rate bands were laid down between countries which, subject to agreed adjustments, were maintained until the 1960s. For example, the £/USD exchange rate was initially fixed at £1/$4.03. It remained at that level until 1949 when economic circumstances forced a repegging of sterling at a new rate of £1/$2.80. It was not until the Wilson devaluation of 1967 that rates were altered again. Of course even under a regime of fixed exchange rates there were daily fluctuations in the rates, however, under the IMF rules such fluctuations were minimal and were within tight specified bands.

Another example of an increased volatility environment can be found in the interest rate arena. Following the end of the Second World War the British Labour Government of the day followed a policy of 'cheap' money. It was thought that low and stable interest rates would create a state of confidence and optimism that would encourage firms to invest and, over time, pull the economy back into prosperity. Interest rates were fixed at 2 per cent in 1945 where they remained until 1950.

In both cases outlined above the object was to remove as much uncertainty as possible from the economic scene in an attempt to enable economies to stabilize and grow. Contrast that position with that in existence today where interest rates are used as a means of regulating the UK economy and were changed four times from 10 to 6 per cent between Tuesday 21 September 1992 and Wednesday 27 January 1993; a total of just 128 days. Moreover, on several occasions recently financial markets have been taken by surprise by such changes. Two such examples are:

1   The decision to join the Exchange Rate Mechanism (ERM) on Friday 5 October 1990 coupled with a 1 per cent reduction in base rates.
2   The decision to cut base rates by 1 per cent on 26 January 1993.

The impact of such unexpected changes creates headlines for the financial press— *The Financial Times* of 27 January 1993 has many examples. The 26 January decision to cut base rates by 1 per cent resulted in sharply higher share prices and, predictably, a weaker sterling foreign exchange rate.

The reported figures support the headline claims reported in the press. The FT-SE 100 Index stood at 2771.9 at the close of business on 25 January and at 2835.7 at close of business on 26 January, a rise of 2.3 per cent. The £/USD spot rate moved in the opposite direction, on 26 January the spot rate was quoted at 1.5595, one day later at 1.5380, a fall of approximately 1.4 per cent value in sterling in one day. These changes are by no means isolated. The impact of the unanticipated 1 per cent cut affected all of the domestic financial markets, as will be seen in later chapters of this text, and spilled over into European markets. Although this example presents an extreme case, it is this type of uncertainty about where markets might be moving and how they might be driven by domestic economic policy, and the economic policies of other countries, that has created a climate in which the need for risk management has become increasingly recognized.

Lotus demo   MKT_VOL.WK3
Reference has already been made in Chapter 1 to the concept of volatility, which has been demonstrated using the spreadsheet RISK_RET.WK3. The spreadsheet entitled MKT_VOL.WK3 displays the daily log returns of several variables over a period of time. Graphs of the natural log returns ($\log_e$) can be accessed by using the special menu activated via the Alt+A keys. The choices shown in Table 3.1 are available.

The graphs of each of the variables: Abbey National plc, FT-SE 100, yen/sterling, Treasury stock, and risk–return are presented as Figs 3.1–3.5.

Table 3.1.   Menu of MKT_VOL.WK3

ABNAT	Abbey National plc daily share price $\log_e$ returns (02/01/1992–31/12/1992)
FT_SE	FT_SE 100 Share Index daily $\log_e$ returns (02/01/1992–31/12/1992)
Yen_Ster	Yen/Sterling exchange rate (02/01/1992–31/12/1992)
Treas_Stock	Daily $\log_e$ returns of a Gilt edged bond (02/01/1992–31/12/1992)
Comparison	FT-SE 100 returns compared with Abbey National plc returns (02/01/1992–31/12/1992)
Risk_ret	Risk-Return profile for the four assets
Quit	Exit Macro

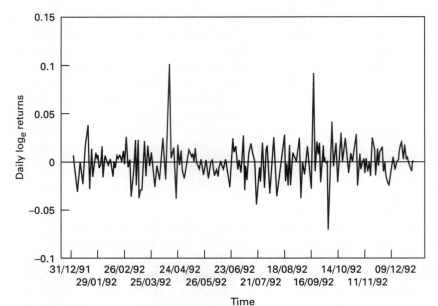

Fig. 3.1. Abbey National plc: daily log$_e$ returns

To enable direct comparison between the instruments, Figs 3.1–3.5 have been drawn to the same scale. Even the most cursory inspection of the figures reveals that the daily natural logarithmic returns oscillate far more in respect of the Abbey National data than the FT-SE 100 Index data which in turn oscillates far more than the data on the 12 per cent Treasury gilt of 1995. Figure 3.5 illustrates the

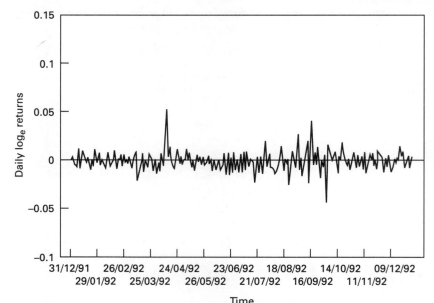

Fig. 3.2. FT-SE 100 Index: daily log$_e$ returns

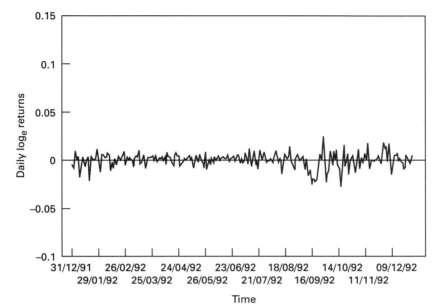

Fig. 3.3.   Yen–sterling exchange rate: daily $\log_e$ returns

annualized risk–return profiles for each of the data sets. The yen profile for this period is far from satisfactory from an investment point of view as the annualized return is negative and the annualized risk is extremely high. At the other extreme the Treasury stock shows a positive low return but also exhibits low risk.

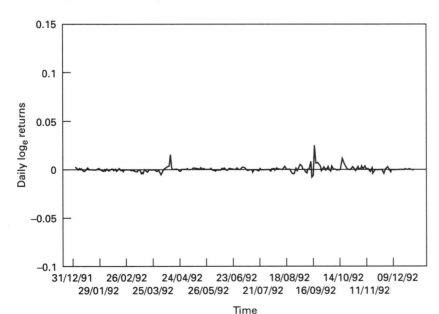

Fig. 3.4.   Treasury 12 per cent 1995: daily $\log_e$ returns

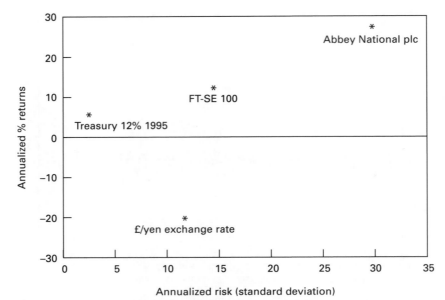

Fig. 3.5.   Risk–return profile (based on daily observations)

3.2 Forwards

Forward contracts have a well-established background as risk management or
hedging instruments. They have been used for many years in commodity and
financial markets. The contracts themselves are very simple. They represent an
agreement between two parties (usually two financial institutions or an institution
and a corporate client) to undertake a transaction of some agreed future date at a
price agreed now. The party agreeing to buy at the future date is said to be taking
a *long* position. The counterparty agreeing to make delivery at the future date is
said to be taking a *short* position. The price which appears in the contract is termed
the *delivery price*. A benchmark for these prices is provided by the FT and takes
the form shown in Table 3.2.

The spot rate quote is the current rate for (almost) immediate delivery. All of
the other rates quoted in the table refer to delivery at some future date and will
provide a benchmark for forward contracts of the specified maturity. Note that, in
this example, the further ahead the forward deal the lower the exchange rate.
There is a sound economic reason for this: it is known as 'covered interest rate
parity'. To avoid the possibility of a shrewd market participant making a risk-free

Table 3.2. $/£ spot and forward rates

Spot	1 month	3 month	6 month	12 month
1.5380	1.5339	1.5266	1.5176	1.5055

Source: The Financial Times, 27 January 1993.

(arbitrage) profit, calculation of the forward exchange rate must take account of the differences in the interest rates prevailing in each country at the time that the deal is struck. Equation (3.1) sets out a basic relationship for calculating forward currency rates:

$$F = S\left(1 + \frac{\langle r_f - r_d \rangle}{100} \times \frac{t}{T}\right) \tag{3.1}$$

where:

> F represents the forward exchange rate;
> S represents the spot price of £1 in units of a foreign currency;
> r_f represents the risk-free rate of interest in the foreign currency;
> r_d represents the domestic risk-free rate of interest;
> t represents the number of days until maturity of the contract;
> T represents the number of days in the year.

Using Equation (3.1) together with the spot rate £1 = \$1.5380, drawn from the FT's Exchange Cross Rate Table (or Pound–Dollar Table), and the UK and US Eurocurrency rates, it should be possible to calculate the forward rates reported in Table 3.2. For the six month forward rate:

$$F = 1.5380(1 + \langle 0.03375 - 0.06125 \rangle 0.5)$$

$$F = 1.5169 \tag{3.2}$$

The interpretation is that £1 can be exchanged for 1.5169 dollars in six months' time. (Looking at it from the dollar point of view \$1 = £0.6593 (1/1.5169) in six months' time.) This figure is close to the reported figure of £1.5176 in Table 3.2. Similar calculations would yield the three month and one year forward rates which also appear in that table.

Lotus demo   FORWARDS.WK3 demonstrates the calculation of forward rates for currency and interest rates at an introductory level. More will be said about this spreadsheet towards the end of this section.

It must be stressed that the quotes in Table 3.2 are only indicative, they do not reflect any of the transactions' costs that will be incurred between the parties, nor any risk premium which one party may be required to pay, and it must be remembered that the published rates are a snapshot of the exchange rates prevailing in the market at that time. The New York quoted rates and the London money rates will have been recorded at different times. Given the high volatility of currency and interest rate markets these rates could be quite significantly different from those actually achievable even on an intra-day basis. Nevertheless, the participants in Cases 1.3 and 1.4 could well be looking to such rates when contemplating a forward contract as a way of managing their identified currency risk.

Before turning to consider how the quoted forward rates are arrived at, it will be

Table 3.3.   Advantages and disadvantages of using forward contracts

Advantages	Disadvantages
Forwards are over-the-counter instruments	The contracts are not subject to an exchange's regulation
Contract amounts are flexible	Contracts may be difficult to cancel if a party wishes to close the transaction
Contract delivery dates are flexible (they can range from a few weeks to a number of years)	There may be a penalty clause if one party wishes to close the contract early
Dealings are not limited to exchange trading times	Bid–offer spreads may make forward contracts expensive
Payment of the delivery price takes place at the specified future date	A credit line needs to be established
No basis risk–exact interbank interest rates are used to price a contract	There is a risk of counterparty default

useful to offer a review of the general advantages and disadvantages of using forward contracts to manage or hedge an identified exposure. Table 3.3 provides a useful summary.

On the advantages side forward contracts are over the counter (OTC), that is, instruments which can be bespoken to fit the exact needs of a party dealing with a financial institution. As an illustration take the Case 1.3 scenario.

Case 1.3 revisited

The UK company is committed to exchanging ¥250,000,000 in six months' time when, if the worst fears of the managing director are realized, the exchange rate might have fallen to £1/¥215 from the £1/¥192. This is the type of situation in which the managing director may talk to his or her bank about entering a (short) forward contract in which the company would sell yen to the bank at a contracted delivery price on maturity on the contract. A delivery price and a delivery date corresponding exactly to the date on which the moneys are to be received would be agreed now and the company would thus be protected from any exchange rate fluctuations that might occur. Note, however, that the agreement only covers this first payment, what happens after that date could remain a problem for the company in the future.

The fact that the contract amount (¥250,000,000) is a round figure and that the date when it is required is in exactly six months should not be interpreted as the norm. As an OTC transaction a contract can be devised to suit the exact requirements of a financial institution's client. A transaction could have been arranged for an odd amount, say ¥187,692,314, and for an odd period of time, say 7½ weeks.

Another attractive feature of forwards is the fact that the contract can be entered into and then forgotten. Figure 3.6, which relates to Case 1.3, demonstrates this idea from the point of view of the UK company which will be

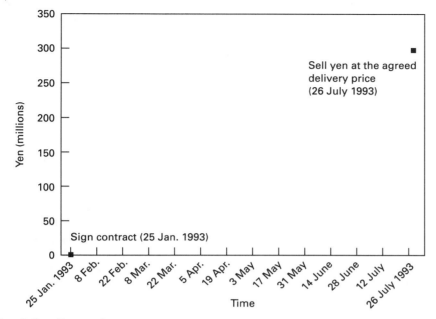

Fig. 3.6.   Forward contract

receiving yen in six months' time. There is no need to monitor what is happening to yen on a daily, weekly, monthly or indeed any other basis. The delivery price has been fixed (locked into) and will be received when the contract matures.

If the position is reversed, as in Case 1.4, the Japanese company may consider taking out a forward contract to buy (long) sterling at a pre-agreed rate on the forward date. The same advantages discussed above would accrue to the Japanese company under this scenario but in each case there would also be disadvantages.

One of the problems associated with forward contracts can be the very fact that the delivery price is known with certainty. So long as the movement of the exchange rate is adverse, as is anticipated in the cases discussed above, the use of a forward contract can be quite beneficial. However, if the movement of the rates is in a direction opposite to that expected in either of Cases 1.3 and 1.4 the parties would have been better off had they not entered into a forward contract. Clearly from the UK company's point of view, if the £/¥ rate in six months' time stands at £1/¥185, the amount of sterling received would be £1,351,351 (ignoring all other costs) almost £50,000 more than the amount which could have been expected had rates remained fixed at £1/¥192. Additionally, the UK company would also have saved the institutional costs that it would have incurred by entering a forward contract.

Following this example through, assume that the UK company realizes one month into the forward contract that rates are not going to move as it had previously anticipated. Under these circumstances the company may decide to try to release itself from (unwind), sell or reverse the forward contract. When this decision is taken the bespoke transaction set up by its bank may no longer appear as attractive as it did at the outset of the contract. There may be a stipulation in the contract that release in advance of the maturity date by either of the parties will incur a penalty. If the company seeks to reverse the transaction by taking another forward contract but in an opposite position a new counterparty must be found (this may be the bank that initiated the deal originally). The company could also try to find a buyer to take the existing contract off its hands. For this it would probably have to return to the bank market where the pool of likely buyers for such a contract may prove to be very small. The contract could thus prove to be illiquid and the position unwound only at a high cost.

If a reversing contract is the course of action decided upon, the bid–offer spread would probably be highly disadvantageous. Assume that the forward transaction was set up on the basis of an ¥8 bid–offer spread, say (£1/¥194±¥4), which means that the bank would buy yen from its clients at ¥198 for each £1 and sell yen to its clients at ¥190 for each £1. Even if in the intervening month—between entering the original contract and now deciding to enter a new contract—no movements have taken place in the exchange rate this would mean that at maturity of the contracts the client would receive £1,262,626 from the first contract (£1/¥198) which it would then use to buy yen in the second contract (£1/¥190), ¥239,898,989, which could then be taken to the spot market to convert at current spot rates. Obviously this represents a very messy transaction and it is not without risk. After the reversing contract has been signed exchange rates could move adversely leaving the company much worse off.

Although from the company's viewpoint there is little risk of the bank as a counterparty defaulting (failing to honour the contract at maturity) on the transaction there is a real risk in the other direction. A company's creditworthiness will need to be established and a line of credit authorized. The likely consequences of being regarded as a high risk borrower are wider bid–offer spreads and higher front-end processing costs.

Apart from forward currency contracts another very popular arena for forward transactions is the interest rate market. Contracts struck in this market are frequently termed forward rate agreements (FRAs). FRAs are in essence contracts in which the parties agree to pay the present value of the difference between a contracted rate and the market rate of interest holding at a specified date in the future, multiplied by the notional principal specified in the contract.

Cases 1.1 and 1.2 would be ideal candidates for an FRA should the parties involved be interested in a 'one-period' only contract.

Case 1.2 revisited

Recall that the current rate for deposits is 7.5 per cent and that the company's financial director feels that interest rates may have fallen by 1 per cent by the time that a large tranche of money is received from the sale of machine tools. In this case the company could enter into an FRA. Assume that the contracted rate is 7.00 per cent, that the specified date in the contract matches the date when the money is due to be received, and that the deposit rate has fallen to 6.5 per cent. The company will then receive the present value of:

$$(7.00 - 6.50)\% \times \text{nominal principal}$$

The basic idea behind the calculation of forward rates is not difficult to grasp. Imagine the scenario where an investor has a sum of money to invest for up to a period of six months. Assume further that the possibilities open to the investor are that the principal can either be deposited with a bank for the full six months from the outset or be invested for a period of three months followed by a reinvestment, at the end of three months of principal plus interest accrued during the first three months, for a second three month period. The question is: what rate in three month's time will make the investor indifferent when choosing between the two investment possibilities?

Calculation of a benchmark for this unknown forward rate can be achieved by using quoted spot rates on the basis of the following formula:

$$(1 + \{_0r_6/100\} \times 0.5) = (1 + \{_0r_3/100\} \times 0.25)(1 + \{_3r_6/100\} \times 0.25) \tag{3.3}$$

where:

> $_3r_6$ represents the forward interest rate for money to be placed on three months' deposit in three months' time;
> $_0r_6$ represents the spot rate for six month money;
> $_0r_3$ represents the spot rate for three month money.

This formula simply states that the nominal principal received at the end of a six month horizon will be the same as the product of the two sequential, three month investments.

Using the FT's London Money Market Table, illustrated in Table 3.4, the three and six month middle rates can be picked up by taking the average of the interbank bid and offer rates. It is important to note that these interbank rates provide an indication of short-term interest rates between large banking institutions. One oft quoted rate is LIBOR (London Interbank Offer Rate) which serves as a benchmark for many instruments including swaps about which more will be written later in this chapter. On 27 January 1993 these rates were those shown in Table 3.4.

The unknown in Equation (3.3) is $_3r_6$. Rearranging gives:

$$_3r_6 = [(1 + \{_0r_6/100\} \times 0.5)/(1 + \{_0r_3/100\} \times 0.25) - 1] \times 400 \tag{3.4}$$

Solution of equation (3.4) yields a rate of 6.0244 per cent. This rate is a benchmark forward rate and is the three month, three month forward rate.

In general for periods of up to one year the formula can be written as:

Table 3.4. The FT's London Money Market Table

26 January	Three month	Six month
Interbank offer	7.1875	6.8125
Interbank bid	6.1875	6.0000
Interbank average	6.6875	6.4063

Source: The Financial Times.

$$x r_{TL} = [((1 + \{_0 r_{TL}/100\} \times TL/DY)/(1 + \{_0 r_{SL}/100\} \times TS/DY)) - 1]$$
$$\times DY/(DY - TS) \tag{3.5}$$

where:

> $x r_{TL}$ represents the unknown forward rate from period X to the end of the investment horizon (TL);
>
> $_0 r_{TL}$ represents the spot rate of interest until the far period investment horizon;
>
> $_0 r_{SL}$ represents the spot rate of interest until the near period investment horizon:
>
> TL represents the number of days from now until the end of the far investment horizon;
>
> TS represents the number of days in the shorter investment horizon;
>
> DY represents the number of days in the year (360 or 365 depending on the market convention).

Equation (3.5) forms the basis of the formula used in the FORWARDS.WK3 spreadsheet which provides some examples of the forward pricing mechanisms in action.

Lotus demo   FORWARDS.WK3

This spreadsheet offers the menu shown in Table 3.5 when the Alt + A keys are simultaneously depressed on the keyboard:
The D (d) key should be selected if new rates of interest and spot currency rates are to be input. When D is pressed the cursor highlights cell B29 and waits for the user to input the three month Eurocurrency[1] interest rate. (The spreadsheet makes use of the FT quoted Eurocurrency rates for calculating forward exchange rates and of the FT Money Market Tables for the calculation of forward interest rates; in the latter case, the average of the interbank bid and offer rates needs to be input.) Once a number has been typed and the [ENTER] key pressed the cursor moves down automatically to cell B30 where the relevant six month Eurocurrency rate is expected. This process is repeated for the one year rate after which the cursor jumps to cell C29 where the three month foreign interest rate is expected, again a numerical entry is made and [ENTER] pressed. The cursor moves then through the six month, one year foreign rates before finally moving to E29 where the user must

Table 3.5.   Menu of FORWARDS_WK3

Data_Input	Input interest rates and spot currency rates
Interest	Calculates forward interest rates
Currency	Calculates forward currency rates
Quit	Exit Macro

type in the number which reflects the amount of *spot* sterling that has to be paid to obtain one unit of the foreign currency.

After setting up the forward currency table the cursor moves to highlight the first cell of the forward interest rate table. In this table the inputs required are those from the London Money Market Table. Once the new entries have been made, or [ENTER] typed if no change is required, the special menu reappears at the top of the spreadsheet.

Note: [ENTER] must be pressed after each number is typed. *Do not* steer the cursor through cells B29–E29. If no change is required for a particular cell press [ENTER] and the existing value in that cell will then be taken as the current input.

● Selecting I (i) from the menu toggles the user to the forward interest rate table. If new interest rates have already been updated by selecting the D key the new rates will appear automatically in this table.
● Selecting C (c) toggles the user to the forward currency rate table.
● Selecting Q (q) exits the special menu and places the cursor at cell A1 and returns Lotus to normal operating mode.

Tables 3.6, 3.7 and 3.8 illustrate the initial set-up of the currency and interest rate tables based on data reported in *The Financial Times* on 27 January 1993.

Table 3.6.   Forward currency table using Eurocurrency interest rates of 27 January 1993

	UK interest rates (Bid–Offer averages %)	Foreign interest rates (Bid–Offer averages %)
3 Month	6.25	3.25
6 Month	6.13	3.38
1 Year	6.00	3.69

Table 3.7.   Forward currency table, 27 January 1993

Amount of sterling per unit foreign currency (spot rate)	Foreign currency forward rates
1.5380	1.5265
	1.5169
	1.5025

Table 3.8.   Forward interest rates using London money rates, 27 January 1993

	UK interest rates (Bid–Offer averages %)	Forward rates	Period	Forward rates	Period
3 Month	6.69				
6 Month	6.41	6.0244	3–6		
1 year	6.31	6.0257	6–12	6.1822	3–9

3.3 Futures

Futures contracts are in concept fundamentally the same as forward contracts. They represent an agreement between two parties to undertake a transaction at some agreed future date at a price agreed now. There are, however, important operational differences in the way that the two markets operate. In the previous section Table 3.3 listed the major advantages and disadvantages of a forward contract; one of the disadvantages notes that 'contracts are not subject to an exchange's regulation'. The opposite is true for futures contracts: futures are exchange-based instruments and, as such, contracts are tightly specified so that market participants know exactly what they are agreeing to buy or sell. The contracts have standard delivery dates and fixed nominal values. Table 3.9 illustrates a typical contract specification from the London International Financial Futures Exchange (LIFFE).

It should be noted that dealing in any of the contracts offered by LIFFE—or any other exchange—is restricted to members of that exchange, large international

Table 3.9.   Typical contract specification from LIFFE

	Three Month Sterling (Short Sterling) Interest Rate Future*
Unit of Trading	£500,000
Delivery Months	March, June, September, December
Delivery Day	First business day after the Last Trading Day
Last Trading Day	11.00
	Third Wednesday of delivery month
Quotation	100.00 minus rate of interest
Minimum Price Movement	0.01
(Tick Size & Value)	(£12.50)
Trading Hours	08.05–16.02
APT Trading Hours	16.27–17.57

* **Three Month Sterling Interest Rate Future Contract Standard**   Cash settlement based on the Exchange Delivery Settlement Price.
Exchange Delivery Settlement Price (EDSP)   Based on the British Bankers' Association Interest Settlement Rate (BBAISR) for three-month sterling deposits at 11.00 on the Last Trading Day. The settlement price will be 100.00 minus the BBAISR (rounded accordingly).
Source: LIFFE. Reproduced by kind permission.

financial institutions and some individuals, who will have paid for the privilege of membership. The normal mode of operation will then be one where contracts are bought and sold on behalf of parties through brokers.

Apart from the existence of an exchange regulating and ensuring the integrity of the market, there is also a clearing house with which matched buy/sell deals will be registered and which will take on the contractual obligation of delivery. In the case of LIFFE the clearing house is the London Clearing House (LCH).

Table 3.9 introduces new jargon and ideas which warrant some interpretation and explanation.

3.3.1 LIFFE LTOM Short-term interest rate futures contract

The unit of trading for the illustrated contract is £500,000. This is the standard nominal value of *one* contract. To enable market participants to know when the contract reaches maturity a fixed cycle of expiry months has been designated. The cycle runs:

March, June, September, December

and fixed delivery dates laid down in the contract specification in 1993, for example, are:

Thursday 18 March
Thursday 17 June
Thursday 16 September
Thursday 16 December

Market participants are aware of these facts and can arrange their transactions accordingly.

In addition to this idea of predefined, standard delivery dates and amounts there are several other features of the contract which need explanation:

1 *Quotation 100 minus rate of interest.* Table 3.10 is an extract from the 27 January 1993 issue of *The Financial Times*. It reports some useful information about the way that the three month sterling contract traded on the Exchange on 26 January.

   The quotation for the contract is (100−rate of interest). Table 3.10 provides the futures' quotations which if subtracted from 100 will yield an implied rate of interest. Taking the March close quote the implied rate of interest will be:

   (100−94.08) = 5.92 per cent

   Similarly the December close quote would imply:

   (100−94.39) = 5.61 per cent

   In both cases the implied rate of interest refers to a rate applicable for three months on expiry of the contract. This means that 5.92 per cent is the implied

Table 3.10.   Three Month Sterling

	£500,000 points of 100%			
	Close	High	Low	Prev.
Mar	94.08	94.16	93.50	93.55
Jun	94.38	94.50	93.90	93.93
Sep	94.49	94.56	94.00	94.03
Dec	94.39	94.43	93.95	93.98

Source: The Financial Times, 27 January 1993.
Est. vol. (inc. figures not shown) 1378 (2172)
Previous day's open interest (i.e. matched, long and short positions active in the contract) 258,397 (252,582)

rate for three month money effective from March 1993. Note that if the current date is close to a futures delivery date then the three month rate found from the futures contract should be close to the $_3r_6$ forward rate found by using the formula presented in the previous section together with the appropriate interbank rates from the FT's London Money Rates Table. For Example:

Current date: Thursday 24 September 1992.
(September futures contract matured 17 September 1992)
London Interbank Bid Rates
3 Months 9.000 per cent
6 Months 8.625 per cent
$_3r_6 = 8.07$ per cent

The December futures contract closed at 91.80 implying a rate of 8.20 per cent.

Forward rates and the interest rates implied by the price of a futures contract will be similar but will not necessarily be equal even if they are quoted on an identical basis and for the same period of time.

Recall from the previous section that the forward market is likely to be a relatively opaque market and that this may lead to problems of contract liquidity should one of the parties wish to unwind his or her position. In connection with the 'short sterling' contract the estimated volume statistics show that 1378 contracts were entered into on 26 January and 2172 on the previous day. Since each contract is for a standard £500,000 and requires two parties (one with a long position, one with a short position) this represents total money values of £344.5 million and £543 million, respectively, over all the available short sterling contracts. Statistics from LIFFE show an average daily volume over all contracts in excess of 210,000 in 1992. Of course not all contracts that were bought and sold on any day will be held until maturity: some positions will have been opened by buying a contract, possibly for speculative reasons, and closed, perhaps, a few minutes later by selling a contract of the same maturity. In practice only a very small percentage of futures contracts are held until maturity, the majority of positions are cleared before delivery day arrives.

The *open interest* statistic for the short sterling shows how many contracts with matched long and short positions are still active. Over all contracts the figure for 26 January is quoted at 258,397. These figures give a good idea of just how much in demand the contracts are. The exchange matches buyers and sellers, the market is very liquid and as a result bid–offer spreads for trading are very tight. Any apparent mis-pricings will be short-lived, being seized upon by the market professionals as an opportunity of making a quick profit, with the effect of pushing the price of a contract back to its perceived 'fair' level. The end effect of these active, transparent transactions is that the futures market can provide a useful benchmark for the forward market in its determination of delivery prices for forward contracts.

It must be mentioned, however, that the trading day is limited. From the contract specification in Table 3.9 two types of trading are identified: floor trading driven by open-outcry (08.05–16.02) and automatic pit trading (APT) (16.27–17.57). This does not compare as favourably with the forward market where, since no exchange is involved, 24-hour global trading is a possibility.

2 *Minimum price movement 0.01.* Tick size and value (£12.50)
This regulation sets the smallest permissible price movement. The jargon used to describe this movement is one *tick*, this is also often referred to as a basis point or a bp. The £12.50 is not an arbitrary figure but is derived from the construction of the contract itself. The movement refers to 1/100 (0.01) of 100. Since the standard trading unit is £500,000 the formula for finding the value of one tick can be set up as:

({Nominal contract value/100} × 0.01)/(No. of periods in year)

Hence:

({£500,000/100} × 0.01}/4 = £50/4 = £12.50

3 *Margin.* In order to buy or sell a futures contract an account must be opened with the exchange and a defined amount must be posted (i.e. deposited) into that account. (Certain interest-bearing bonds may also be used as a deposit. The interest accruing on these bonds will be paid to the holder of the bonds not to the exchange.) This deposit is known as *margin* and is a mechanism for controlling potential default by a party to the contract. From the contract specification above initial margin is set at £750 per contract.[2] This is not necessarily the final payment that is made into the margin account. There is a warning limit set at a certain level of the initial margin which is known as maintenance margin and, for example, may be set at 75 per cent of initial margin. At the close of business each day the client's position in futures contracts is market-to-market. If the day's trading has resulted in a loss to the client's total position in futures contracts the net amount of the loss is subtracted from the margin account. If the new balance in the account is below the maintenance level then the margin account must be topped-up to the original initial margin level. Should a client fail to meet the margin call the position will be closed at the market price.

The way in which an exchange's potential default risk is managed via the margin account represents a significant difference between a forward and futures contract. In connection with Cases 1.1–1.4, Fig. 3.6 illustrated how a forward contract can, in general, be signed today and then filed until required. If a futures contract were available for these same interest rate or currency transactions then every day, for as long as the futures contract is held, the position would be marked-to-market and adjustments made to the margin account with additional calls for maintenance margin as and when required. The need to post and maintain margin may well lead to an appropriate long-term, well hedged position being liquidated because of the short-run movements running against the position. This process is referred to as a squeeze.

Figure 3.7 illustrates the operation of a margin account, and spreadsheet MARG_AG.WK3 facilitates the simulation of the operation of a margin account for up to 20 days on the LIFFE three month sterling interest rate contract.

Lotus demo   MARG_AC.WK3
This spreadsheet enables the user to simulate the margin account transactions for both long and short positions for a period of up to 20 days. By using the Alt+A keys the special menu is activated to reveal the menu shown in Table 3.11.

If the spreadsheet is required simply to demonstrate the operation of a margin account using the data provided typing L (l) or S (s) will display the graphs of the long or short futures positions respectively. Table 3.12 shows the hypothetical, initial futures prices for days 1–20.

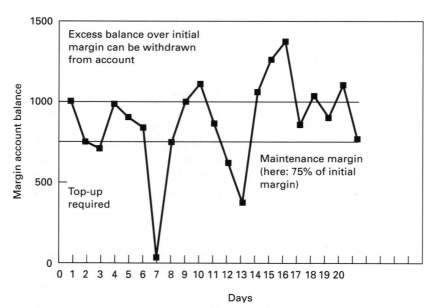

Fig. 3.7.   Hypothetical margin account behaviour: short futures position over 20 days

Table 3.11. Menu of MARG_AC.WK3

Input	Input No. Of Contracts, Initial Margin, Tick value, etc.
Long_Graph	Graph of the margin account position
Short_Graph	Graph of the margin account position
Data	Input the daily closing prices for up to 20 days
Table	Profit/Loss Table for Long and Short positions
Quit	Exit Macro

It is possible, however, to modify the basic inputs by typing I (i) or D (d). Selecting I moves the user to the first input cell of the input frame where the number of contracts is required. Type in the number of

Table 3.12. Hypothetical initial futures prices for days 1–20

Input table				Futures price
No. of contracts	1			90.80
				91.00
Contract size	500000			91.03
				91.04
Margin				91.10
required (%)	20			91.15
				91.80
Tick value (£)	12.5			92.00
				91.80
Purchase at	90.8			91.70
				91.90
				92.10
Profit/loss				92.60
Short	Long	Margin calls		92.54
				92.38
−2475	2475	2250	0	92.29
				92.70
				92.56
				92.67
				92.50
				92.78

contracts and press [ENTER]. The cursor moves automatically to the margin required. This value must be entered as a number greater than 0 but less than 100, once the number has been entered press [ENTER]. The next input required is the purchase/selling price of the futures contract. Note that both the contract size (£500,000) and tick value (£12.50) are fixed and require no input from the user. Table 3.12 displays the initial contents of the input table.

To change to a new set of futures prices the user selects D (d) from the menu. The cursor highlights the day 1 cell (initially set at 91.00) and waits for the user to type in a new value. After the new value has been entered (and [ENTER] pressed) the remaining cells in the column are altered to the last value entered. Thus if only one input is required the new value can be input as described above and then [ENTER] pressed for every other new futures price requested. This means that the D selection is not suitable for editing purposes if an entry has been entered incorrectly. Editing of individual inputs can be performed by exiting the special macro and highlighting the necessary cells in the usual spreadsheet way.

The profit/loss resulting from the positions can be examined by selecting T (t) from the menu. The left-hand side of the table displays the short and long positions profit/loss. Apart from the case where the futures price has not moved, one value should be positive and the other an equal amount but negative. On the right-hand side of the table the margin calls for the short and long positions, respectively, are shown.

Graphs relating to the newly created positions can be viewed by choosing L (l) or S (s) on the special menu.

Intuitively, if the corporate treasurer in Case 1.1 wishes to hedge the interest rate exposure that has been identified one way of achieving this would be to take out a futures contract opposite to the position that has been identified. In Case 1.1 the exposure was on the liability side of the company's accounts which a rise in interest rates would hurt. The company's position in the cash market can be interpreted as a short position and to counteract this a short position could be taken in the futures market.

In Fig. 1.1, higher interest rates were reflected by movements from left to right along the horizontal axis. However, the interest rate futures contract discussed above is indexed off 100 so that a progression from smaller (left) to larger (right) values along the horizontal axis would reflect decreases in interest rates. Diagrammatically both cash and futures positions can be displayed on a graph which has the price of the futures contract on the horizontal axis. Note that a move from right to left along the horizontal axis (falling futures price) indicates rising interest rates.

Figure 3.8 depicts the long position, which was identified in Chapter 1 and

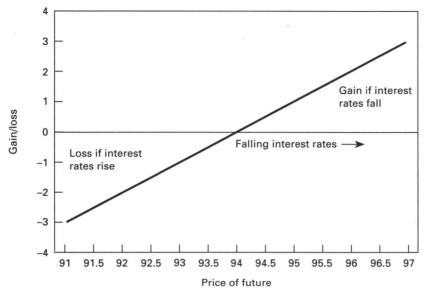

Fig. 3.8.   Interest rate risk (liability) for futures price — long position

appeared as Fig. 1.1, but with the horizonal axis modified to show the futures price rather than interest rates directly. As the price of the futures contract rises interest rates fall and servicing any borrowing will become cheaper. Conversely, a fall in the price of the futures contract will imply rising interest rates and an increase in the cost of borrowing.

Figure 3.9 superimposes the short futures position on to the graph in Fig. 3.8 and

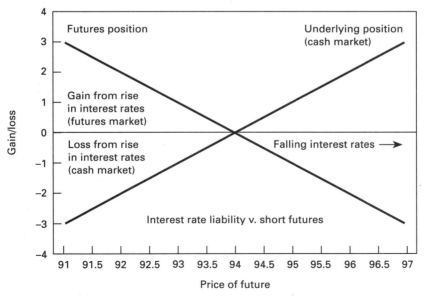

Fig. 3.9.   Interest rate risk (liability) for futures price — long and short position

illustrates the offsetting nature of the two positions in the event of interest rate movements. If interest rates rise the borrower will face a higher charge when servicing the debt. This higher cost is offset, however, by a gain from the short position in the futures market. Having sold the futures contract at a price of, say, 94 today the borrower can buy back the contract (close the position) when the futures contract has fallen to, say, 92. This would represent a 200 basis point gain which can be used to offset the increase faced in the cash market. Had interest rates moved in the opposite direction the borrower, having bought at 94 may now be faced with closing the position by buying a contract at, say, 96. This would generate a loss on the futures side of 200 basis points but would be offset on the cash side by lower interest rates on the outstanding debt. The idea introduced above will receive more thorough attention in Chapter 8.

In principle, the company is hedged for the next period at least. The figure seems to suggest that the gain in one market will be exactly counterbalanced by a fall in the other market whatever happens to interest rates. There are, though, a number of reasons why this might not be the case in practice. One problem is that of *basis*. Generally the term basis describes the difference between the price of two different instruments. In the current context basis is the difference between the cash (spot) market price of the underlying security and the price of the corresponding futures contract on that security. This is often written as:

(a) Basis = Futures price − Spot price

but can also appear as:

(b) Basis = Spot price − Futures price

In either (a) or (b) basis can be positive, negative or zero. If (a) is adopted, basis will be positive when the futures price is greater than the spot price. This situation is termed contango. The currently quoted futures price is greater than the currently quoted spot and will tend to fall over time to equal the spot price on delivery day. Still using (a), should the futures price be less than the spot price, basis will be negative. This situation is termed backwardation and describes the case where the futures price will tend to rise over time to equal the spot on delivery day—a feature of commodity markets in London in recent years, for example.

The prices of these two instruments at any time, although related, are not perfectly correlated. Apart from delivery day when the basis is zero, accurately predicting basis is virtually impossible. There are a number of reasons why this is the case:

1 Both prices respond to news entering the markets, but the impact of this news may be different on each market.

2 The operational rules in each market can be substantially different. One particular example of this would be where an exchange imposes a maximum allowable price movement on a futures contract on any day (e.g. CME: Chicago Mercantile Exchange): opening limits in place on all currency contracts, 8 December 1992). Where such a limit exists and the specified limit is reached,

the exchange can close business in that contract. This, theoretically, should help to reimpose the semblance of an orderly market in that instrument. However, closing down the futures market, effectively freezing prices and making contracts temporarily illiquid, does not stop business on the spot market where transactions in the underlying security continue. Far from giving the market a chance to settle down, this course of action can allow a widening of the basis to creep in between the two instruments.

3   The technical construction of indexes, the updating of those indexes to reflect price movements, and the reporting of those indexes. On the technical side a futures index quote will include some premium. This typically will include a cost of carry which will be the amount of interest that must be paid to finance the purchase of the underlying security (plus storage costs in the case of commodities) less dividends, interest or other income received from the underlying security during the life of the futures contract.

Basis can be interpreted in different ways and to an extent the interpretation depends on the context in which the word is being used. Later chapters will use basis to describe differences between the prices of cash instruments in different market sectors.

As mentioned above, on delivery day the basis between the spot and futures instruments will be zero. The price at which the futures contract closes is known as the Exchange Delivery Settlement Price (EDSP). In the case of the Short Sterling Interest Rate Future described earlier the contract specifies that the EDSP will be: 'based on the British Bankers' Association Interest Settlement Rate (BBAISR) for three-month sterling deposits at 11.00 on the Last Trading Day. The settlement price will be 100.00 minus the BBAISR (rounded accordingly).'

A real disadvantage of the use of futures contracts also becomes apparent if the currency example used in Cases 1.3 and 1.4 is examined. In those examples, it will be recalled that both companies have identified £/¥ currency exposure. While the establishment of a forward contract is unlikely to cause many problems, finding a matching futures contract will—primarily no exact contract exists. A position could possibly be engineered by the companies' treasury departments by taking out the appropriate number of USD/¥ (IMM)[3] and £/USD (IMM) contracts maturing at the same time and on or as close after the yen delivery date as possible. This process necessitates converting the yen first into USD and then proceeds that contract from USD into sterling. Not only is there no direct £/¥ contract available but it may also be the case that the fixed delivery dates fail to coincide with the date on which the yen are received (paid) and the transaction required.

The dynamic policies adopted by exchanges worldwide have resulted in many new contracts being created for market consumption—1992 saw the introduction of LIFFE's three month Eurolira futures contract and the medium term German government bond (Bobl). However, contracts also have a tendency to disappear. In 1989/90 CME introduced interest rate spread contracts; by 1991 the contracts had been withdrawn. In 1991 LIFFE introduced the FT-SE Eurotrack 100 Index futures contract only to withdraw it by the end of 1992. Likewise LIFFE's ECU bond futures contract introduced in 1991 had disappeared by 1993. So, for example, an institution which had decided to create an Eurotracking equity porfolio in 1991 knowing that an exchange-based hedge instrument would be readily available must now decide to abandon the portfolio or seek an alternative method of hedging the risk of that portfolio.

Table 3.13 summarizes the major advantages and disadvantages of using futures contracts to hedge risk.

Appendix 3.A at the end of this chapter lists some of the major contracts available through LIFFE, CME, CBOT as at 31 January 1993.

```
(Long_Graph,Short_Graph);
```

a final macro exits the special menu returning the spreadsheet back to normal Lotus operating mode:

```
(Exit).
```

Table 3.13.   The major advantages and disadvantages of using futures contracts to hedge risk

Advantages	Disadvantages
Standardized contract sizes and delivery dates	Margin required
Market transparency	Exchange trading hours may be limited
Highly liquid market which generates small bid–offer spreads	If maximum price movement limits operate, futures contracts may become totally illiquid at short notice
Market regulated by rules laid down by the exchange	Basis difference between spot (cash) market and futures market instruments
Ease of buying and selling contracts	Contracts may be withdrawn from the market
	Dealing restricted to members of the exchange

3.4 Swaps

Swaps in all but name have been around for many years. Originally conceived to help stabilize currencies and facilitate financial activities between governments as long ago as the 1920s, in recent years they have taken on a major role in the corporate sector. Although swaps basically fall into two main categories, interest rate and currency swaps, within these categories there are many divisions, sub-categories, refinements and derivatives. The market for swaps is global, enormous and highly liquid. Every major financial institution has its swap book which will be passed from centre to centre as trading closes in one market and opens in another elsewhere in the world. The true scope of swaps and an in-depth consideration of their many features is beyond the scope of this text, nevertheless, the basics of interest rate and currency swaps as hedge instruments, the mechanics of their operation, and their advantages and disadvantages will be examined.

3.4.1 Interest rate swaps

In essence interest rate swaps are a *strip* of FRAs over a long period of time. To obtain an idea of the mechanics of such swaps it is perhaps best to start with an interest rate example where only two markets exist: the fixed interest rate market and the floating interest rate market. It will also be assumed that there is no *basis* risk between the coupons being swapped, and that the length of the swap transaction is the same for both of the parties involved. The example will be looked at from the point of view of the corporate treasurer in Case 1.1 where, it will be recalled, that he or she is concerned that interest rates may rise before the next interest rate reset date thereby adversely affecting profits. If the corporate treasurer suspects that rising interest rates are likely to be the scenario for the coming months (or years maybe), he or she may decide that a longer term view of the company's interest rate exposure is in order. So, rather than put in place a hedge for the next reset only, he or she may examine the possibility of entering a swap agreement which may run for the remaining lifetime of the loan. It must be emphasized at this point that swaps are normally for periods of greater than two years, and as such provide a vehicle for managing interest rate (or currency) exposure over a long period of time; unlike futures and forwards which are generally used as short-term instruments.

In practice, having identified a swap possibility for a client, a financial institution will search for a counterparty to that transaction. For a company wishing to swap from a floating payment regime to a fixed payment regime this requires finding a party interested in swapping from fixed to floating. If such a counterparty can be found, and given the size and liquidity of the market this should not normally prove to be a problem, then when interest payments fall due the parties involved in the swap will meet each other's payments; the floating rate payer will pay fixed and the fixed rate payer will pay floating where all cash flows are being calculated from a notional principal. If interest payments fall due on the same date and are both paid at the start of each period a diagram of the swap would appear as:

Now	Quarter 1	Quarter 2	Quarter 3	Quarter 4
	1st FRA due	2nd FRA due	3rd FRA due	Final FRA due

An exchange of principal is not involved only the appropriate interest rate payments need to be met by each of the parties at the start of each quarter. It is essential to realize that at the commencement of a swap agreement the present values of each party's payments are equal and that the swap will have a net value of zero. (This is true for all swaps. If the arithmetic yields a value other than zero then a sum equal to the difference must be paid by the, otherwise, benefiting party.) An example of the way in which swaps can be valued can be obtained from the SPOT_PAR.WK3 spreadsheet—included at this point to illustrate some of the arithmetic involved in swap transactions, it will receive full attention in the context of yield curves and bond risk in Chapter 7. By entering the necessary spot zero rates and copying them to the relevant cells in the spreadsheet (this is easily achieved using the Alt +A key routine selecting S, typing in the spot zero interest rates followed by C to copy those rates to the par and forward rate tables, and finally typing F to move the cursor to the forward table section of the spreadsheet).

Example 3.1

Assume that the swap is required for a five year period with interest being paid at the end of each six month period. If the notional principal involved is for 100 monetary units—thus allowing interest rate swaps to be analysed for any sum in any currency—and the swap is a straightforward fixed–floating agreement then the present values of the fixed and floating payments can be seen at the foot of the fixed and floating columns shown in Table 3.14(b). Note that the figures are equal, no advantage accrues to either party at the start of the transaction. The picture will certainly change as time elapses and interest rates move either up or down.

In this demonstration the five year par yield curve coupon, 7.6918 per cent (see bold, boxed value in Table 3.14(a)) will provide the total to be paid by the fixed side of the deal each year. The calculations are based on semi-annual payments so the amount to be discounted every six months will be 7.6918/2 = 3.8459. The actual amount that will be paid by the floating side of the deal is obviously unknown at the commencement of the swap but recall that the forward rates indicate a point of indifference between a straight one long period investment and a matching time period investment comprising a short period investment rolled over so that the forward rates calculated in the spreadsheet will provide today's notion of what the future payments will be.

Table 3.14(a).   Interest rate swaps

Years	Deutschmark Rates (%) Spot Zero	Par
0.50	7.450	7.31618
1.00	7.680	7.53384
1.50	7.690	7.54444
2.00	7.750	7.59978
2.50	7.780	7.62758
3.00	7.810	7.65482
3.50	7.820	7.66446
4.00	7.835	7.67797
4.50	7.840	7.68297
5.00	7.850	**7.69180**

Table 3.14(b).   Interest rate swaps

Monthly periods	Spot rate labels	Current spot rates %	Forward rate labels	Forward rates %	Swap floating rate	Swap fixed rate
6	0.R. 6	7.450			3.529	3.710
12	0.R.12	7.680	6.R.12	7.910	3.603	3.572
18	0.R.18	7.690	12.R.18	7.710	3.385	3.441
24	0.R.24	7.750	18.R.24	7.930	3.350	3.313
30	0.R.30	7.780	24.R.30	7.900	3.213	3.189
36	0.R.36	7.810	30.R.36	7.960	3.115	3.069
42	0.R.42	7.820	36.R.42	7.880	2.970	2.955
48	0.R.48	7.835	42.R.48	7.940	2.880	2.844
54	0.R.54	7.840	48.R.54	7.880	2.752	2.738
60	0.R.60	7.850	54.R.60	7.940	2.669	2.636
				PV:	31.467	31.467

The current six month spot rate is known (7.45 per cent—see Table 3.14(b)) the annualized forward rates run 7.91 per cent, 7.71 per cent, etc. These rates also need to be modified to reflect the semi-annual interest rate charge involved and this is achieved by:

$$\text{Interest payment} = \text{principal} \times ([1 + \text{Forward rate}/100]^{0.5} - 1) \qquad (3.6)$$

where the notional principal is taken to be 100, the 0.5 represents semi-annual payments, and the (Forward rate/100) simply turns the percentage figure into a proportion (see Chapter 7 for fuller coverage).

Once each of the cash flows have been calculated they can be discounted and summed to provide the present value of the transaction from each interest rate payer's perspective. The results for this example show 31.467 for each counterparty. The net value is thus zero as expected.

Having established how the value of a swap can be calculated, attention can now be focused on how a swap can be arranged. The example below provides a demonstration of the mechanics of an interest rate swap.

Example 3.2

Taking an extended version of Case 1.1 assume that the corporate treasurer has decided that the interest rate outlook over the coming months is bleak and suspects that more than one increase will be accounted over the next 12 months. The loan that the company has taken out to finance the development project is due to be repaid in one year and the company's bank is in a position to set up a floating to fixed swap on the company's behalf. A counterparty has been found with a matching profile who requires a floating rate on the same amount of principal and for exactly the same length of time. The interest rate profiles of the two companies are shown in Table 3.15.

Table 3.15.   Interest rate profiles of two companies

Company	Swap term	Fixed rate	Floating
Case 1.1	1 year	9.80%	LIBOR+160 bps
B	1 year	10.00%	LIBOR+260 bps
Absolute advantage		0.20%	1.00%
Comparative advantage			0.80%

The figures in the fixed rate column can be thought of as the rates of interest that the companies would have to pay if they raised the required funding on the corporate bond market. The company in Case 1.1 would have to pay 9.80 per cent on paper that it issued in that market. Company B would have to pay 10.00 per cent. In the bank sector (floating market) the company in Case 1.1 can raise funds at LIBOR+160 bps (i.e. 1.60 per cent above spot LIBOR) currently they are paying 9.60 per cent. Company B would have to pay LIBOR+260 bps. The absolute advantage row shows that the company in Case 1.1 has a 20 bp advantage over Company B in the fixed rate market and a 100 bp advantage in the floating market. The bottom right-hand corner cell reveals that by subtracting 20 bp from 100 bp an 80 bp (0.80 per cent) comparative advantage exists to the company in Case 1.1. The strategy to adopt here is for Company B to raise funds in the fixed market and the company in Case 1.1 to raise funds in the floating sector and then to swap their interest payments. If this is done then the 80 bps can be split between the two parties to reduce the overall cost of borrowing.

To analyse how this might be achieved assume that there is no financial intermediary involved in the transaction, that the 80 bps will be split equally between the parties and that currently LIBOR is at 8.00 per cent. The cash inflows and outflows over the lifetime of the agreement can be summarized as shown in Table 3.16.

The transaction has been beneficial to both parties. Case 1.1 wanted to pay fixed but could only do so at 9.80 per cent by going directly to the bond market. The rate achieved in the swap, as shown in Table 3.16, is 9.40 per cent representing a saving of 40 bps over the going market rate. Company B wanted a floating rate but would have been faced with a rate of 10.60 per cent when going directly to its bank. By entering the swap transaction it has achieved LIBOR+220 bps = 10.20 per cent.

Table 3.16.   Cash inflows and outflows with no financial intermediary

	Cash flow	Case 1.1	B
Debt issue	Out	LIBOR+160 bps	10.00%
Swap receipt	In	LIBOR+160 bps	9.40%
Swap payment	Out	9.40%	LIBOR+160 bps
Result	Out	9.40%	LIBOR+220 bps

Table 3.17. Cash inflows and outflows giving LIBOR without bp risk premium add-on

	Cash flow	Cash 1.1	B
Debt issue	Out	LIBOR+160 bps	10.00%
Swap receipt	In	LIBOR	7.80%
Swap payment	Out	7.80%	LIBOR
Result	Out	9.40%	LIBOR+220 bps

Normally, of course, a financial intermediary will be involved who would also require a fee to arrange the transaction which would have to be deducted from the comparative advantage figure, thereby reducing the gain to the parties. Convention, too, requires that LIBOR swap receipts and swap payments are shown *flat*, that is to say, LIBOR without the bp risk premium add-on. If that is done for the example above then the table would appear as shown in Table 3.17. Clearly the end result is the same, given the assumptions made earlier, Case 1.1 pays 9.40 per cent fixed while Company B pays LIBOR +220 bps floating.

The story does not end there. It is most unlikely that the parties to the transaction will put the deal in place themselves; a financial intermediary will be involved and will be responsible for facilitating the deal and its ongoing management. This will not be a costless service and the example illustrated in Fig. 3.10 assumes that a 10 bp charge is split equally between the two counterparties. Figures 3.10 and 3.11 show how the swap might appear both with and without the presence of an intermediary.

Example 3.2 is often referred to nowadays as a *plain vanilla swap*. It is a

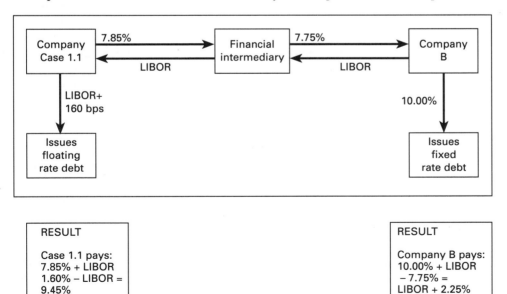

Fig. 3.10. Plain vanilla interest rate swap with financial intermediary

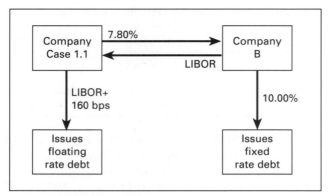

Fig. 3.11. Plain vanilla interest rate swap

straightforward fixed–floating interest rate arrangement with no embellishments. Later in this section, more will be said about the way that swaps have developed with an outline discussion of some other types of swaps available. However, returning for a further look at the swap described above its appears at first glance that the corporate treasurer has succeeded in putting an extremely beneficial hedge in place. The interest rate payable for the lifetime of the loan is now fixed at 9.40 per cent which will allow the company to plan in the knowledge that its interest rate charges for the next four quarters, in connection with this particular loan, are known. Of course, should his or her forecast of rising interest rates prove incorrect the company will find itself paying a higher income charge than that which would have been faced had the company stayed with the floating rate loan.

   The whole process described above appears very attractive; all parties to the transaction, in theory at least, manage to raise capital at rates better than would otherwise be achievable, and are paying the interest rates they wished to at the outset, and the financial intermediary which arranged and implemented the deal has generated an income. Unfortunately, setting up a long-term contract of this nature brings with it different risks. The first of these can be described as *default risk*, that is the risk that the counterparty to the swap might fail to honour the transaction when the cost of replacing the swap on the market has risen considerably. The second is called *clean risk* and is the risk that the agreed interest payments into the swap will not be made when they fall due. When the swap has been arranged by a financial intermediary it will often be that institution which bears the brunt of these new risks. Both types of risk are very real and can lead to substantial losses for the managing institution; it is not unheard of in recent years for financial intermediaries with good credit standing and reputation to cease trading. When such an event occurs, substantial losses may be experienced by the parties with whom they had been trading. It is for the financial institutions to hedge the positions that they created for themselves by acting as an intermediary. This they may achieve by netting out their exposure and hedging using the instruments described in this chapter.[4] Table 3.18 summarizes the major advantages and disadvantages of interest rate swaps.

Table 3.18. Advantages and disadvantages of interest rate swaps

Advantages	Disadvantages
Allow counterparties to take advantage of interest rate differentials between markets	Introduce counterparty default risk with legal implications
Achieves structured borrowing at reduced cost	Risk of non-payment of individual coupons by counterparty
Enables borrowers to tap into new sources of funds	OTCs not subject to exchange controls
May enble issuing queues to be bypassed	
Achieves a long time period, hedged interest rate position	
Tight bid–offer spreads resulting from global market trading	
Standardized quoting conventions	
Customized transactions	

3.4.2 Currency swaps

The best documented currency swap is that undertaken by the World Bank and IBM in 1981 where the World Bank swapped US dollars for Deutschmarks and Swiss francs and also took on IBM's Deutschmark and Swiss franc debt obligations in return for IBM's commitment to honour its US dollar charges. Just as in the case of interest rate swaps, comparative advantage was the driving force behind the transaction.

The scenario in 1981 was simply that the World Bank had approached the German and Swiss capital markets on many occasions and its paper was no longer an attractive proposition for institutional buyers; ensuring a successful take-up of any new issue required increasing the paper's yield at the expense of the issuer. On the other hand IBM, an existing DM and Swiss franc borrower of some years' standing, noted that the then prevailing US dollar/DM and US dollar/Swiss franc exchange rates were very favourable compared with those that had prevailed at the time when the original debt had been issued, this meant that a foreign exchange rate gain could be locked into by entering a swap agreement. The success of that transaction is popularly regarded as being the catalyst that led to the development of the global currency swap market.

Unlike the interest rate swap discussed earlier, the currency swap involves more steps and it is usually more complex for an intermediary to find an exact match. Common practice is to enter a customized transaction with a client offsetting as much of the currency and interest rate risk as possible using a complementary sway—possibly one that had been held on the institution's books until a suitable match could be found (often referred to as *warehousing*)—and covering the exposure which remains by going into the spot market or using standard exchange-based instruments. There are in fact three steps involved in arranging a currency swap:

1 *Exchange of principal.* Most but not all currency swaps involve the raising of new capital. This capital is raised in one currency and then swapped into a foreign currency at an agreed rate of exchange.
2 *Exchange of interest.* If the swap is constructed around the issue of debt the counterparties will take on each other's debt service commitments.
3 *Re-exchange of principal.* On reaching the maturity date of the swap—a date agreed on entry into the contract—the principals will be re-exchanged at a pre-agreed exchange.

These three steps represent the fundamental basis of the transaction. As the discussion in Sec. 3.4.1 illustrated, the analysis of any swap becomes a process of identifying all the cash flows involved in a transaction over time, discounting and equating those cash flows and ensuring that, when the contract is entered into, no excess value is enjoyed by either counterparty.

The actual mechanics of any swap agreement and, indeed, the final form that a swap agreement takes will depend upon the currencies that are being swapped, over what period of time, the negotiating strength of each counterparty, etc. An example will help to clarify how the procedure can work in practice.

Example 3.3

Assume that Company A is looking for US$50,000,000 financing over a five-year period and that a European branch of an American bank is willing to act as financial intermediary to the transaction. Acting in the capacity of an intermediary to such a transaction, without any counterbalancing position, would put the bank in the situation of, potentially, having exposure in currency movements, interest rate movements, as well as default and clean coupon risk. To hedge the currency and interest rate risks the bank would be looking for a counterparty with a requirement for a similar amount of financing and willing to take on the settlement of Company A's interest rate liabilities. Consider the data that has been collected (Table 3.19).

Spot market exchange rate: $1 = DM1.66
Current DM swap rate 8.25–8.35 per cent (bid–offer)

The borrowing requirements of the two companies appear to be exactly matched from the intermediary's point of view. Company A issues

Table 3.19. Data for US$50,000,000 financing

	Company A	Company B
Deutschmarks	8.25%	8.55%
US dollars	LIBOR+75 bps	LIBOR
Requires	DM83,000,000	US$50,000,000
Term	5 Years	5 Years

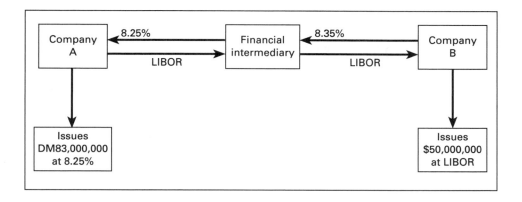

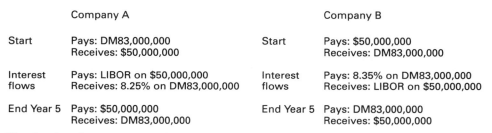

Fig. 3.12. Currency swap between two companies with a financial intermediary

DM83,000,000 at 8.25 per cent while Company B issues US$50,000,000 at LIBOR.

The full structure of the resulting deal is summarized in Fig. 3.12.

Of course Example 3.3 is a vastly simplified version of the real world. In practice, swap quotes would have to take into account the interest rate conventions adopted in different markets in different countries—day counts, annual, semi-annual interest payments, etc.—and the basis difference that exists indicates risk premiums between paper in distinct segments of markets. Additionally, as previously emphasized, it may not be possible to find a counterparty with exactly matching funding requirements and the intermediary must take some action to hedge its position.

Table 3.20 summarizes the major advantages and disadvantages of using currency swaps.

3.5 Spreadsheets

There are three demonstration spreadsheets used in this chapter:

1 MKT_VOL.WK3 which is described in Sec. 3.1 and whose special menu is illustrated in Table 3.1.

2 `FORWARDS.WK3` which is discussed in Sec. 3.2 and whose special menu appears as Table 3.5.

3 `MARG_AC.WK3` which is described in Sec. 3.3 and whose special menu appears as Table 3.11.

Table 3.20.   Advantages and disadvantages of currency swaps

Advantages	Disadvantages
Allow counterparties with foreign capital requirements to reduce their international borrowing costs over substantial periods of time	More complex to arrange than interest rate swaps—from the intermediary's point of view currency swaps may need to be warehoused until a matching deal can be found
Allow counterparties to take advantage of interest rate differentials between markets	Riskier than interest rate swaps—both currency and interest rates are involved
Achieve structured borrowing at reduced cost and without exchange rate risk	From the intermediary's point of view swaps introduce counterparty default risk with legal implications
Enable borrowers to tap into new sources of funds	From the intermediary's point of view swaps introduce a risk of non-payment of individual coupons by counterparty
May enable issuing queues to be bypassed	OTCs not subject to exchange controls
Can enable the circumvention of exchange controls	OTC may prove difficult to unwind particularly in the case of less popular currencies
Provide forward foreign exchange cover for less demanded currencies	Bid–offer spreads are larger than interest rate swaps
Enable the management of the currency denomination of assets and liabilities on a customized basis	
Can lock in currency gains on existing debt	
Intermediary guarantees performance in the swap	

3.5.1 `MKT_VOL.WK3`

The special menu, which appears as Table 3.1, provides users with an opportunity of viewing graphical profiles of the daily $\log_e$ returns on four different types of security over a one year period:

```
(ABNAT,FT_SE, Yen_Ster, Treas_Stock);
```

and two graphical comparisons:

(Comparison, Risk_ret);

a seventh macro exits the special menu returning the spreadsheet back to normal Lotus operating mode:

(Quit).

3.5.2 Forwards.WK3

The special menu, which appears as Table 3.5, provides users with an opportunity of inputting up-to-date interest and spot exchange rates:

(Data_Input);

and performing two sets of calculations for forward interest rates and exchange rates:

(Interest, Currency);

a fourth macro exits the special menu returning the spreadsheet back to normal Lotus operating mode:

(Quit).

3.5.3 MARG_AC.WK3

The special menu, which appears at Table 3.11, provides users with an opportunity of inputting the number of contracts, the initial percentage margin required (as a figure between 1 and 99), the value of 1 tick, and the price at which the contract has been purchased:

(Input);

as well as daily closing prices for up to 20 days:

(Data);

three output macros one of which provides a profit/loss table of the long and short positions:

(Table);

and two of which provide a graphical representation of the path of the margin account over a period of up to 20 days:

(Long_Graph, Short_Graph)

Questions

3.1 Outline the main difference between forward and futures contracts.

3.2 Under what circumstances might a company be happy to see interest rates rise?

3.3 If a company is currently paying floating interest on an outstanding loan that it has with its bank, what might be its reaction to a scenario of:

(a) likely increases in interest rates?

(b) likely reductions in interest rates?

3.4 What action could a US dollar company take to protect sterling funds due to be received by them in three months' time?

3.5 Using the appropriate rates in today's *Financial Times* together with the `FORWARDS.WK3` spreadsheet, calculate:

(a) UK forward interest rates;

(b) US dollar forward currency rates.

3.6 Use the notion of comparative advantage and the data provided below to assess whether an interest rate swap is desirable:

		Fixed	*Floating*
(a)	Company A	8.00%	LIBOR
	Company B	9.50%	LIBOR + 75 bps
(b)	Company C	9.50%	LIBOR
	Company D	9.50%	LIBOR + 90 bps
(c)	Company E	10.00%	LIBOR + 0.50%
	Company F	11.50%	LIBOR + 2.00%
(d)	Company G	8.00%	LIBOR
	Company H	9.00%	LIBOR + 150 bps
(e)	Company I	9.75%	LIBOR + 1.20%
	Company J	10.75%	LIBOR + 40 bps
(f)	Company K	8.75%	LIBOR + 1.00%
	Company L	9.00%	LIBOR

3.7 For those cases in Question 3.6 where an interest rate swap appears attractive describe how the swap might be arranged assuming that the comparative advantage is split equally between the parties.

3.8 If a financial institution acts as an intermediary in arranging the swaps identified in Question 3.6 and charges 5 bps to each of the parties concerned will the swap still be attractive?

Appendix 3A

Futures contracts on LIFFE (December 1992):

Short-term interest rate
Three Month Sterling
Three Month Eurodollar
Three Month Euromark
Three Month Euroswiss

Three Month Eurolira
Three Month ECU

Bonds
Long Gilt
German Government Bond (Bund)
German Government Bond (Bobl)
US Treasury Bond
Italian Government Bond
Japanese Government Bond

Stock Index
FT-SE 100
Source: London International Financial Futures Exchange.

Futures contracts on CME (December 1992):

Currency against US dollar
Australian Dollar
British Pound
Canadian Dollar
Deutschmark
Japanese Yen
Swiss Franc

Cross-rate foreign currency
Deutschmark/Yen

Short-term interest rate
Eurodollar Time Deposit
13-Week US Treasury Bills
One-Month LIBOR

Stock Index
Standard & Poors 500
Standard & Poors MidCap 400
Nikkei 225 Stock Average
Goldman Sachs Commodity Index
FT-SE 100 Share Index

Source: Chicago Mercantile Exchange

Notes

1 A Eurocurrency deposit indicates that the instrument in question is a deposit which is not
   subject to domestic banking regulations.

2 This sum is the amount required by the exchange and may vary with market volatility. Since 1991 the London Clearing House has operated a margining system known as LONDON SPAN—an explanatory booklet entitled *Understanding LONDON SPAN* is available from them. Moreover, if a buyer or seller is dealing through a broker that broker may require a margin deposit above that required by the exchange.

3 International Monetary Market, a division of the Chicago Mercantile Exchange.

4 One aspect not discussed here is the exposure that UK banks have built up to adverse movements in property prices following their entry to the mortgage markets in the 1980s. There are no exchange based instruments available with which they can hedge their positions and mortgagee default coupled with falling property prices have left them possessing properties with a market value less than original loan. At the same time that the banks were readily meeting the consumer demand for long term credit, the banks should have been considering ways in which the exposure they were creating for themselves could be managed. The exchange based instruments, abortively, introduced by the Futures and Options Exchange, London (FOX) might have gone some way to meeting this requirement, mortgage backed swaps might have provided another avenue worth exploring.

References and further reading

Blake, D. (1990), *Financial Market Analysis*, McGraw-Hill, London.

Dubofsky, D. (1992), *Options and Financial Futures: Valuation and Uses*, McGraw-Hill, New York.

Hull, J. (1993), *Options, Futures and other Derivative Securities* (2nd edn), Prentice-Hall, Englewood Cliffs, NJ.

4 Options

4.1 Option Pay-off profiles

The forward and futures risk management instruments introduced so far were very similar in respect of their operational profiles. Both enabled the user to lock into a rate today that would be deliverable at some future date. Options provide a special tool for hedging risk with an operational profile that is quite different from those developed for the other instruments. There are a number of features of options that have caught the attention and imagination of the financial community. These features have generated a vast amount of literature from both academic and marketing sources. In essence, options offer great flexibility and enable the construction of complicated financial positions related to equity, interest rate, currency and commodities in both the cash and futures markets. What makes the application of options so attractive is that they can be used as a set of easily understood building blocks with risk-managed positions being engineered step by step.

Features which attract participants and have generated a great deal of literature relate to the following:

1 Pricing of options—selling a product.
2 Mis-pricing of options—undertaking arbitrage.
3 Using naked option positions—speculation and hedging.
4 Combining options and underlying instrument positions—hedging.

This chapter concentrates mainly on points 3 and 4 in the list above, i.e. the use of options as hedge instruments. However, before developing the fundamental operational profiles of options, and applying them to risk management cases in detail, it is essential to examine and understand some basics about options.

In Chapter 3, Secs 3.2 and 3.3 the use of forwards and futures was discussed in relation to the managing of identified interest rate and currency risk. Although an explanation of the use of options could be developed along the same lines here, this section will revert to the idea of equities and will examine the use of options in managing the specific risk of a particular share within a portfolio. The arguments used in this discussion can be carried over almost completely to the uses of options in the management of risk involved in interest rates, bonds, currencies, and indeed commodities contexts.

Basically there are two types of options available: calls and puts. A call option gives the holder (the purchaser of the option) the right to buy an underlying instrument while a put option gives the holder the right to sell an underlying instrument. Initially this section will concentrate on the idea of call options, and on developing an understanding of option terminology. Put options will be examined later in the chapter.

To start with a working definition of a call option is required:

Call options (European). The holder of a call option has the right, but not the obligation, to buy a fixed number of shares of a named company at a fixed price on a specified date.

The title European does not refer to where the option is traded, London, Frankfurt/Main, Paris, Amsterdam, etc., but to the fact that the right to buy the shares at a fixed price is only applicable on the date specified in the contract. Although it may be possible to trade the option on an exchange or over the counter as an instrument in its own right, actual transfer into the underlying shares can only take place on the date specified in the contract. The specified date is the *expiration* date of the contract. The purchaser of a call option is taking a long position and is called the *holder* of an option.

The fixed price at which exercise takes place is called either the *strike* or the *exercise* price. Making use of this right to buy is called exercising—exercising the right to buy the shares at the strike price. If an option contract is held under expiration but the holder chooses not to exercise the right to buy on that date the contract expires worthless.

Call options (American). In this case the holder of a call option has the right, but not the obligation, to buy a fixed number of shares of a named company at a fixed price on or before a specified date.

The title American indicates the flexibility that the holder of the option has in deciding *when* to exercise the right to take up the underlying instrument at the strike price. Equity options on LIFFE LTOM exchange are American style options. Currently (February 1993) there are 66 options available on major companies, these are displayed in Table 4.1. Each contract, with the exception of that in respect of Val Reefs, is for 1000 shares in the company concerned. The standard contract specification appears in Table 4.2.

From the contract outline there are three main cycles listed: January, February and March. This does not mean that each and every share will have options expiring in each of those months. Shares in a particular company belong to a specific cycle. For example: Allied Lyons belongs to the January cycle. It has options with expiry dates in January, April, July and October. British Aerospace belongs to the February cycle. It has options which expire in February, May, August and November. Abbey National belongs to the March cycle. It has options which expire in March, June, September and December. Last trading day and settlement day are defined and can be ascertained by reference to the Stock Exchange calendar.

Table 4.1. Companies in which equity options are available (February 1993)

Company	Expiry cycle	Company	Expiry cycle
Abbey National	M	Ladbroke	J[2]
Allied Lyons	J	Land Securities	J
Amstrad	M	Lasmo	F
Argyll Group	J	Lonrho	M
ASDA Group	J	Lucas Industries	F
BAA	F[1]	Marks & Spencer	J
Barclays Bank	M	National Power	M
Bass	J	National Westminster Bank	J
BAT	F	P&O	F
Blue Circle	M	Pilkington	F
Boots	J	Prudential	F
BP	J	Redland	F
British Aerospace	F	Reuters	M[1]
British Airways	J	Rolls-Royce	M[2]
British Gas	M	Royal Insurance	F
British Steel	J	RTZ	F
British Telecom	F	Sainsbury	J
BTR	F	Scottish Power	M
Cable and Wireless	J	Sears	M
Cadbury Schweppes	F	Shell	J
Commercial Union	J	Smithkline Beecham	J
Courtaulds	J	Storehouse	J
Dixons	M	Tarmac	M
Eastern Electricity	F	Tesco	F
Fisons	J[3]	Thames Water	F[1]
Forte	M	THORN EMI	M
GEC	F	Tomkins	M
Glaxo	M[1]	Trafalgar House	J
Grand Metropolitan	J[2]	TSB	M
Guinness	F	Unilever	J
Hanson	F	United Biscuits	J[2]
Hillsdown Holdings	M	Vodafone	F
HSBC	M[1]	Wellcome	M
ICI	J	Williams Holdings	F
Kingsfisher	J	Zeneca Group	J

Source: LIFFE. Reproduced with permission.
[1] Changing to January expiry cycle.
[2] Changing to February expiry cycle.
[3] Changing to March expiry cycle.

As an example of the way in which equity option quotes are reported in the financial press the data in Table 4.3 reflect the closing prices of Sainsbury plc options for three expiration months at strikes of 550 and 600 pence per share on 26 January 1993.

In Table 4.3 the underlying instrument in question is the stock (shares) of Sainsbury plc. The contract is a standard LIFFE LTOM contract which is to say that the buyer or holder of the call option is paying for the right to buy 1000 shares in

Table 4.2. Standard contract specification for equity options

Unit of Trading	1 option normally equals rights over 1000 shares
Expiry Months	January Cycle (J): Means the 3 nearest expiry months from Jan., Apr., Jul., Oct. cycle February Cycle (F): means the 3 nearest expiry months from Feb., May, Aug, Nov. cycle March Cycle (M): means the 3 nearest expiry months from Mar., Jun., Sep., Dec. cycle
Exercise/ Settlement Day	Exercise by 17.20 on any business day,* extended to 18.00 for all series on a Last Trading Day. Settlement Day is the relevant Stock Exchange Account Day following the day of exercise/Last Trading Day.
Last Trading Day	16.10† Two days prior to the last day of dealings of the last Stock Exchange Account ending within the relevant expiry month.
Quotation	pence/share
Minimum Price Movement (Tick Size & Value)	0.5 pence/share (£5.00)
Trading Hours	08.35–16.10†

Source: LIFFE. Reproduced with permission.

Equity Options
Contract Standard Delivery will be 1000 shares (for other such number of shares as determined by the terms of the contract).
Delivery will be make through the London Stock Exchange's TALISMAN settlement system.
Option Premium Premium is payable in full by the buyer on the business day following a transaction.
Exercise Price and Exercise Price Intervals Pence, e.g. 240, 260, 280. The interval between exercise prices is set according to a fixed scale determined by the Exchange.
Introduction of New Exercise Prices Additional exercise prices will be introduced on the business day after the underlying share price has exceeded the second highest, or fallen below the second lowest, available exercise price.
*Except the last day of dealings of a Stock Exchange Account.
†Commencement of Closing Rotation.

Sainsbury plc. As described in the contract specification the option prices quoted are all in pence per share. The price quoted for an option is known as the *premium*.

The potential buyer of the call option can choose either the 550 pence per share

Table 4.3. Closing prices of Sainsbury plc call options

Strike	Calls		
	Jan.	Apr.	July
550	24	42	53
600	1	15	29
Current share price	571		

Source: The Financial Times, 27 January 1993.

or the 600 pence per share strike prices as the fixed price in the contract. These reported strikes will move automatically to stay in line with movements in the underlying share price. It would not be very useful for a potential hedger to know the option price of a 800 strike when, say, the current price of the underlying share is 200. The mechanism for creating new strikes is described in the contract specification (Table 4.2).

Additionally, the potential buyer can also choose to contract for different expiration dates as shown in Table 4.3, these could be January 1993, April 1993, July 1993. The actual expiry date of a contract is normally two days before the last day of dealings for the last complete Stock Exchange account of the expiry month. Since the Stock Exchange account closes on 29 January this means that the quoted January contract will cease trading at 16: 10 on 27 January. On 28 January the cycle of available options will be reported with the April contract as the *nearby* contract. *The Financial Times* will then report quotes for April, July, and October for this option.

When a call option is purchased a long position is taken up, and this may result in the *holder* of that option taking delivery of 1000 shares at or before a specified date in the future. Clearly, from the discussion above, there are a number of contracts on offer at any time—different strike prices and different delivery months—however, the contract(s) selected for purchase will depend on a number of factors not least the role being played by the buyer—speculator, hedger or arbitrageur—with an eye on the current market price and the time remaining to expiration. To provide an example take the case where the call contract entered into relates to April, 550. Bearing in mind that one contract is for 1000 shares the cost of a contract will be :

$$\frac{42 \times 1000}{100} = £420$$

Before considering the call table (Table 4.3) and the figures it contains in any more detail, it will be useful to examine another type of option that is available : a *put* option.

Put options (European). The holder of a put option has the right, but not the obligation, to sell a fixed number of shares of a named company at a fixed price on a specified date.

Like their counterpart the European call option, European puts can only be exercised on a specified date.

Put options (American). Again in this case, as with the call option, the holder of a put option has the right, but not the obligation, to sell a fixed number of shares of a named company at a fixed price on or before a specified date.

The title American once again indicates the flexibility that the holder of the option has in deciding when to exercise the right to sell the underlying instrument at the selected strike price.

The interpretation of the put table (Table 4.4) is analogous to that of the call

Table 4.4.   Closing prices of Sainsbury plc put options

	Puts		
Strike	Jan.	Apr.	July
550	2	13	25
600	32	41	52
Current share price	571		

Source: The Financial times, 27 January 1993.

table. The contract size is for 1000 shares. The quotes are all in terms of pence per share. So, by way of example, The premium for an April, 550 put is 13 pence per share and the contract for 1000 shares would cost £130.

Returning now to a more detailed look at the contents of the call and puts tables, the question can be raised: what accounts for the differences in the costs of each contract?

It would appear that at £130 the April, 550 *put* contract is a bargain compared to the £420 that has to be paid for the April, 550 *call* contract. One answer to this is quite simply that the instruments being compared are different. Although the strike prices and contract dates are the same the functional characteristics of the two contracts are not offering the same transaction, one instrument refers to the right to buy while the other refers to the right to sell.

Example 4.1

Assume in connection with the current market price of 571p, that the April, 550 call costs the same as an April, 550 put, namely 13p per share. If this case were to hold then a shrewd investor would buy a call contract for £130, and immediately exercise the right to buy the underlying share at 550 (£5500) and immediately sell the shares at the market price of 571 (£5710). This would result in a risk-free profit of:

(£5710 − £5500 + £130) = £80 per contract

Obviously this type of recipe for getting rich quick does not exist in the market. The different premiums for call and put options reflect the different characteristics of the instruments.

This argument is in part a satisfactory but incomplete answer to why all the premium differentials exist. Perhaps a fairer comparison would be to consider either call or put options with the same expiration dates but with different strikes. Take the case April call contracts:

the April, 550 costs 42
the April, 600 costs 16

why should this 26 pence per share option premium differential exist?

The answer lies in the position of the strike price, whether it lies above or below the current price of the underlying security and how distant the strike is from the current price of the security. In this example the 550 strike is below the current market price of 571 while the 600 strike is above the current market price. Hence the purchaser of the April (July), 550 contract must expect to pay a higher premium than the purchaser of the April (July), 600 contract.

Example 4.2

If no premium differential existed between the April, 550 and 600 call strikes a good strategy would be to purchase 550 for £160, immediately exercise into the underlying share at the contracted 550 (£5500) and immediately sell on to the market at the current 571 (£5710). This would enable the investor to make a risk-free profit of:

(£5710 − £5500 + £160) = £50 per contract

Clearly then the premium of a call option with a strike price below the current market price of the security will be higher than the premium of an option with a strike closer to the current market price, while an option with a strike price above the current market price will have a lower premium. *Note that in the case of put options the reverse will be true.* This difference between the current market price and a strike price is known as the *intrinsic value* of an option. For a call option this can be found by:

(Current market price − Strike price) = Options intrinsic value

So for the April, 550 the intrinsic value will be:

(571 − 550) = 21, an intrinsic value of 21 pence per share.

For the April, 600 the intrinsic value will be:

(571 − 600) = 0

The option has no intrinsic value and a rational investor would not choose to exercise if this situation holds an expiration. (*Note:* although arithmetically an intrinsic value of −29p can be calculated for this option, since there is no obligation to buy the underlying security the worst possible case that needs to be considered is where the option is allowed to expire worthless. The lowest intrinsic value of an option is thus zero.

Special labels are attached to call and put options as indicators of an option's position in relation to the underlying security. Options which have a positive intrinsic value are referred to as *in-the-money* options, if they have a large intrinsic value they are said to be *deep* in-the-money. Options with zero (or very small or negative) intrinsic values are referred to as *at-the-money* options, those with high negative intrinsic values are referred to as *out-of-the-money* options.

The process of calculating intrinsic values, can easily be extended to cover the July strikes in a similar manner. However, another premium differential still needs to be explained : why is the July, 550 call contract more expensive than the April, 600 call contract. The reason for the existence of this difference lies in the fact that an option has time value. A portion of the premium that has to be paid for an

Table 4.5.   Sainsbury plc, intrinsic values of call options

	Calls		
	Jan.	Apr.	July
Current market price	571	571	571
Strike	550	550	550
Intrinsic value	21	21	21

option covers the time remaining until expiration. Setting up a table of call option premiums for different expiry dates facilitates the calculation of that portion of an options premium which relates to time value.

Note that each of the expiry months displayed in Table 4.5 has the same intrinsic value of 21 pence per share.

Having identified the intrinsic value, the time value can now be identified. To achieve this separation the intrinsic value is subtracted from each of the quoted option premiums. This is illustrated in Table 4.6 where the time values of 3p, 21p and 32p are calculated for the January, April and July contracts, respectively.

The 600 strike can be considered in a similar manner.

In this example for a strike of 600 there is no intrinsic value as the zeros along the bottom row of Table 4.7 indicate. The current price of the underlying security is below the strike price and, therefore, exercise would not be desirable.

The arithmetic in Table 4.8 demonstrates that, although no intrinsic value exists, each option has a time value, even in the case of the January option which is due to expire on the day after this quote.

Table 4.6.   Sainsbury plc, time values of options

	Calls		
	Jan.	Apr.	July
Premiums	24	42	53
Intrinsic value	21	21	21
Time value	3	21	32

Table 4.7.   Sainsbury plc, no intrinsic values for 600 strike

	Calls		
	Jan.	Apr.	July
Current market price	571	571	571
Strike	600	600	600
Intrinsic value	0	0	0

Table 4.8. Sainsbury plc, time values of call options

	Calls		
	Jan.	Apr.	July
Premiums	1	15	29
Intrinsic value	0	0	0
Time value	1	15	29

Over the life-span of an option the underlying security's price may move up or down and in consequence may generate a positive intrinsic value for options which had previously been out-of-the-money. This possibility, however small, must be paid for. From Tables 4.6 and 4.8 it is clear that the closer an option is to expiration the smaller will be its time value.

Until now the discussion of options has centred on the holder's position, i.e. a long position. In order for a long position to be taken a short position has to be created; in the case of an equity call option some financial institution, company or individual must agree to the terms of the contract, namely, to deliver 1000 shares at a contracted price on or before a specified date in the future. The seller of the option is known as the option *writer* and, not surprisingly, the opening up of a short position is known as *writing* an option. There are two types of writing options needed to cover the bought option positions discussed above: they are written calls and written puts. Unlike the holder of an option the writer *must* meet an obligation to sell or buy shares at the agreed strike price as soon as the holder decides to exercise. More will be said about written options as this section develops.

Having considered some of the basic terminology it is now time to consider the potential pay-off profiles that holders (writers) of call or put options face when using options. It is these operational profiles that set options apart from other instruments and make them so flexible and attractive to a wide variety of market participants.

As a concrete example use will again be made of the call and put prices quoted for the Sainsbury plc share.

Example 4.3

Assume that the current market price of the Sainsbury share is 571p. A fund manager may decide to enter the options arena for several reasons:

1 The price of the share is expected to rise or fall substantially. In this case a fund manager who is not holding the share in a portfolio, would probably be looking to enhance the returns on the portfolio by either buying calls or puts. If the share price rises or falls as expected profit will be generated and realized either through an increase in the relevant option's price and selling the option on the market, or by exercising the option and buying the underlying shares at a lower price than the current market price (call) or selling the underlying shares at a higher market price than the current market price (put).

2 A fund manager intends to buy the underlying share at some point in the near future to add it to a client's portfolio but currently lacks sufficient funds to do so. Moreover, there is an expectation that the price of the share is about to move up significantly. Call options would allow the fund manager to lock into a favourable price now, and will provide insurance against the expected price rise.

3 A fund manager may suspect that a share is about to fall in price and wishes to insure the current value of the stock being held in a portfolio. By purchasing put options with a strike close to the current market price of the share, the fund manager is able to lock into a figure close to the value required.

The potential pay-off profiles that can be constructed to reflect the scenarios listed above depend upon whether the options are used by themselves—without the backing of an underlying security (a *naked* or *uncovered* position)—or in conjunction with an underlying security (a *covered position*). In this present introductory context an *options only* framework will be used.

As an example consider point 1 above. The fund manager does not hold the underlying share but enters the option market and buys an April, 550 call on the expectation that the market price of the share will rise. A hypothetical set of outcomes can be obtained by assuming a set of share prices that might hold on expiration of the contract. The pay-offs obtained from these assumed share prices, displayed in Table 4.9, can be used to construct a figure of possible outcomes that may result from the purchase of an option. An example of such a profile is shown in Fig. 4.1.

The hypothetical profit figures in the final column of Table 4.9 are obtained

Table 4.9. Possible outcomes from purchase of an April, 550 call option

Assumed price on expiration	Strike price	premium	Hypothetical pay-off profile
490	550	42	−42
500	550	42	−42
510	550	42	−42
520	550	42	−42
530	550	42	−42
540	550	42	−42
550	550	42	−42
560	550	42	−32
570	550	42	−22
580	550	42	−12
590	550	42	−2
600	550	42	8
610	550	42	18
620	550	42	28
630	550	42	38
640	550	42	48
650	550	42	58

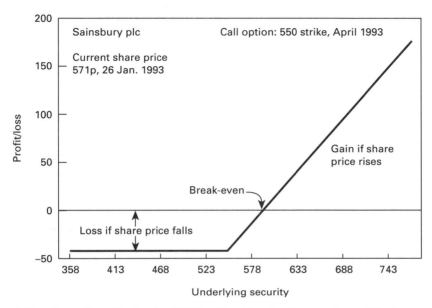

Fig. 4.1. Pay-off profile for April 550 call option (options only position)

easily by following a simple decision rule and using some arithmetic. A holder's decision rule for call options that is universally used is:

Max.[(Share price − Strike price), 0]

In other words exercise should take place if the difference between the share price and the strike price is greater than zero. If the current share price is equal to the strike price an investor should be indifferent between exercising the option and allowing it to expire worthless. If the current share price is less than the strike, at expiration, an investor should allow the option to expire worthless. In this case it would be cheaper to buy the underlying security directly from the market than to pay the higher contracted strike price.

Using figures relating to the hypothetical market prices of the share on expiration, the strike price and the option premium the following formula can be set up:

Pay-off = Share price − (Strike + Premium)

The beauty of options lies in the fact that the holder has the right but not the obligation to buy the shares, hence the maximum loss faced by the call option holder in this case will be the up-front premium of 42 pence per share.

Example 4.4

Assume a share price on expiration of 490:

Pay-off = 490 − (550 + 42) = − 102

This would only result if the option were to be exercised. In this case it would not be rational to do so. A better strategy here would be to allow the option to expire unexercised costing 42p and, if so desired, buy the share in the market at 490.

This scenario also holds for all of the hypothetical share prices from 490 up to 550. Once the share price moves above 550 the call holder reduce the premium outlay by taking advantage of the fact that the market price of the share lies slightly above the strike price; a portion of the premium can be recouped by exercising the option. If this is done the resulting cost is reduced.

Should the market price of the share close out at 592 (break-even point on Fig. 4.1) or higher, the pay-off on the position moves more and more into the black. The pay-off profile of this position is illustrated in Fig. 4.1.

When the premium that has to be paid is taken into account the choices facing the holder of a call option can be summarized in the following way:

Maximum [Share price − (Strike + Premium) or − Premium]

If [Share price − (Strike + Premium)]> − Premium then an option holder, acting rationally, will exercise the option and the pay-off will be:

Share price − (Strike + Premium)

If [Share price − (Strike + Premium)]< − Premium (i.e. more negative) then, acting in a rational manner, the holder should not exercise the option in which case the cost involved in this entire transaction will be the *premium*.

If [Share price − (Strike + Premium)] = − Premium then the holder will be indifferent. Whether exercise takes place or not the cost of the position to the holder will be the initial premium outlay.

In Lotus the call option decision rule can be handled by making the use of the @if function. Suppose that the assumed 490 share price is housed in cell J5, the strike of 550 in cell K5, and the premium in L5, cell M5 could be used as the decision rule cell and one way in which the rule could be applied would be:

M5 = @if(J5 − K5<0, − L5, J5 − (K5 + L5))

Consider now the case where the price of the underlying share is expected to fall. Table 4.10 summarizes outcomes for the use of options alone (i.e. no underlying security in the analysis) in this situation.

As an example consider once again Example 4.3, point 1. The fund manager does not hold the underlying share but now decides to enter the option market to buy an April, 550 put on the expectation that the market price of the share will fall. A hypothetical set of outcomes can be obtained by assuming a set of share prices that might hold on expiration of the contract. The pay-offs obtained from these assumed share prices are reported in Table 4.10 and can be used to construct a graph of possible outcomes resulting from the purchase of the option. Figure 4.2 illustrates this position.

The hypothetical pay-off figures in the final column of Table 4.10 are obtained by modifying the formula adopted in the call example. A holder's decision rule for

Table 4.10. Outcomes from put option where share price expected to fall

Assumed price on expiration	Strike Price	Premium	Hypothetical pay-off profile
490	550	13	47
500	550	13	37
510	550	13	27
520	550	13	17
530	550	13	7
540	550	13	−3
550	550	13	−13
560	550	13	−13
570	550	13	−13
580	550	13	−13
590	550	13	−13
600	550	13	−13
610	550	13	−13
620	550	13	−13
630	550	13	−13
640	550	13	−13
650	550	13	−13

put options that is universally used is:

Max [(Strike price − Share price), 0]

In other words exercise should take place if, on expiration, the difference between the strike price and share price is greater than zero. If the share price at that time is

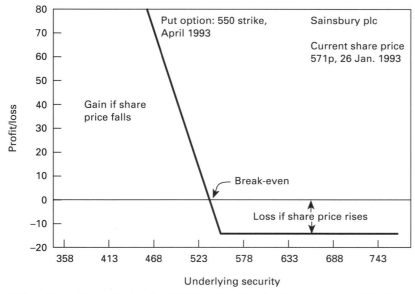

Fig. 4.2. Pay-off profile for April 550 put option (options only position)

equal to the strike price, an investor should be indifferent between exercising the option and allowing it to expire worthless. If the share price is greater than the strike an investor should allow the option to expire worthless; in this case it would be more profitable to sell the underlying security directly in the market rather than exercise and realize the lower strike price.

Using the same figures relating to the hypothetical market prices of the share on expiration and strike price used in the call example, and bringing in the option premium, the following formula can be set up:

Payoff = Strike − (Share price + Premium)

Just as in the previous example the holder has the right but not the obligation to sell the shares, hence the maximum loss faced by the put option holder in this case will be the up-front premium of 13 pence per share.

Example 4.5

Assume a share price on expiration of 650:

Pay-off = 550 − (650 + 13) = − 113

This would only result if the option were to be exercised. In this case it would not be rational to do so. A better strategy would be to let the option expire unexercised incurring a cost of 13p premium and if so desired sell the share in the market at 650.

This scenario also holds for all of the hypothetical share prices from 550 up to 650. Once the share prices moves below 550 the put holder can reduce the premium outlay by taking advantage of the fact that the market price of the share lies below the strike price; a portion of the premium can be recouped by exercising the option. If this is done the resulting loss is reduced.

When the market price of the share closes out at 537 (break-even point on the graph; Fig. 4.2) and below the pay-off on the position moves more and more into the black. Figure 4.2 illustrates the pay-off profile of this position.

Taking the premium that has to be paid into account, the choices facing the holder of a put option can be summarized in the following way:

Maximum [Strike − (Share price + Premium) or − Premium]

If [Strike − (Share + Premium)]> − Premium then an option holder, acting rationally, will exercise the option and the pay-off will be:

Strike − (Share price + Premium)

If [Strike − (Share price + Premium)]< − Premium (i.e. more negative) then, acting in a rational manner, the holder should not exercise the option in which case the cost involved in this entire transaction will be the premium.

If [Strike − (Share price + Premium)] = − Premium then the holder will be indifferent. Whether exercise takes place or not the cost of the position to the holder will be the intial premium outlay.

In Lotus the put option decision rule can be handled by making use of the @if function. Supposing that the assumed 490 share price is housed in cell J5, the strike of 550 in cell K5, and the premium in L5, cell M5 could be used as the decision rule cell and one way in which the rule could be applied would be:

```
M5 = @if(K5 - J5<0, - L5, K5 - (J5 + L5))
```

In the examples used to illustrate the situations described above, no account has been taken of the cost of money, taxes, transactions' costs and company balance sheet implications—all of which could have a not insignificant role to play in a real-life situation.

From the option writer's point of view the decision rules need only slight modification. Recall that the writer has an obligation to meet the contract requirements. The decisions are being taken by the option holder, the writer is playing a passive role so that the pay-offs will be the mirror images of those already obtained for the call and put positions. The pay-offs faced by the call writer will be:

− Maximum [Share price − (Strike + Premium) or − Premium]

and for the put writer:

− Maximum [Strike − (Share price + Premium) or − Premium]

Thus the decision not to exercise the Sainsbury plc April, 550 call option when the underlying share price is at 490 would result in a 42p per share profit to the writer of that option. A decision to exercise at a share price of 650 would result in a 58p per share loss to the option writer of that option.

In that case of the put option writer a decision on the part of the holder not to exercise at a price of 650 would result in a 13p per share profit to the writer of that option. While a decision on the part of the holder to exercise at a share price of 490 would result in a 47p per share loss to the put option writer.

In general, an option writer can be in a much more vulnerable position than an option holder. Whereas the option holder is fully aware of the maximum loss he or she faces from the outset, the loss faced by an option writer is unknown and can be huge if the underlying share price falls rapidly to zero.

The graphs relating to the call and put writers' positions appear as Figs 4.3 and 4.4, respectively.

Lotus demo   OPT_BAS.WK3

This spreadsheet enables the user to examine the pay-off profiles of a variety of options-only positions. Pressing the Alt+A keys simultaneously will activate the special menu which will display the possibilities shown in Table 4.11.

The initial entries are presented in Table 4.12.

By selecting I (i) from the menu the initial settings can be altered to suit a case of the user's own choosing, if the value in any highlighted cell is to be left unaltered the [ENTER] key must be pressed. Having

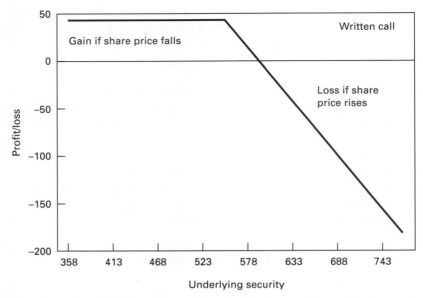

Fig. 4.3.   Pay-off profile for written call option (options only position)

selected I the cursor will highlight the cell relating to the 'Current price
of the underlying security', type the number required and press the
[ENTER] key. (Just as with other macros presented in this text *do not*
steer the cursor through the input cells while the special menu is active,
use the automated input sequence described below. The cursor will

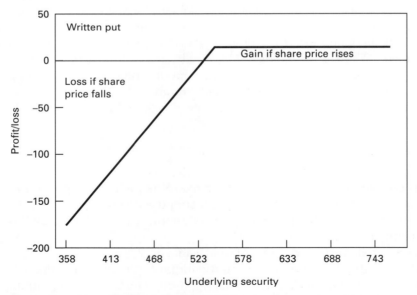

Fig. 4.4.   Pay-off profile for written put option (options only position)

Table 4.11. Mean of `OPT_BAS.WK3` spreadsheet

Input	Input Strike Prices, Premia, etc.
Table_Profits	Profit profiles for options only
Graphs	Graphs of the payoff profiles
Quit	Exit macro

now proceed to work through the required data inputs one at a time. In each case a number is entered and the [ENTER] key pressed. The sequence of inputs runs as follows:

Strike price* [ENTER]
Call Premium [ENTER]
Put Premium [ENTER]
Number of Long (bought)
Call options [ENTER]
Number of Written (sold)
Call options [ENTER]
Number of long (bought)
Put options [ENTER]
Number of Written (sold)
Put options [ENTER]

* Note that the other strike price cells in the rest of the spreadsheet will automatically be updated when this entry is typed and entered.

On completion of the data input procedure the special menu reappears.

Table 4.12. Initial entries

Current Price of the underlying security: 571

Srike Price		Premiums		
	CALLS		PUTS	
550	42		13	

LONG OPTIONS		Number of Contracts		
	CALLS		PUTS	
Strike 550		1		0

WRITTEN OPTIONS		Number of Contracts		
	CALLS		PUTS	
Strike 550		0		0

- A pay-off table for hypothetical share prices is displayed on selection of T (t).
- A graph of the current combined options position will be displayed on selection of G (g).
- To exit the special menu and return to normal Lotus operating mode, type Q (q).

The initial example used by this macro has current share price set at 571, a strike price of 550, call and put premiums of 42 and 13, respectively, and one long call option. If no changes are made to this set-up the initial graph display will illustrate the pay-off of a call option. Once the data has been altered to examine the user's own example the graph and pay-off table will be updated automatically to illustrate the new position.

Using this spreadsheet the generation of graphs of written call and written and long put options positions is a straightforward process. To do so select I (i) and press [ENTER] until the cell requesting the number of long call contracts is reached. At that point type 0 and press [ENTER], the previous entry of 1 will now be replaced by a zero. The cursor moves to highlight the cell which requests the number of short call contracts, type 1 and the previous entry of zero will be replaced by 1. Pressing the [ENTER] key twice will leave the zero long and short put contract values unchanged and will reactivate the special menu at the top of the spreadsheet. G (g) can be entered now to display the graph of the call writer's pay-off profile. As suggested above this will appear as the mirror image of the call holder's position. The graphs for written calls and puts appear as Figs. 4.3 and 4.4, respectively.

4.2 Option strategies

Section 4.1 concentrated on the use of options as stand-alone instruments. Initially, in this section, the stand-alone idea is built upon in order to demonstrate how the kinked shape of options' pay-off profiles can be used to structure special positions. Finally, combinations of underlying security and options positions are considered to emphasize further the flexibility of options. Throughout this chapter it will be assumed that all the situations discussed represent positions that will be held until expiration of the option's contract. To retain an element of continuity the equity framework developed in the previous section will be maintained. Later chapters in the text will discuss the use of options in the context of underlying interest rate and currency exposures.

It was suggested earlier that the four pay-off graphs introduced in Sec. 4.1 could be regarded as the basic set of building blocks that facilitate the engineering of seemingly complicated risk management positions. It should be emphasized that one of the big differences between the futures and forward contracts discussed in

Chapter 3, is that for the holder of an option the downside risk is limited. Should the market move in the opposite direction to that expected, the maximum loss involved in a transaction will be the initial contract premium that was paid to engineer the position, multiplied by the number of contracts bought. An important point here is that the holder of an option—a call or a put—must have held a view about where the market was going when the transaction was entered into. However naive, some method of forecasting will have been used to gain that view. In the futures and forwards arena this might have been the case but any forecast is, to an extent, irrelevant because the price at some future time is fixed at the point in time when the contract is formally agreed. After that point whatever happens to the market price—whether it rises or falls—the future price is assured. Any gain (loss) in the spot market will be offset by a loss (gain) in the futures or forward market, ensuring absolute price stability. Options, on the other hand, protect against anticipated downside risk but allow participation in the market at favourable prices, if the anticipated downside risk disappears.

To gain an idea of some of the basic strategies that can be constructed use will continue to be made of the spreadsheet introduced in Sec. 4.1 : OPT_BAS.WK3.

Strategy 1   Straddle

Assume that a portfolio manager does not hold shares in a particular company in a portfolio under his or her control. He or she feels—perhaps on the basis of a controversial press report—that the price of that share is about to move dramatically but is not sure in which direction. To make the most of this situation the portfolio manager decides to buy one call and one put option with the same strike price and the same expiration date. This strategy is known as a *straddle*.

To give this example a real-life flavour consider the shares in Sainsbury plc. The share price at close of business on 26 January 1993 was 571p, the price of the April, 550 call was 42p and the April, 550 put was 13p. This data is presented on the OPT_BAS.WK3 input sheet as shown in Table 4.13. The

Table 4.13.   Input sheet for OPT_BAS.WK3

Current Price of the underlying security: 571			
Strike Price		Premiums	
	CALLS	PUTS	
550	42	13	
LONG OPTIONS		Number of Contracts	
	CALLS	PUTS	
Strike 550	1	1	
WRITTEN OPTIONS		Number of Contracts	
	CALLS	PUTS	
Strike 550	0	0	

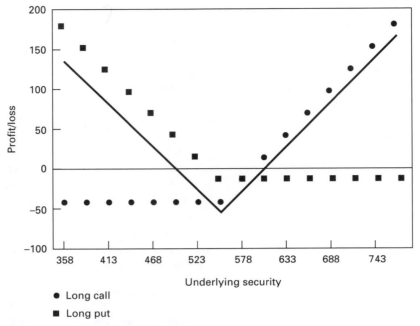

Fig. 4.5.   Pay-off profile for long call and long put in Sainsbury plc, 26 January 1993 (options only position)

pay-off profile that is derived from this data is shown as a continuous line on Fig. 4.5 and is formed from a combination of the diamond symbols and the triangle symbols. Figure 4.6 annotates what happens should the price of the share rise or fall significantly from the 571p position.

It is worth noting that by 26 March 1993 the price of a share in Sainsbury plc had fallen to 494p. If the portfolio manager does not wish to wait until expiration to exercise into the shares, he or she may well decide to sell the put option on LIFFE LTOM at a higher premium than the 13p paid originally. The call option will now be worth less than the 42p at which it was bought but will still have time value. The portfolio manager may decide to sell the call option too or to leave it in place in case the share price stages a revival.

Strategy 2   Creating a synthetic short position
Assume in this example that a portfolio manager feels that the price of the Sainsbury plc share is about to fall in price as bad news is released on to the market. He or she, under house 'rules', is not permitted to take a short position in any security that is not currently held in a portfolio. Buying a put option would be the answer but the current price seems too high. The portfolio manager can overcome this problem by using options to create a synthetic position.

Using the same data as for Strategy 1, a strategy that the portfolio manager could now adopt is to buy a put option and sell a call option with the same

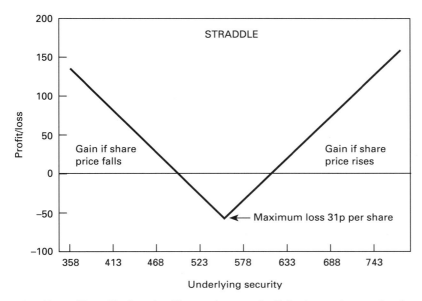

Fig. 4.6. Pay-off profile for significant changes in Sainsbury share price (options only position)

strike and same expiration date. The control OPT_BAS.WK3 inputs appears in Table 4.14 and the graph of this pay-off profile appears as Fig. 4.7. In this case the diamonds show the short call position at various share prices while the triangles illustrate the long put position. The continuous line is the synthetic short position that has been created.

Although these strategies alone do not really demonstrate the idea of risk management they do give an insight into the attraction and power of options as risk management tools. It will become clearer at this stage that the spreadsheet being used to develop these pay-offs is very restricted. It allows only one strike to

Table 4.14. OPT_BAS.WK3 inputs

```
Current Price of the underlying security: 571
Strike Price                    Premiums
                    CALLS               PUTS
          550               42                   13

LONG OPTIONS                    Number of
                                Contracts
                    CALLS               PUTS
Strike    550                0                   1

WRITTEN OPTIONS                 Number of
                                Contracts
                    CALLS               PUTS
Strike    550                1                   0
```

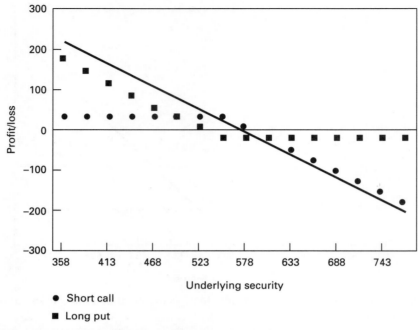

Fig. 4.7.   Pay-off profile for buying a put option and selling a call option—same strike and same date (options only position)

be input, takes no account of the different expiration dates that are available for each option, nor does it take any account of—what is crucial from this text's point of view—the identified risk exposure in respect of the underlying security in a portfolio. The following tables portray other types of strategies which make use of some of the characteristics just mentioned. Although Tables 4.15–4.17 illustrate vertical, horizontal and diagonal strategies using call options, it must be stressed that similar strategies are also available using puts.

Strategies 1 and 2, described above are examples of the application of vertical strategies.

To illustrate the way in which puts with differing expirations could be used consider Example 4.6.

Table 4.15.   Examples of possible *vertical strategies*

Sainsbury plc	Calls	Strategies	
Strike	Jan.	Apr.	July
550	●24	○42	■53
600	● 1	○16	■29
	Vertical	Vertical	Vertical

●, January vertical strategies.
○, April vertical strategies.
■, July vertical strategies.

Table 4.16. Examples of possible *horizontal strategies*

Sainsbury plc	Calls			
Strike	Jan.	Apr.	July	
550	●24	●42	●53	Horizontal
600	○ 1	○16	○29	Horizontal

●, Horizontal strategies spread over the January, April and July expirations at a strike of 550.
○, Horizontal strategies over the same cycle of expiration months at a strike of 600.

Table 4.17. Example of possible *diagonal strategies*

Sainsbury plc	Calls			
Strike	Jan.	Apr.	July	
550	●24	○42	53	
600	1	●16	○29	
		Diagonal	Diagonal	

●, Possible diagonal strategy at strikes of 550 and 600 for the January and April expirations.
○, April 550 together with July 600 diagonal strategies.

Example 4.6

A fund manager suspects that the Sainsbury plc share, which is currently held in a portfolio, may fall slightly over the next *few days* when a competitor announces a small increase in its share of the market. For a number of reasons, however, the fund manager does not expect the fall to be dramatic. The current share price is 571p. To capitalize on the situation the following position is created (theoretical option prices have been obtained from the option pricing spreadsheet in Chapter 5):

Today: Sell *one* 550 Jan. *put* at 2.5
          Buy *one* 550 Apr. *put* at 13
Jan. expiration scenario 1: *Share price falls to 560*
          Jan. put expires worthless to the buyer thus a gain of 2.5 to the seller (the fund manager)
          Fund manager sells Apr. put for 16
Overall profit = 16 − 13 + 2.5 = 5.5
Jan. expiration scenario 2: *Share price rises to 580*
          Jan put expires worthless to the buyer thus a gain of 2.5 to the seller (the fund manager)
          Fund manager sells Apr. put for 10
Overall profit = 10 − 13 + 2.5 = − 0.5

In effect the fund manager has taken advantage of the rapid decay in time value that occurs when an option approaches expiration. Selling an at- or close-to-the-money option close to expiration in a quiet market is likely to result in the option expiring worthless to the holder. Thus the income from this sale can be used to offset the cost of buying a longer term option. In the hypothetical example above, if the market falls to 560 the fund manager realizes an overall profit (excluding bid–offer spreads and transactions' costs, etc.) of 5.5 (£55 per contract) as compared to a profit of 3 (£30 per contract) had an accompanying put not been written. In the second scenario a rise in the ρrice of the share to 580 results in a loss of 0.5 (£5 per contract) as opposed to 3 (£30 per contract) that would have resulted had no accompanying put been written.

Note that the position created used written options close to expiration, close to or at-the-money options with the same strike price, and assumed only small changes in the price of the underlying security. Had the fund manager been more bearish on the impact of news on the share price then a diagonal spread could have been constructed by purchasing an option with a strike price higher than the option being written and with an earlier expiration date.

If long or short positions in the underlying security are to be introduced into the picture, a spreadsheet will need to take that underlying position into account along with all options' positions when deriving the combined pay-off profile at expiration. Cases 1.1–1.4 would all serve as useful vehicles for discussing options in the context of risk management, however, for consistency this section will continue to make use of an equity framework and will revert to the use of the Sainsbury plc share as a focal point to the discussion.

At this point it is essential to introduce a spreadsheet that extends the capabilities of OPT_BAS.WK3. This new spreadsheet, OPT_STR1.WK3, introduces some additional features: it enhances the analysis of *vertical* strategies by permitting the input of low, middle and high strike prices, and facilitates the illustration of expiration pay-off diagrams for options' positions alone, with a short position in the underlying security, or a long position in the underlying security. Table 4.18 shows the choices available on the special menu. Note that this spreadsheet will also be of use when considering the use of options in the currency and interest rate arenas later in this text.

Lotus demo   OPT_STR1.WK3
Pressing the Alt + A keys simultaneously will activate the special menu which displays the possibilities shown in Table 4.18. Typing I (i) will select the input mode (this should be the first selection if the user wishes to input or update the option information. Any changes to the strikes made here will be automatically updated throughout the spreadsheet). The user will be prompted to enter the following information sequentially (remember to press the [ENTER] key after each value has been typed):

Current price of the underlying security
Low strike price

Table 4.18.   Mean of `OPT_STR1.WK3` spreadsheet

Input	Input Strike Prices, Premiums and Current Security Price
Calls	Input Number of CALLS to be BOUGHT or SOLD
Puts	Input Number of PUTS to be BOUGHT or SOLD
Graphs	Graphs of the profit profiles
Table_Profits	Payoff profiles for options only and option+ underlying security positions
Scale	Allows the scale of a graph to be altered to provide a better view of the payoff profile
Quit	exit menu

Middle strike price
High strike price
Premiums for calls with low, middle and high strike prices
Premiums for puts with low, middle and high strike prices.

As with the other macros presented in this text *do not* steer the cursor through the input cells while the special menu is active, use the automated input sequence programmed into the macro.

Table 4.19 illustrates the initial data supplied with the text.

If no changes are to be made to the data then [ENTER] can be pressed repeatedly until the special menu reappears at the top of the screen. Otherwise input each new value remembering to press [ENTER] after each value has been typed in.

● Selecting C (c) enables the user to input the number of call contracts to be bought (long position) or written (short position), the cursor

Table 4.19.   Initial data supplied with text

Input the following information:
Current Price of the underlying security: 571

Strike Prices:	CALLS	PUTS
	Premiums	
Low* 500	80.00	2.50
Middle 550	42.00	31.00
High 600	16.00	41.00

* The call and put prices used here were estimated using the options pricing spreadsheet discussed in Chapter 5. The prices were established using 23% volatility and 7% risk-free interest rate for the April 500 contract.

initially highlights the low call number of contracts cell. A value must be typed and [ENTER] pressed (or [ENTER] pressed if no change is to be made), the cursor will move automatically through the middle and high strike contract cells.

- Selecting P (p) enables the user to input the number of put contracts to be bought or sold and operates in the same way as C (c) above.

- Typing G (g) allows the user to select a graph of the pay-off profile he or she wishes to view. There are three possibilities: *options only*, *options* together with *short underlying position*, or *options* together with *long underlying position*. To select the appropriate graph highlight the name of the graph to be viewed by guiding the cursor with the left or right arrow keys and then pressing [ENTER].

- Selecting T (t) from the special menu enables the user to view the pay-off table for each of the positions available in G (g). To allow the user to browse through the table the special menu is automatically exited when T is selected. Alt+A needs to be typed again to reactivate the menu.

- Typing S (s) enables the user to scale the graph and pay-off table in order to obtain a closer picture of the interaction of the different instruments. This facility is particularly useful for considering interest rate and equity index options where the input values are likely to be very small compared to their equity counterparts. For example, an equity option may have premiums of 80p, as in the control example used here, but in an interest rate context the premiums will be measured in basis points and may be input as 0.61, such a case could well result in the pay-off graph being readable. By selecting an appropriate scaling factor the user can zoom in to obtain a better view of the situation. The scale for the control examples used in this section of the text is 2.

- Typing Q (g) exits special menu, and returns the user to normal Lotus operating mode.

To demonstrate the use of this spreadsheet a number of examples have been constructed and are presented below. In each example a scale of 2 has been used so that the closing price of the underlying security always ranges from 342.60p to 799.40p. The basic input data is the control data described above. The examples examined are cases where a portfolio has been constructed using options either alone or together with an underlying security. Each of Strategies 3 to 6 may be regarded as risk management situations. The examples used as illustrations are not an exhaustive list and the diagrams obtained using the strategies suggested may equally well have been obtained by using other combinations of options and/or the underlying security; Strategy 7 illustrates this point in connection with the construction of a straddle.

Strategy 3 Bullish vertical spread—options only

In this example a portfolio manager suspects that the price of the Sainsbury share is about to rise and would like to benefit from that rise but feels that the price of a long call is too expensive. In order to recoup some of the cost of the long call with a low strike (500) the portfolio manager writes a call with a high strike (600). Assuming no bid–offer spread the cost of the long call is reduced from 80p to 64p. Notice that should the forecast of a rise in the price of the share prove incorrect the potential loss faced by the portfolio manager is limited to this 64p premium. There is, however, a downside to this strategy, namely, if the forecast proves correct the maximum pay-off to the portfolio manager will be limited to 36p (refer to table of results on the spreadsheet). Some of the upside profit potential has been forgone by writing the call with a high strike and thereby obtaining the long call at a cheaper premium.

The OPT_STR1.WK3 basic data, closing price of the underlying security and the graphs on this strategy appear in Table 4.20 and Figs. 4.8 and 4.9.

Strategy 4 Butterfly spread—options only

This strategy would enable a portfolio manager to benefit from a market where little movement is taking place; a case where volatility is very low. In a

Table 4.20. The OPT_STR1.WK3 basic data and closing prices for strategy 3

				Closing Price (Underlying)
Input the following information:				
Current Price of the underlying security: 571				
				342.60
		Premiums		365.44
Strike Prices:		CALLS	PUTS	388.28
Low	500	80.00	2.50	411.12
Middle	550	42.00	31.00	433.96
High	600	16.00	41.00	456.80
				479.64
				502.48
LONG OPTIONS		Number of		525.32
		Contracts		548.16
		CALLS	PUTS	571.00
Low	500	1	0	593.84
Middle	550	0	0	616.68
High	600	0	0	639.52
				662.36
				685.20
SHORT		Number of		708.04
		Contracts		730.88
		CALLS	PUTS	753.72
Low	500	0	0	776.56
Middle	550	0	0	799.40
High	600	1	0	

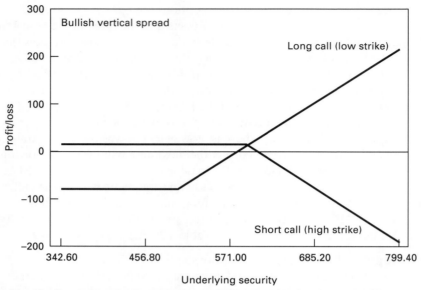

Fig. 4.8.   Profit profile of long call (low strike) and short call (high strike)

risk management context it is a strategy which could be adopted by option market-makers/traders as a way of minimizing the downside risk of their exposure.

Adopting the viewpoint of a portfolio manager and assuming that the Sainsbury plc share price is moving sluggishly on the market, he or she can pick up a profit in the form of premiums received from writing calls (puts)

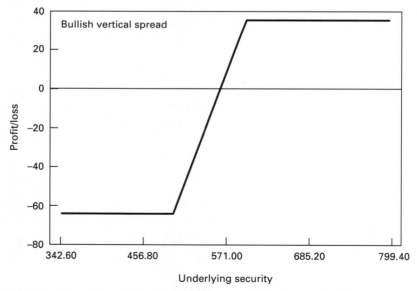

Fig. 4.9.   Profit profile of combined options position (no underlying security)

while, at the same time, minimizing any downside risk by buying calls (puts) as illustrated in Table 4.21.

If the strategy suggested in Table 4.21 (buy one call with a low strike, one call with a high strike, and write two calls with a strike in between the two) is adopted the maximum pay-off will be approximately 36p, and the maximum loss will be limited to 12p (refer to the `Table_Profits` on the spreadsheet) whether the share price unexpectedly moves sharply up or down. Should the share price move sharply lower and drop, say, to below 500p all of the long call options held by the portfolio manager will expire worthless and premiums of 96p will have been lost. On the other hand the written options, of which the portfolio manager holds two, will also have expired worthless to their holder but will have generated an income of 84p (again assuming no bid–offer spread) to the writer; a difference of 12p. Should the share price move sharply upwards, to 600p or over, the portfolio manager stands to gain from the position held in long calls but will lose out on the two written calls. The gains on the long positions will offset the loss on the written position and the worst case scenario, again, is a loss of 12p.

The `OPT_STR1.WK3` basic data, closing price of the underlying security and the graphs of this strategy appear in Table 4.21 and Figs. 4.10 and 4.11.

Table 4.21.   The `OPT_STR1.WK3` basic data for strategy 4

Input the following information:			Closing Price (Underlying)
Current Price of the underlying security: 571			
			342.60
			365.44
	Premiums		388.28
Strike Prices:	CALLS	PUTS	411.12
Low 500	80.00	2.50	433.96
Middle 550	42.00	31.00	456.80
High 600	16.00	41.00	479.64
			502.48
LONG OPTIONS	Number of		525.32
	Contracts		548.16
	CALLS	PUTS	571.00
Low 500	1	0	593.84
Middle 550	0	0	616.68
High 600	1	0	639.52
			662.36
			685.20
SHORT	Number of		708.04
	Contracts		730.88
	CALLS	PUTS	753.72
Low 500	0	0	776.56
Middle 550	2	0	799.40
High 600	0	0	

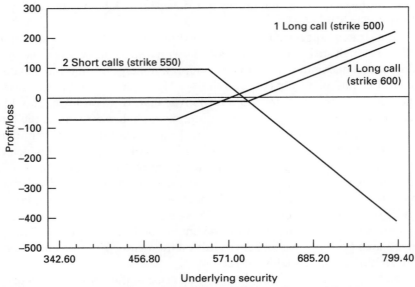

Fig. 4.10.   Profit profile of butterfly spread (options only position)

Strategy 5   Long the underlying security and long put option
In this example the portfolio manager holds the Sainsbury plc share in a
portfolio and suspects that the share price is about to fall. To protect the
value of the portfolio a put option is bought at a strike of 550. The
long underlying position and the long put are shown in Fig. 4.12. The
synthetic call position created by combining the long put and long

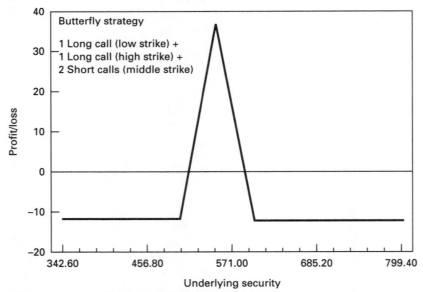

Fig. 4.11.   Profit profile of butterfly spread (options only position)

underlying position is illustrated in Fig. 4.13.

If the forecast of a falling share price is incorrect the maximum loss faced by the fund manager is the cost of the put premium, namely 31p per share (refer to the `Table_Profits` on the spreadsheet to see the numerical outcomes of this position). The share, however, will still be held in the portfolio and will benefit from the rise in the share's price in the market. If the forecast proves to be correct the portfolio manager has a hedged position and can put the shares onto the market at, in this example, the contract strike price of 550 (see Table 4.22 for the control data for this example).

The `OPT_STR1.WK3` basic data, closing price of the underlying security and the graphs of this strategy appear in Table 4.22 and Figs. 4.12 and 4.13.

Strategy 6   Short the underlying security and long call option

Here the portfolio manager has sold the Sainsbury plc share in anticipation that the share's price will fall. To hedge the position, in case the forecast proves incorrect, he or she purchases a call option at a 550 strike and effectively creates a synthetic long put. If the share price falls the combined position on Fig. 4.15 shows the gain to the portfolio manager. If the share price rises, exercise of the long call ensures that the share can be bought for 550 to

Table 4.22.   Control data for Strategy 5

Input the following information:				Closing Price
Current Price of the underlying security:		571		(Underlying)
				342.60
		Premiums		365.44
Strike Prices:		CALLS	PUTS	388.28
Low	500	80.00	2.50	411.12
Middle	550	42.00	31.00	433.96
High	600	16.00	41.00	456.80
				479.64
				502.48
LONG OPTIONS		Number of		525.32
		Contracts		548.16
		CALLS	PUTS	571.00
Low	500	0	0	593.84
Middle	550	0	1	616.68
High	600	0	0	639.52
				662.36
				685.20
SHORT		Number of		708.04
		Contracts		730.88
		CALLS	PUTS	753.72
Low	500	0	0	776.56
Middle	550	0	0	799.40
High	600	0	0	

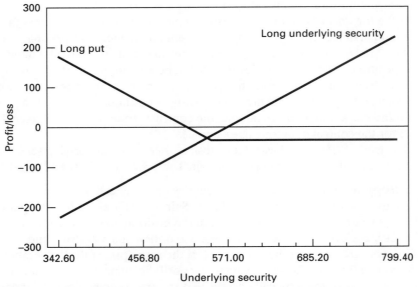

Fig. 4.12.   Profit profile of long put and long underlying position

be delivered into the short contract as required. The maximum downside loss
is thus limited to the call's premium of 42p per share (refer to
`Table_Profits` on the spreadsheet for details of the numerical pay-off of
this position).

The `OPT_STR1.WK3` basic data, closing price of the underlying security and
the graphs of this strategy appear in Table 4.23 and Figs. 4.14 and 4.15.

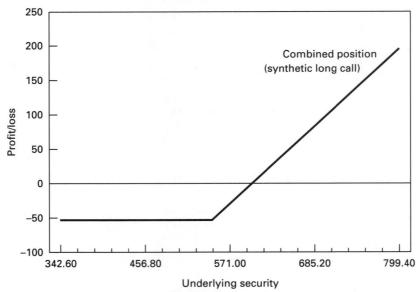

Fig. 4.13.   Profit profile of combined options and long underlying position

Table 4.23.   Basic data for Strategy 6

```
Input the following information:              Closing
                                               Price
Current Price of the underlying security:  571 (Underlying)
                                               342.60
                          Premiums             365.44
Strike Prices:      CALLS      PUTS            388.28
Low        500      80.00      2.50            411.12
Middle     550      42.00     31.00            433.96
High       600      16.00     41.00            456.80
                                               479.64
LONG OPTIONS              Number of            502.48
                         Contracts             525.32
                    CALLS      PUTS            548.16
                                               571.00
Low        500        0          0             593.84
Middle     550        1          0             616.68
High       600        0          0             639.52
                                               662.36
SHORT                    Number of            685.20
                         Contracts             708.04
                    CALLS      PUTS            730.88
                                               753.72
Low        500        0          0             776.56
Middle     550        0          0             799.40
High       600        0          0
```

Strategy 7   Long the underlying security and long two puts (with the same
strike)—straddle

In this case the portfolio manager suspects that the share price is about to
move dramatically but is unsure in which direction. The purchase of two puts
with a middle strike price replicates the same position, graphically, as Strategy
1 above. If the share price moves sharply higher the long position in the
underlying security will show a profit and the puts will expire worthless. If the
share price falls sharply the underlying security will lose value but two
contracts can be put on to the market at a strike of 550 and will show a profit.
For detailed numerical results of the pay-offs refer to the `Table_Profits`
section of the special menu.

The `OPT_STR1.WK3` basic data, closing price of the underlying security and
the graphs of this strategy appear in Table 4.24 and Figs. 4.16 and 4.17.

The entries in Table 4.25 summarize the advantages and disadvantages of using
exchange-based options to hedge an underlying position.

Perhaps the most important disadvantage in the use of options is the effect on
premiums in a volatile market. Like most investment decisions timing is crucial. In
some cases markets react sluggishly to news, good or bad, giving a shrewd, or

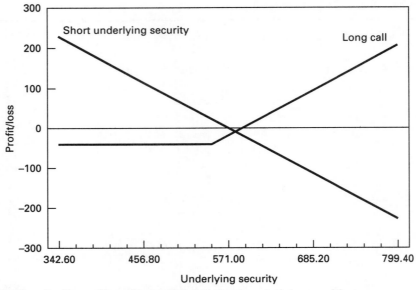

Fig. 4.14.   Profit profiles of long call and short underlying position

simply lucky, investor the opportunity to get in or out of a position before the true impact of that news is felt. More often than not though markets will have anticipated events and the market prices prevailing for affected instruments will, at the moment the news is released, already reflect the fact. Given the high gearing of options this can be most unfortunate for the hedger since premiums will rise very rapidly.

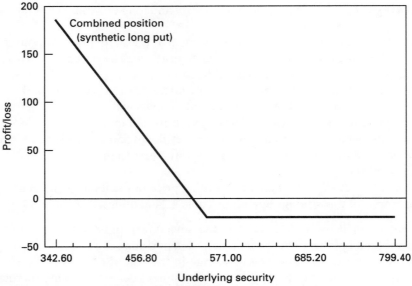

Fig. 4.15.   Profit profile of combined options and short underlying position

Table 4.24.   Basic data for Strategy 7

				Closing Price (Underlying)
Input the following information:				
Current Price of the underlying security:		571		
				342.60
	Premiums			365.44
Strike Prices:	CALLS	PUTS		388.28
Low	500	80.00	2.50	411.12
Middle	550	42.00	31.00	433.96
High	600	16.00	41.00	456.80
				479.64
				502.48
LONG OPTIONS	Number of Contracts			525.32
				548.16
	CALLS	PUTS		571.00
Low	500	0	0	593.84
Middle	550	0	2	616.68
High	600	0	0	639.52
				662.36
				685.20
SHORT	Number of Contracts			708.04
				730.88
	CALLS	PUTS		753.72
Low	500	0	0	776.56
Middle	550	0	0	799.40
High	600	0	0	

Example 4.7

During the breakfast briefing session a fund manager is advised by his or her economists that the latest round of international arms talks is likely to conclude in an agreement that expenditure on armaments be reduced worldwide. It is felt that subsequent cuts will be large and that shares in several arms-related companies, already trading nervously, will fall dramatically. One share which the fund manager holds in his or her portfolio and about which he or she is concerned is currently priced at 544p, technical analysts suggest a first support level of 520p and suggest that once that level is breached a drop to as low as 425p is quite probable.

Immediately following the briefing session the fund manager checks the put option price for the contract with the closest expiry date. The premium is 1.5p, calculated on the basis of an interest rate of 8 per cent, 25 days to expiration of the contract, strike of 525 and annualized volatility of 15 per cent. Later in the morning the share price has fallen slightly to 538p but the option premium has now risen to 7p. Two things have worked against the fund manager here: the option has moved closer to an at-the-money position and options' traders have anticipated the outcome of the talks and have lifted

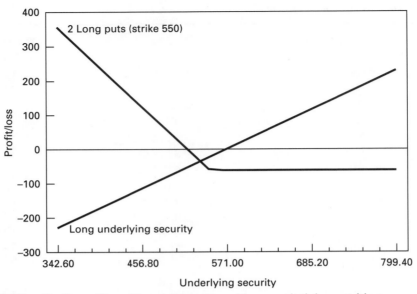

Fig. 4.16.   Profit profiles of two long puts and long underlying position

volatility from 15 per cent to 25 per cent. If the bid–offer spread is also taken into account the position will be even worse. Initially at a premium of 1.5p the spread might have been 0.5–2.5p, later in the day the bid–offer spread might look more like 5–9p. Taking a negative view and assuming that the decision to buy a put option is delayed, one contract, at a later point in the day, may cost £90 as opposed to £15 at breakfast time. Of course, from a more positive point

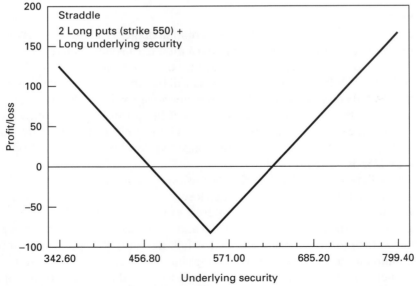

Fig. 4.17.   Profit profile of combined options and long underlying position

Table 4.25. Exchange-based options

Advantages	Disadvantages
Very flexible instruments, can be combined easily to create desired pay-off strategies	Highly geared, premiums can be lost rapidly in a volatile market
Limit downside risk but allow participation in gains from a rising or falling market	Premiums increase in a volatile market
Many strike prices and delivery dates available	Bid-offer spreads widen in a volatile market
Risk-neutral positions can be maintained using dynamic hedging strategies (refer to Chapter 5)	Dynamic hedging can be expensive, especially in transaction costs
Most contracts are highly liquid	Margin is required on written (short) positions
Market regulated by an exchange	Written options may suffer from early assignment

of view, a large profit would have accrued very quickly had the option been bought immediately at breakfast time.

Chapter 5 will look in depth at how the option premiums used in Example 4.7 were obtained.

4.3 Spreadsheets

There are demonstration spreadsheets used in this chapter:

1 OPT_BAS.WK3 which is described in Sec. 4.1 and whose special menu is illustrated in Table 4.11.
2 OPT_STR1.WK3 which is discussed in Sec. 4.2 and whose special menu appears as Table 4.18.

4.3.1 OPT_BAS.WK3

The special menu, which appears as Table 4.11, provides users with an opportunity of inputting call and put premiums, a strike price, current underlying price, and number of long and short contracts:

(Input);

obtaining graphs of the pay-off profiles:

(Graphs);

or output in the form of numerical results:

(Table_Profits);

and a final macro which exits the special menu returning the spreadsheet back to normal Lotus operating mode:

(Quit).

4.3.2 OPT_STR1.WK3

The special menu, which appears as Table 4.18, provides users with an opportunity of inputting call and put premiums for high, middle and low strike prices and current underlying price:

(Input);

number of long and short call contracts:

(Calls);

number of long and short put contracts:

(Puts);

output in the form of numerical results:

(Table_Profits);

obtaining graphs of the pay-off profiles:

(Graphs);

obtaining a good pictorial representation of the pay-off profile by scaling the graph:

(Scale);

and a final macro which exits the special menu returning the spreadsheet back to normal Lotus operating mode:

(Quit).

Questions

4.1 Using the spreadsheet OPT_STR1.WK3 and the control data that it contains obtain:
(a) a put writer's profile;
(b) a call writer's profile.

4.2 Explain whether the following calls are in-, at- or out-of-the-money:

	Strike	Oct.
ABC plc	460	45
(502)	500	10
	550	2.5

4.3 Given the information below calculate:
(a) the option's intrinsic value;
(b) the option's time value (time value over parity).

Current	Strike	Apr.	July	Oct.
Share	300	43	46	57
Price: 339	330	19	27	36
	360	5	14	21

4.4 What is a short straddle? Under which circumstances might it be used?

4.5 Using OPT_STR1.WK3 and the control data that it contains:
(a) Construct a short butterfly with the following strategy: buy two calls with a strike of 550, write one call with a strike of 500, write one call with a strike of 600.
(b) How could a similar strategy have been constructed using puts?
(c) What might have been the scenario underpinning the adoption of this type of strategy?

4.6 Using the additional data at the end of this question find the numerical pay-off profiles of the following strategies:
(a) Buy one call with a low strike and write one call with a high strike.
(The combined result is a bullish vertical spread.)
(b) Buy one call with a high strike and write one call with a low strike.
(The combined result is a bearish vertical spread.)
(c) Buy one put with a low strike and write one put with a high strike.
(What name would you give to this combination?)
(d) Buy one put with a high strike and write one put with a low strike.
(What name would you give to this combination?)

Additional information:

	Premiums	
Strike	Calls	Puts
80	23	½
100	5	5
130	½	33

Current price of the underlying security is 100.

4.7 Use OPT_STR1.WK3 to obtain graphs of the vertical strategies described in Question 4.6(a)–(d) above.

4.8 Again using the data provided in Question 4.6, find the numerical pay-off of combining a long position in the underlying security with a short put option for different closing prices of the underlying security.

4.9   Obtain a graph of the pay-off in Question 4.8.

4.10 A call ratio backspread has a particularly interesting profile. It may be constructed in a number of ways, for example, writing one call with a low strike price and buying two calls with a high strike price. Using the control data on OPT_STR1.WK3 obtain this profile and discuss in what situations it might be employed.

4.11 From the financial pages of one of today's newspapers select one share and construct a vertical options only strategy around a price scenario that you feel appropriate for that share.

4.12 Describe what is meant by a 'horizontal strategy'? How might this work in practice?

4.13 Describe what is meant by a 'diagonal strategy'? How might this work in practice?

References and further reading

Cox, J.C. and Rubinstein, M. (1985), *Options Markets*, Prentice-Hall, Englewood Cliff, NJ.

Dubofsky, D. (1992), *Options and Financial Futures: Valuation and Use*, McGraw-Hill, New York.

Elton, E.J. and Gruber, M.J. (1991), *Modern Portfolio Theory and Investment Analysis* (4th edn), New York.

Hull, J. (1993), *Options, Futures and other Derivative Securities* (2nd edn), Prentice-Hall, Englewood Cliffs.

5 Options pricing and hedge ratios

5.1 Black–Scholes option pricing

Most certainly the best known option pricing model is that developed by Fischer Black and Myron Scholes and which first appeared in academic literature in 1973. Since it was first introduced to the financial community the basic Black–Scholes (BS) option pricing model has been followed by other pricing models developed by other researchers. The reason for this is simply that, like many pathfinders before them, the basic model that they published was based on some quite restrictive assumptions in order to advance an understanding of the processes involved and establish an effective starting point solution. Researchers following after have been able to relax some of the underlying assumptions, which appeared in the original work, and develop their own 'better' option pricing models (for thorough coverage of options pricing models see Hull, 1993). It is not the intention here to derive the BS option pricing model from first principles and then to compare it algebraically with other models. It is, however, worth getting an intuitive appreciation of the BS option pricing model, the inputs it requires, the assumptions which underpin it, and some useful by-products that it generates.

The BS model for pricing either a call or a put option on a share requires the following *inputs*:

1 The current price of the share.
2 The strike price.
3 The time remaining until expiration.
4 The risk-free rate of interest.
5 A measure of the standard deviation of the continuously compounded annual rate of return on the share—this input is crucial to the pricing model and is known as *volatility*.

The *assumptions* on which the model is built are:

1 The option is only exercisable at expiration (European-style).
2 The market operates continuously.
3 The share pays no dividend over the lifetime of the option.
4 The risk-free rate of interest is constant over the lifetime of the option.
5 There are zero taxes, no transactions' costs, and no bid–offer spread.

6   The underlying share can be shorted without penalty and short-sellers receive the cash benefits from the short sale in full.
7   Share prices are continuous and are not subject to precipitous changes in prices either up or down—shares are assumed to follow an *Ito process* (see Appendix 5B).

Obviously this list presents quite a mixture of inputs and a very demanding set of assumptions some of which will seldom, if ever, be satisfied.

Considering first of all the required inputs it should be clear that the user of the option will have a great degree of control over some of them, for example, the strike price that is to be adopted will be chosen by the user. In the case of the Sainsbury plc option, discussed in Chapter 4, from the quotes published in *The Financial Times* the user can choose between strikes of 550 and 600. In reality there will be many other strikes that the user could choose, DATASTREAM and the BBC'S CEEFAX pages, for example, will provide options prices on more than just two strikes for this and other shares. The user is also, within limits, able to decide for what period of time the option will be held. In addition to having the possibility of trading and option (buying or selling the option before expiration), the user can decide which expiration date is to be purchased or sold. Recall that in the case of the Sainsbury plc option this would be somewhere in the cycle: January, April, July, October. (In some cases blue chip equity options in the United States can have much longer time periods to expiration. In 1991 the Chicago Board Options Exchange (CBOE) introduced Long-term Equity AnticiPation Securities (LEAPS) which are in fact American style call and put options with expiration dates up to two years ahead.)

On the other hand there are also inputs required over which the option user can exercise little or no influence. The current price of an underlying share will, however, be determined by market forces. It is an input whose value is likely to vary throughout each and every day, and over which the user of the option has no direct control. Moreover, since movements in the share's price determine returns which in turn account for volatility of the share's price, the user can do little about the value chosen to represent volatility apart from, perhaps, the choice of formula used to estimate the input's value (see Appendix 5A). In the same way the risk-free rate of interest is an input whose value is determined by factors outside the option user's control.

Turning now to the assumptions on which the model is based, it is clear that in some respects they are untenable. Markets do not operate continuously: they close at weekends and for bank, religious and other public holidays, and national exchanges are not open for 24 hours a day. These factors will have an impact on the measure of the time to expiration input. A problem arises in day counting; should this input be represented by counting the number of *calendar days* (365, 366 or money market 360) to expiration or the number of *trading days* (between 255 and 265) to expiration? The assumption concerning constancy of the risk-free rate of interest is also a problem. As pointed out in Chapter 3 interest rates have a tendency these days to change quite dramatically and unexpectedly. However, even if the user is prepared to overlook this in the case of equity options pricing models when the underlying security on which an option is being used is an interest rate product, making use of a constant risk-free rate of interest to price an option, while at the same time taking out an option to insure against loss arising from a change in interest rates, would seem to be a dubious procedure. Assuming away dividends is also questionable, owners of shares do receive dividends at certain times in the year—in the United Kingdom this normally takes place on a semi-annual basis, but in the United States on a quarterly basis—so the chances are that for some options series dividends will fall due and will be paid during the life span of the option. If this is the case the share price could experience a discrete jump, bringing into question the assumption about the behaviour pattern that share prices are supposed to follow and, in consequence, the way in which the volatility input is estimated. Clearly, question marks can also be put next to the remaining inputs: zero transactions' costs, no bid–offer spread, etc. However, despite the many criticisms that can be made, from a practical and a philosophical standpoint, and some documented systematic biases that exist in certain applications of the formula, the fact remains that the BS option pricing model was the pioneer in the field and, as an estimator of options prices, is a quite robust performer. It provides an excellent vehicle for exploring the uses to which options can be put in the area of risk management.

The BS formula for the pricing of a call option based on the assumptions outlined above and the inputs described above can be written as:

$$C(S, t, X, R, \sigma) = SN(d_1) - X\exp^{-rt}N(d_2) \tag{5.1}$$

While the price of a put option (P) can be written as:

$$P = C - S + X\exp^{-rt} \tag{5.2}$$

from the put–call parity theorem. (The put–call parity relationship states that the value of a European put (call) with a given strike price and given expiration date can be found from the known value of a European call (put) with the same strike price and expiration date.)

Where:

S represents the current share price;
X represents the strike price;
t is the time to expiration as a proportion of a year;
r represents the risk-free rate of interest as a proportion;
σ represents the standard deviation of the continuously compounded annual rate of return on the share—volatility;
$d_1 = [\log_e(S/X) + (r + \sigma^2/2)t]/\sigma\sqrt{t}$
$d_2 = [\log_e(S/X) + (r - \sigma^2/2)t]/\sigma\sqrt{t}$ or
$d_2 = d_1 - \sigma\sqrt{t}$
$\log_e$ represents logarithms to base e (natural logarithms).

Example 5.1
An intuitive understanding of the BS formula (5.1) can be gained as follows.

Assume that it is known with 100 per cent certainty that the share price will close in-the-money on expiration. Under this scenario a call option holder, acting rationally, will at expiration take delivery of the contracted number of shares at the contracted strike (X). To take delivery the call option holder will need to pay X. The price of the share on expiration will be S, so that the intrinsic value of the call option at that time will also be the call option's premium and will be given by:

$$C = S - X > 0$$

At any time between initially buying the call option and expiration the call's price can be regarded as being determined by a situation where the holder is short the share at the current price S and has deposited a sum of money that will grow at a rate r to ensure that a sum X is available to meet the strike at expiration. The present value of X assuming continuous compounding at t will be given by:

$$\exp^{-rt} X$$

This implies that the call's price at any time up to and including expiration will be given by:

$$C = S - \exp^{-rt} X \tag{5.3}$$

Take the case where an option has 90 days until expiration which together with a 365-day year yields a value of $t = 0.2466$, assuming also a risk-free rate of interest of 8 per cent, which converts to a value of $r = 0.08$, a fixed share price of 110p, a strike of 100. Using these figures in Equation (5.3) will yield:

$$C = 110 - \exp^{-(0.08 \times 0.2466)} 100 = 110 - (0.9805)(100) = 11.9535\text{p}$$

which represents the call's price with 90 days to expiration.

Assuming now that today is expiration day, the value of $t = 0/365 = 0$, all other inputs remain unchanged and Equation (5.3) yields:

$$C = 110 - \exp^{-(0.08 \times 0)} 100 = 110 - 100 = 10\text{p}$$

which again represents the call's price but at expiration.

The assumption that the share's price at expiration will close above the strike price is untenable. There is, of course, a great deal of uncertainty about where the share price will close—it could close below, at, or above the strike price. It is to take account of this uncertainty that the terms $N(d_1)$ and $N(d_2)$ appear in Equation (5.1), these terms represent the values of the cumulative normal distribution and, in essence, capture the probability that the option will be exercised.

5.2 Option premium sensitivities

In addition to providing a formula for pricing calls (Equation (5.1)) and puts (Equation (5.2)), the equations can be taken further in order to examine how sensitive the options price is to changes in the value of the other inputs. From the bracketed section on the left-hand side of Equation (5.1) or from Equation (5.2) it should be clear that the following possibilities could be considered:

$\partial C/\partial t$ or $\partial P/\partial t$ estimates an option's sensitivity to the passing of time. The term $\partial C/\partial t$ or $\partial P/\partial t$ is often referred to as an option's *theta* (Θ).

$\partial C/\partial X$ or $\partial P/\partial X$ estimates an option's sensitivity to the strike price.

$\partial C/\partial r$ or $\partial P/\partial r$ estimates an option's sensitivity to changes in the risk-free rate of interest.

$\partial C/\partial \sigma$ or $\partial P/\partial \sigma$ estimates the sensitivity of an option's price to changes in the volatility of the underlying share. The term $\partial C/\partial \sigma$ or $\partial P/\partial \sigma$ is often referred to as an option's *vega*.

$\partial C/\partial S$ or $\partial P/\partial S$ estimates the sensitivity of an option's price to changes in the price of the underlying share. The term $\partial C/\partial S$ is known as the option's *delta* (Δ), and plays an important role as a hedge ratio in risk management (see Appendix 5B for mathematics of risk-neutral portfolios). The formula for calculating Δ is given by:

$$\Delta_c = \partial C/\partial S = N(d_1) > 0$$

while that of a put is given by:

$$\Delta_p = \partial P/\partial S = N(d_1) - 1 < 0$$

These values can be readily found once the option's price has been calculated since the expression $N(d_1)$ occurs in the BS formula, too.

Another important hedge ratio is that given by the second derivative of $\partial C/\partial S$, namely, $\partial^2 C/\partial S^2$. This derivative measures the rate at which the option's delta is changing and is known as an option's *gamma* (Γ). The formula for calculating gamma is given by:

$$\Gamma_c = \Gamma_p = \partial^2 C/\partial S^2 = \partial\Delta/\partial S = N'(d_1)/S\sigma\sqrt{t}.$$

In all these formulae reference is made to the normal distribution [N] and the cumulative standard normal distribution inputs $N(d_1)$ and $N(d_2)$. There are a number of ways in which these values can be approximated on Lotus (see Abramowitz and Stegun, 1972). The method used in spreadsheet B&S.WK3 provides accuracy to about four decimal places and is based on:

$$N(x) = 1 - (1/\sqrt{2\pi})\exp^{-x^2/2}(b_1c + b_2c^2 + b_3c^3) \quad \text{for } x \geq 0 \qquad (5.4)$$

where:

$c = 1/(1 + 0.33267x)$
$b_1 = 0.4361836$
$b_2 = -0.1201676$
$b_3 = 0.9372980$

and

$$N(x) = \frac{1}{\sqrt{2\pi}} \exp^{-x^2/2}$$

(5.5)

For $x < 0$ calculate for $x > 0$ then subtract the result from 1.

Lotus demo B&S.WK3

This spreadsheet enables the user to calculate options' prices, calls and puts, for several types of options (equity, stock index, currency and futures) using the basic BS methodology and some simple modifications to the formula which will be explained as the chapter progresses. To facilitate the introduction of hedging, based on the sensitivity values obtained from the BS formula, this chapter will concentrate on the use of the equity option pricing model. Table 5.1 illustrates the facilities offered by this spreadsheet. The special menu from which these facilities can be selected is activated via the Alt+A keys. The initial data used in B&S.WK3 is that of the Sainsbury plc option data from Chapter 4, Table 5.2 displays this initial control data.

Note: It is possible on first entering this spreadsheet that the cells in which calculations for premiums, deltas and gammas are performed all show ERR. This is easily rectified by entering an expiration date greater than that currently shown in the input (Table 5.2). This is achieved by moving the cursor to the appropriate date cell and entering a date in the form: DD-MMM-YY where DD will be numerical values, MMM will be literal characters representing the first three letters of a month's name, and YY will be numerical values. Alternatively the F2 key can be used to edit the entered date. The label identifier ' or ^ or " is required otherwise the first character entered is taken to be a number on which numerical operations can be performed, this will result in the spreadsheet failing to execute correctly. *This spreadsheet assumes that the date has been*

Table 5.1. Facilities offered by B&S.WK3 spreadsheet

Data_Input	Input basic data
Equity	Table of Option Prices, Deltas, and Gammas
Stock_Index	Option Pricing for Stock Indexes (FTSE100, S&P500, etc.)
Currency	Option Prices for Currency Options
Futures	Options on Futures
Quit	Exit Macro

Table 5.2.   Sainsbury plc option data used in B&S.WK3

```
INPUT DATA
Input the following values:


Expiration Data                    15-Apr-93
Days to expiration                     79.00
Strike price                             550
% Volatility p.a.                      22.53
Current Underlying Price                 571

Rate of Interest (%) p.a.                  7
Approx. dividend yield (%) p.a.            3
(Required for pricing Stock
Index options)

Risk-free Rate of Interest (%)          3.22
p.a. in Foreign Country
(Required for pricing
Currency options)
```

correctly entered on the user's PC, errors in computation will occur if this is not the case.

- Typing D (d) will enable the user to input the data for pricing an option of his or her choice. The cursor will highlight each variable in turn (see paragraph above for entering expiration date) but will skip the number of days to expiration, this will be calculated automatically. After each input has been typed press [ENTER] to move the cursor to the next input cell.
- Once the user has input the required data E (e) may be selected to view the Black–Scholes option premiums, deltas and gamma.
- The tables for stock (share) index, currency, and options on futures can be accessed via S (s), C (c) and F (f), respectively.
- Selecting Q (q) exits the special menu and places the cursor at cell A1.

Table 5.3 displays the calculated premiums, deltas and gammas for the initial data.

The European-style, option premiums calculated in Table 5.3 are fairly robust. However, research work has documented systematic biases in the BS option pricing model particularly for in- and out-of-the-money options. The reader should be aware that the option pricing formula used here is for demonstration purposes and will not give accurate prices in all cases. The option prices quoted for the Sainsbury plc control data are 41 for a call and 11 for a put given a strike of 550, a

Table 5.3. Calculated premiums, deltas and gammas for initial data of BS European options pricing formula

	Call	Put
Premium	41	12
Delta	0.71	0.29
Gamma	0.0057	0.0057

current price of 571, volatility of 22.53 per cent p.a. (estimated from spreadsheet TA_DEMO.WK3 using the Sainsbury plc share price data), a risk-free rate of interest of 7 per cent and 80 days to expiration. This compares with the premiums of 42 and 13 for calls and puts, respectively, quoted in *The Financial Times* on 27 January, 1993.

The second line of Table 5.3 refers to the option's delta and, as emphasized earlier, this is an important concept in hedging when using options. A contrived example is useful at this point to compare the 'hedge-and-forget' forward-type strategy discussed in Chapter 3 with *delta hedging* strategy.

Example 5.2

Although unrealistic, imagine the scenario where an investment bank has agreed to buy 500,000 shares in a large plc at £4.90 per share in six weeks' time as part of a financial restructuring package; currently the share price stands at £5.00. One way in which the bank's position could be hedged is to short the 500,000 on the market for delivery in six weeks' time at, say, £4.90 per share (the best price achievable given the impact of such a large sale on the market), so that in six weeks' time there would be sufficient to pay the amount agreed with the plc. The deal is fully hedged on a one-long for one-short basis. The delta in this case is 1, any change in the long position will be equally offset by a change in the short position. To clarify this, ignoring any potential growth in the value of the underlying security, the transaction can be expressed as:

$$F = S + g$$

where:

F represents the forward price;
S represents the spot price;
g represents the gain or loss to the buyer of the forward contract.

If g is fixed at the beginning of the transaction (in this case $g = 10$p per share: $500 - 490$) then the rate of change of the price of the derivative security with respect to changes in price of the underlying security is unity:

$$\partial F/\partial S = 1$$

Now consider the case where an option is used. In this case the investment bank agrees to write an OTC European-style put option on 500,000 shares with a strike of 490, to expire in six weeks' time, for a premium of 13.99p per share. This will generate an immediate income from the premium of £69,950 and interest at 7 per cent over the 42 day period over the life span of the option, £563. From the option pay-off profiles in the previous chapter there can be little doubt that this position potentially carries with it a great deal of risk. The income is fixed at £69,950, however, this can be rapidly swallowed up if the share price moves downwards and against the put option writer. Suppose for example that the share price falls to £4.70 by the end of the day on which the put was written, if the option could be exercised at that time the investment bank would be faced with a situation where it has to pay £4.90 for a share which will fetch only £4.70 on the market. This loss of 20p per share translates into a loss of £100,000 against which a premium income of only £69,950 can be set. Fortunately for the bank the option is an OTC and is European-style and, therefore, may not be exercised until expiration, which allows time for the market to move in the bank's favour over the coming weeks.

Assume now that six weeks have elapsed and that the share price has fallen to £4.00 per share. The loss to the bank at this stage will be:

$$500{,}000 \times - \max.[\pounds 4.90 - \pounds 4.00] + \pounds 69{,}950 + \pounds 563 = -\pounds 450{,}000 + \pounds 70{,}513$$
$$= -\pounds 379{,}487$$

The premium received is certainly no compensation for the large loss incurred. As an alternative to this naked put option position the bank might attempt a hedge where a short position in 500,000 shares is established (shorted either immediately or as a forward transaction as described above). The resulting option plus underlying position would then be that of a synthetic written call which itself introduces renewed downside risk exposure should the share price climb above the 490 strike. (This can easily be verified by using the OPT_STR1.WK3 spreadsheet described in Chapter 4.) To clarify this consider the scenario where the underlying share price closes on expiration at £5.30p per share. The put option thus expires worthless to the holder but provides a clear income of £69,950 to the bank as option writer, having shorted the share at, say, £4.90, as in the previous case above. The bank must now find 40p per share to buy back and deliver the required number of shares into the short contract. This represents a sum of £200,000, and even taking into account the income from the put premium it still means a loss of £130,050. Clearly this is not a satisfactory hedge at all.

At this point the delta from the option pricing formula comes in to its own. Black and Scholes demonstrated as part of their model's derivation process that, on a written option, only a fraction of the underlying shares need to be held in order to set up a *risk-neutral* portfolio; the proportion of shares which needs to be held is given by the option's delta. (From Table 5.3 the delta in respect of the written put option on the Sainsbury plc share is 0.29.) In this current example the put delta is calculated as 0.372 which means that for every put option written on one share 0.372 shares need to be shorted to set up a risk-neutral portfolio. Thus with 500,000 being the contract size 0.372 × 500,000 yields 186,000 shares which will need to be shorted to put on the delta hedge.

Reconsidering the outcome achieved during the discussion above in respect of the naked put position, if the share falls from £5.00p to £4.70p at the end of day one and exercise were possible at that time, the bank would stand to lose £100,000. However, in the case where a fraction of the shares have been shorted to create a delta hedged position there will be a gain achieved by closing out the short position. If the shares were shorted at £4.90 (the best price achievable given such a large placement on the market at one time), they can now be bought back at £4.70 to deliver into the short contract. This realizes a profit of £37,200 which together with the £69,950 premium income generates £107,150. Although not a perfect hedge, in the sense that the gain on one position is equally offset by the losses on the opposite position, the sums almost match, there is a small profit of £7150 for the bank on the transaction.

A problem with delta hedging is the fact that it may need to be frequently reviewed, just how frequently depends on the calculated value of gamma—the larger the gamma the more frequently must the portfolio be rebalanced. The gamma calculated for this example is 0.007 which implies that for each unit change in the underlying security the delta of the option will change by around 0.007 of a unit and is relatively small.

Tables 5.6 and 5.7 trace the development of the delta-hedged portfolio discussed above over a six week period and for two cases; the first example looks at the situation when the option closes out-of-the-money, the second considers the case when the option finishes in-the-money. Each of the delta calculations over time was performed on the spreadsheet B&S.WK3. The initial input data that was used to generate the price of the option, deltas and gammas appears in Table 5.4. Table 5.5 displays the calculated values of those variables at the start of the analysis.

The first row of Table 5.6 shows the bank's position at the start of the hedge on 4 March. The share price stands at 500, the put premium is 13.99, the put delta 0.372. In view of the low value of gamma in Table 5.5 a weekly rebalancing of the portfolio is decided on. As already explained the delta of 0.372 implies that 186,000 shares will need to be shorted in order to put on a delta hedge. Assuming that the proceeds from the short sale are received in full (see assumption 6 at the start of this chapter) this transaction will generate £5.00 × 186,000 = £930,000 (in this example it has been assumed that the full market price can be realized and not the £4.90 used in the earlier example). The risk-free rate of interest assumed in order to generate the put option premium is 7 per cent p.a., and it is further assumed that this £930,000 together with the premium received can be deposited at that rate for the first week. Over that time period interest will accrue in the bank's favour to the sum of approximately £1342.

Table 5.4. Input data to generate price of the option, deltas and gamma

```
INPUT DATA
Input the following values:

Expiration Date                 15-Apr-93
Days to expiration                  43.00
Strike Price                          490
% Volatility p.a.                      30
Current Underlying Price              500
Rate of Interest (%) p.a.               7

Approx. dividend yield (%) p.a.         3
(Required for pricing Stock
Index options)

Risk-free Rate of Interest (%)       3.22
p.a. in Foreign Country
(Required for pricing
Currency options)
```

On 11 March the share price has fallen to 490, the put's premium has increased and the delta has moved up to 0.452 (from B&S.WK3). This means that in order to maintain the hedge a further 40,000 shares have to be shorted at the prevailing market price of 490. The total number of shares now sold equals 226,000. The proceeds from the short position have now moved up to £1,126,000—this amount and the premium can be deposited at 7 per cent p.a. This generates interest income to the value of approximately £1606.

In the third week the share price has risen to 495, the delta has fallen to 0.410 so that 21,000 shares must be bought back at a price of 495. In consequence, the proceeds from the short sale are reduced as is the interest income at the end of that period which will be £1466.

Over the next few weeks the portfolio is balanced in the manner just described so that by the expiration—15 April—when the share price has risen to 530 the bank has to close out the short position in the underlying security by

Table 5.5. BS calculated values for premiums, deltas and gammas

	Call	Put
Premium	28.02	13.99
Delta	0.628	0.372
Gamma	0.0073	0.0073

Table 5.6. Put finishes out-of-the-money

Date	Share Price	Put Premium	Put Delta	Shares Shorted	Proceeds from Short Sales (£s)	Interest received from short sales at end of period
4-Mar-93	500	13.99	0.372	186000	£930,000	£1,342
11-Mar-93	490	16.71	0.452	226000	£1,126,000	£1,606
18-Mar-93	495	12.99	0.410	205000	£1,022,050	£1,466
25-Mar-93	510	6.19	0.262	131000	£644,650	£959
1-Apr-93	500	7.14	0.341	170500	£842,150	£1,224
8-Apr-93	518	1.05	0.095	47500	£205,010	£369
15-Apr-93	530	0.00	0.000	0	(£46,740)	£0

£6,967 Total Interest Received

£69,950 Premium Received
£563 Interest on Premium
(£46,740) Total Proceeds
£0 Delivery Cost

£30,740 Net Profit (Cost)

buying back 47,500 shares at 530p per share which equals £251,750. Since the balance of proceeds from the short transactions is £205,010 this implies that the bank incurs a cost of £46,740 when closing the short side of the position. Taking all income and costs (transaction costs excluded) into consideration results in a £30,740 profit. Delivery cost is zero since the option finishes out-of-the-money and will not be exercised.

Consider now an alternative scenario, displayed in Table 5.7, where the share price follows a different track to arrive at a price of 450p on 15 April. This, of course, means that the put option expires in-the-money and will be exercised. The process of rebalancing the portfolio will be carried out as described above. From the 25 March, however, the option starts to move into-the-money as the share price falls from 490 to 450. As a result of this the number of shares that needs to be sold short in the market rises steadily so that on 15 April when the option is exercised the shares have all been sold. The proceeds from the short position taken together with interest income and the premium received at the start of the transaction yield a sum equal to £2,466,311. The delivery into the options contract means that £2,450,000 needs to be found, setting the £2,466,311 against this figure implies a profit of £16,311 accruing to the bank (once again, however, transactions costs have been ignored).

To illustrate the need for a dynamic approach to the use of delta consider the outcome of the portfolio where the price of the underlying security closes at 450 after 42 days and the initial delta hedge put in place on day 1 was not adjusted over the intervening time period. In that case 186,000 would have been shorted on day 1 generating £930,000, this together with the premium of £69,950 and interest income on some of these two components of £8050 would have resulted in proceeds of approximately £1,008,000. On exercise the bank would have to sell the remaining 314,000 at the prevailing market price of £4.50 providing revenue to the value of £1,413,000. Against these two figures, totalling £2,421,000, the bank would have to set the £2,450,000 payment to meet the contract strike price of £4.90. This results in a loss of £29,000 accruing to the bank.

The dynamic delta hedge put on in Example 5.2 proved to be successful in absorbing movements in the share price either up or down. Agreeing to write a put option on the 500,000 shares for a fixed premium the bank was able to insure itself and leave the value of its overall position virtually unchanged. The weekly delta rebalancing of a portfolio as undertaken in the example may, however, be insufficient to provide adequate insurance against some adverse movements in prices. A large option gamma would indicate that more frequent rebalancing is called for or that the overall position is made simultaneously delta and gamma neutral in order to ensure that the portfolio would be protected against both small price movements in the underlying security (delta) and larger movements (gamma).

Example 5.3

The position delta of a portfolio of instruments can be found by using the formula:

Table 5.7. Put finishes in-the-money

Date	Share Price	Put Premium	Put Delta	Shares Shorted	Proceeds from Short Sales (£s)	Interest received from short sales at end of period
4-Mar-93	500	13.99	0.372	186000	£930,000	£1,342
11-Mar-93	510	9.31	0.293	146500	£728,550	£1,072
18-Mar-93	505	9.34	0.321	160500	£799,250	£1,167
25-Mar-93	490	13.36	0.462	231000	£1,144,700	£1,631
1-Apr-93	485	13.69	0.536	268000	£1,324,150	£1,872
8-Apr-93	480	13.99	0.658	329000	£1,616,950	£2,265
15-Apr-93	450	40.00	1.000	500000	£2,386,450	£0

£9.348 Total Interest Received

£69,950 Premium Received
£563 Interest on Premium
£2,386.450 Total Proceeds
£2,450,000 Delivery Cost

£16,311 Net Profit (Cost)

$$\Delta_p = n_1\Delta_1 + n_2\Delta_2 + \ldots + n_m\Delta_m \tag{5.6}$$

where:

Δ_p represents the delta of the portfolio;
Δ_i represents the delta of the ith instrument ($i = 1, 2, \ldots, m$);
n_i represents the amount of the ith instrument held in the portfolio ($i = 1, 2, \ldots, m$).

In the case of the financial institution discussed above the share in question will have a delta of 1 ($\partial S/\partial S = 1$), the delta of the put option was calculated as 0.372, and there are 500,000 shares in the portfolio. Thus defining instrument 1 to be the underlying share and instrument 2 to be the long put option, delta neutrality can be calculated as:

$$0 = (n_1)(1) + (500{,}000)(0.372)$$

$$n_1 = -186{,}000 \tag{5.7}$$

That is, 186,000 shares should be shorted for delta neutrality and since there are only these two instruments in the portfolio, the portfolio will have a position delta of zero.

The position gamma of a portfolio of instruments can be found by using the formula:

$$\Gamma_p = n_1\Gamma_1 + n_2\Gamma_2 + \ldots + n_m\Gamma_m \tag{5.8}$$

where:

Γ_p represents the gamma of the portfolio;
Γ_i represents the gamma of the ith instrument ($i = 1, 2, \ldots, m$).
n_i represents the amount of the ith instrument held in the portfolio ($i = 1, 2, \ldots, m$).

The underlying instrument (n_1) contained in the portfolio will have a gamma of 0 ($\partial^2 S/\partial S^2 = 0$), the gamma of the put option was calculated as 0.0073, and since there are 500,000 shares in the portfolio the portfolio's position gamma will be:

$$\Gamma_p = (n_1)(0) + (500{,}000)(0.0073)$$

$$\Gamma_p = 3650$$

Since the underlying security cannot be used to manipulate a gamma-neutral position a further position in options (n_3, Δ_3) must be taken out to achieve a Γ_p of zero. The introduction of this third instrument will alter the Δ_p which in turn must be rebalanced to achieve a neutral position delta portfolio. It must also be emphasized that as delta changes, because of changes in the price of the underlying instrument, the risk-free rate of interest and time to expiration, so will gamma change. Although gamma neutrality protects larger movements in the price of an underlying security it, too, must be regularly rebalanced.

5.3 Options on stock indexes, currency and futures

The spreadsheet described above (B&S.WK3) also offers the user the opportunity to calculate options premiums, deltas and gammas for other instruments. The formulae used in this process are all very similar to the basic BS option pricing model used to price equity options but do require some special data inputs that need to be made explicit.

5.3.1 Stock index options

Formulae:

$$C(S, t, X, r, y, \sigma) = S \exp^{-yt}N(d_1) - X \exp^{-rt}N(d_2) \tag{5.9}$$

$$P(S, t, X, r, y, \sigma) = X \exp^{-rt}N(-d_2) - S \exp^{-yt}N(-d_1) \tag{5.10}$$

where:

S represents the current share price:
X represents the strike price:
t is the time to expiration as a proportion of a year:
y represents an average annualized yield on the index over the life span of the option;
r represents the risk-free rate of interest as a proportion;
σ represents the standard deviation of the continuously compounded annual rate of return on the index—volatility;
$d_1 = [\log_e(S/X) + (r - y + \sigma^2/2)t]/\sigma\sqrt{t}$
$d_2 = [\log_e(S/X) + (r - y - \sigma^2/2)t] /\sigma\sqrt{t}$ or
$d_2 = d_1 - \sigma\sqrt{t}$
$\log_e$ represents logarithms to base e (natural logarithms).

Delta

$\Delta = \exp^{-yt}N(d_1)$ for calls

$\Delta = \exp^{-yt}N(d_1) - 1$ for puts.

Example 5.4
Using the spreadsheet B&S.WK3 with the inputs as shown in Table 5.8 and by selecting Stock_Index from the special menu, the price of European-style call can be seen to be estimated at 31.91, which in view of the fact that the FT-SE 100 options contract is priced at £10 per index point, implies a cost of approximately £319 per contract. Table 5.9 shows that to put on a delta hedge for a written call 0.383 of the underlying should be purchased.

Gamma

$\Gamma = \exp^{-yt}N'(d_1)/S\sigma\sqrt{t}$ for both calls and puts.

Table 5.8.   Control inputs

```
Input the following values:
Expiration date               15-Apr-93
Days to expiration                37.00
Strike price                       3000
% volatility pa                      13
Current underlying price           2949
Rate of interest (%) pa               7

Approx. dividend yield (%) pa         3
(Required for pricing stock
index options)

Risk-free rate of interest (%)     3.22
pa in foreign country
(Required for pricing
currency options)
```

Table 5.9.   Call and put premiums

```
STOCK INDEX OPTIONS - EUROPEAN
            Calls          Puts
Premium     31.91          70.65

Delta       0.383          0.614

Gamma       0.0031         0.0031
```

Currency options

Formula:

$$C(S, t, X, r, r_f\ \sigma) = S \exp^{-r_d t} N(d_1) - X \exp^{-r_f t} N(d_2) \qquad (5.11)$$

While the price of a put option (P) can be written as:

$$P(S, t, X, r, r_f\ \sigma) = X \exp^{-r_f t} N(-d_2) - S \exp^{-r_d t} N(-d_1) \qquad (5.12)$$

where:

S represents the current share price;
X represents the strike price;
t is the time to expiration as a proportion of a year;
r_f represents the risk-free rate of interest in the foreign currency as a proportion;

r_d represents the domestic risk-free rate of interest as a proportion (the idea of interest rate differentials between countries was introduced in Chapter 3);

σ represents the standard deviation of the continuously compounded annual rate of return of the exchange rate between currencies—volatility;

$d_1 = [\log_e(S/X) + (r_d - r_f + \sigma^2/2)t]/\sigma\sqrt{t}$

$d_2 = [\log_e(S/X) + (r_d - r_f - \sigma^2/2)t]/\sigma\sqrt{t}$

or

$d_2 = d_1 - \sigma\sqrt{t}$

$\log_e$ represents logarithms to base e (natural logarithms).

Delta

$\Delta = \exp^{-r_f t}N(d_1)$ for calls

$\Delta = \exp^{-r_f t}N(d_1) - 1$ for puts

Note that to fit in with the assumption of continuously compounded returns developed in this chapter the exponential of r_f has been used. This appears at first sight to be fundamentally different to the approach adopted in Chapter 3. In the discussion of forward contracts in that chapter the pricing of a forward contract was estimated using the formula:

$F = S(1 + (r_f - r_d)(t/T))$

(refer to the Equations (3.1) and (3.2) and the spreadsheet FORWARDS.WK3). Had the exponential method been used in Chapter 3 the forward rate would have been calculated as:

$F = 1.5385 \exp^{(0.032 - 0.064063)(0.5)} = 1.5140$

Gamma

$\Gamma = \exp^{-r_f t}N'(d_1)/S\sigma\sqrt{t}$ for both calls and puts

This option pricer can be accessed on the B&S.WK3 spreadsheet by activating the special menu (Alt + A) and selecting C or (c).

Futures options

Formula:

$$C(F, t, X, r, \sigma) = \exp^{-rt}[FN(d_1) - XN(d_2)] \tag{5.13}$$

While the price of a put option (P) can be written as:

$$P(F, t, X, r, \sigma) = \exp^{-rt}[XN(-d_2) - FN(-d_1)] \tag{5.14}$$

where:

F represents the current price of the futures contract;

X represents the strike price;

t is the time to expiration as a proportion of a year;

r represents the risk-free rate of interest as a proportion;

σ represents the standard deviation of the continuously compounded annual rate of return of the futures instrument—volatility;

$d_1 = [\log_e(F/X) + (\sigma^2/2)t]/\sigma\sqrt{t}$

$d_2 = [\log_e(F/X) - (\sigma^2/2)t]/\sigma\sqrt{t}$

or

$d_2 = d_1 - \sigma\sqrt{t}$

$\log_e$ represents logarithms to base e (natural logarithms).

Delta

$\Delta = \exp^{-rt} N(d_1)$ for calls

$\Delta = \exp^{-rt} N(d_1) - 1$ for puts.

Gamma

$\Gamma = \exp^{-rt} N'(d_1)/S\sigma\sqrt{t}$ for both calls and puts.

The option pricer can be accessed on the `B&S.WK3` spreadsheet by activating the special menu (Alt + A) and selecting F or (f).

5.4 Spreadsheets

There is only one demonstration spreadsheet used in this chapter:

1 `B&S.WK3` which is described in Sec. 5.2 and whose special menu is illustrated in Table 5.1.

5.4.1 `B&S.WK3`

The special menu, which appears as Table 5.1, provides users with an opportunity of inputting the option's expiration date, strike price, volatility, current underlying price, domestic rate of interest, dividend yield and foreign rate of interest:

`(Data_Input);`

obtaining option premiums, deltas and gammas for:

`(Equity);`
`(Stock_Index);`
`(Currency);`
`and (Futures);`

and a final macro which exits the special menu and returns the spreadsheet back to normal Lotus operating mode:

`(Quit).`

Questions

5.1   Explain why volatility is such an important concept for options and the use of option strategies:

5.2   Use the data at the end of this question to calculate the call and put premiums of an equity option with 35 days to expiration.

Current price of the underlying security: 300p per share
Short-term rate of interest: 5.5 per cent
Volatility: 25.0 per cent
Strike price: 290p

5.3   From the financial pages of one of today's newspapers select a short-term interest rate futures contract. How would you try to find the volatility of an at-the-money call option premium for that futures contract using `B&S.WK3`?

5.4   What is meant by a delta hedge?

5.5   Why might hedgers need to consider gamma when putting on an options-based hedge?

5.6   Use the data at the end of this question to set up a horizontal strategy (assume appropriate strike prices). Analyse the potential pay-offs in the case where the underlying security:

(a)   falls to 380;
(b)   rises to 440.

Additional data:
The share price is expected to fall in the next few days.
The current underlying security is 390p.
Volatility is estimated at 25 per cent.
Current rate of interest is 5.5 per cent.
The near contract expires in 10 days.

5.7   What other options-only strategy could be employed in order to benefit from the scenario described in Question 5.6?

Appendix 5A   Measuring volatility

Option pricing formulae are highly sensitive to the value attributed to σ. Inevitably, as a consequence of this, a great amount of research has been undertaken in an attempt to obtain the 'best' measure of volatility as an input option pricing formula. This following list is intended to provide the reader with a brief idea of the possibilities that have been suggested:

1   Straightforward statistical estimation based on the variance of:

$$\ln \frac{S_t}{S_{t-1}} \tag{5A.1}$$

as used in several spreadsheets in this text and introduced in Chapter 1.

2   Assume that the option price quoted in the FT, CEEFAX, DATASTREAM or other sources is a fair price and then use that price in the option pricing formula to calculate volatility. The resulting estimate is then called *implied volatility*. One problem with this approach is that the volatility obtained in this way may differ for different option prices in the same series, i.e. the premium on an out-of-the-money option may generate a different volatility figure to that obtained when using the premium on an in-the-money option of the same share. This problem may be overcome by computing a weighted average of the different volatilities giving more weight to those options which are at- or near-the-money and less to those that are deeply in- or deeply out-of-the-money.

3   Use some form of generalized autoregressive conditional heteroskedasticity (GARCH) model which allows for an unconditional homoskedastic (constant) variance:

$$\mathrm{Var}(e_t) = \sigma^2 \tag{5A.2}$$

but a conditional variance that allows for a heteroskedastic (non-constant) variance:

$$\mathrm{Var}(e_t|e_{t-1}) \neq \sigma^2 \tag{5A.3}$$

in connection with a defined regression model. This approach, which is beyond the scope of this text and which needs sophisticated econometric/times series software for computational purposes, has received considerable attention in recent years. So great has been this attention, particularly in the field of option pricing, that the *Journal of Econometrics* devoted a complete supplementary issue of its publication to the use of GARCH models in finance in May 1992.

Appendix 5B   Risk-neutral portfolios

In the derivation of the BS-style option pricing formulae it is assumed that a non-dividend-paying share follows the a stochastic process of the form:

$$dS = \mu S \, dt + \sigma S \, dz \tag{5B.1}$$

or

$$\frac{dS}{S} = \mu \, dt + \sigma \, dz \tag{5B.2}$$

where:

   dS represents a very small change in the share's price;

dt represents a very small time increment;

dz represents uncertainty and d$z = \epsilon\sqrt{dt}$ with $\epsilon \sim N(0, 1)$, i.e. ϵ is a random sample from the standardized normal distribution with mean zero and unit variance;

μ represents the expected return on the share expressed as a decimal;

σ represents share price volatility;

On this basis if p is taken to represent the price of a derivative security which depends on S then p will be determined by some functions of S and t. In such a function as this Ito's lemma can be used to justify Equation (5B.3) where a change in the price of the derivative can be modelled by:

$$dp = \left[\frac{\partial p}{\partial S}\mu S + \frac{\partial p}{\partial t} + \frac{1}{2}\frac{\partial^2 p}{\partial S^2}\sigma^2 S^2 \right] dt + \frac{\partial p}{\partial S}\sigma S \, dz \tag{5B.3}$$

Note that the uncertainty term dz appears in both the equation for the dS and dp. The prices of both securities are subject to the same uncertainty.

In developing the idea of a risk-neutral hedge Equations (5.B1) and (5.B3) will be very useful. To examine the mathematics of a risk-neutral hedge consider the case where an option has been written. Initially the position can be regarded as a portfolio whose value, V, can be denoted by $-p$—the premium received in connection with the sale of the option. To hedge this position a number of shares equal to $\partial p/\partial S$ need to be bought. At this point the value of the portfolio becomes:

$$V = -p + \frac{\partial p}{\partial S} \tag{5B.4}$$

and a change in value, dV, can be written as:

$$dV = -dp + \frac{\partial p}{\partial S} \, dS \tag{5B.5}$$

into which Equation (5B.1) and (5B.3) can be substituted to obtain:

$$dV = -\left(\left[\frac{\partial p}{\partial S}\mu S + \frac{\partial p}{\partial t} + \frac{1}{2}\frac{\partial^2 p}{\partial S^2}\sigma^2 S^2 \right] dt + \frac{\partial p}{\partial S}\sigma S \, dz \right) + \frac{\partial p}{\partial S}[\mu S \, dt + \sigma S \, dz] \tag{5B.6}$$

An interesting and important feature of this equation is that the dz term, which represent uncertainty, cancels, leaving:

$$dV = -\frac{\partial p}{\partial t} \, dt - \frac{1}{2}\frac{\partial^2 p}{\partial S^2}\sigma^2 S^2 \, dt \tag{5B.7}$$

References and further reading

Abramowitz, M. and Stegun, I. (1972), *Handbook of Mathematical Functions*, Dover Publications, New York.

Cox, J. C. and Rubinstein, M. (1985), *Options Markets*, Prentice-Hall, Englewood Cliffs, NJ.

Dubofsky, D. (1992), *Options and Financial Futures: Valuation and Use*, McGraw-Hill, New York.

Elton, E. J. and Gruber, M. J. (1991), *Modern Portfolio Theory and Investment Analysis*, 4th edn, Wiley, New York.

Hull, J. (1993), *Options, Futures and other Derivative Securities* (2nd edn), Prentice-Hall, Englewood Cliffs, NJ.

6 Managing Equity Risk

6.1 Specific risk—the Markowitz approach

In Chapter 1 some time was devoted to demonstrating the way in which specific risk could be managed by diversifying holdings of shares between different sectors of the domestic economy or, if a broader view is taken, diversifying holdings of shares between different countries in an international framework. In that chapter reference was also made to two formal methods that would enable an investor to establish into what proportions it would be best to divide the holdings of equity in that portfolio in order to maximize returns while keeping risk down to a minimum. The first method which will be examined in this chapter is the approach developed by Markowitz, in the early 1950s. A second and strongly related method developed by Sharpe in the 1960s will be examined in Sec. 6.2.

In estimating the optimal proportions both of these methods build on the ideas underlying Equations (1.7), (1.12) and (1.13) of Chapter 1. Limiting an analysis to two risky assets, as does the discussion in Chapter 1, is of course unrealistic. As this chapter develops the methodology will be extended to consider the *potential* inclusion of 'n' risky assets in a portfolio. However, to gain an insight into the Markowitz approach it is worth staying with the two asset case for the time being. Recall that the model used to illustrate the concept of the mean-variance efficient frontier took the form:

Portfolio risk:

$$\text{Var}_p = s_p^2 = x_1^2 s_1^2 + x_2^2 s_2^2 + 2x_1 x_2 s_{12} \tag{6.1}$$

Portfolio return:

$$\bar{R}_p = x_1 \bar{R}_1 + x_2 \bar{R}_2 \tag{6.2}$$

Budget constraint:

$$1 = x_1 + x_2 \tag{6.3}$$

where $\bar{R}_p$, $\bar{R}_1$, and $\bar{R}_2$ represent the return on the portfolio, risky asset 1, and risky asset 2, respectively; x_1, and x_2, are unknown proportions.

The problem faced at this point is that of finding values for x_1 and x_2 that will result in the variance (risk) of the portfolio being a minimum for any given,

150

feasible level of return. To make the problem a little easier to handle another assumption is going to be imposed on the model. This assumption introduces more flexibility to the investor by allowing him or her to divide the £1 budget between investments in risky assets 1 and 2 and, also, the risk-free asset which has a return of r_f. (The variance of the risk-free rate is zero, i.e. no risk. The covariance terms involving the risk-free rate and the risky assets is also assumed to be zero.)

Minimize:

$$\text{Var}_p = s_p^2 = x_1^2 s_1^2 + x_2^2 s_2^2 + 2x_1 x_2 s_{12} \tag{6.1}$$

subject to:

$$\bar{R}_p = x_1 \bar{R}_1 + x_2 \bar{R}_2 + [1 - x_1 - x_2]r_f \tag{6.4}$$

where Equation (6.4) is permitting the return on the portfolio to be a combination of the returns from the two risky assets and the risk-free asset.

These two equations can then be put into Lagrangian and solved as follows:

$$L = x_1^2 s_1^2 + x_2^2 s_2^2 + 2x_1 x_2 s_{12} + \lambda[\bar{R}_p - x_1 \bar{R}_1 - x_2 \bar{R}_2 - (1 - x_1 - x_2)r_f] \tag{6.5}$$

where λ represents the Lagrange undetermined multiplier.

On partially differentiating with respect to x_1 and x_2 and λ the following expressions are obtained:

$$\frac{\partial L}{\partial x_1} = 2x_1 s_1^2 + 2x_2 s_{12} - \lambda \bar{R}_1 + \lambda r_f \tag{6.6}$$

$$\frac{\partial L}{\partial x_2} = 2x_2 s_2^2 + 2x_1 s_{12} - \lambda \bar{R}_2 + \lambda r_f \tag{6.7}$$

$$\frac{\partial L}{\partial \lambda} = \bar{R}_p - x_1 \bar{R}_1 - x_2 \bar{R}_2 - [1 - x_1 - x_2]r_f \tag{6.8}$$

Setting Equations (6.7) and (6.8) equal to zero, and performing some algebraic manipulations, yields the following simultaneous equation model:

$$2x_1 s_1^2 + 2x_2 s_{12} = \lambda(\bar{R}_1 - r_f) \tag{6.9}$$

$$2x_2 s_2^2 + 2x_1 s_{12} = \lambda(\bar{R}_2 - r_f) \tag{6.10}$$

or

$$x_1 s_1^2 + x_2 s_{12} = \frac{\lambda}{2}(\bar{R}_1 - r_f) \tag{6.11}$$

$$x_1 s_{12} + x_2 s_2^2 = \frac{\lambda}{2}(\bar{R}_2 - r_f) \tag{6.12}$$

Then letting:

$$z_1 = \frac{2}{\lambda}x_1 \tag{6.13}$$

$$z_2 = \frac{2}{\lambda}x_2 \tag{6.14}$$

and substituting Equations (6.13) and (6.14) into Equations (6.11) and (6.12) the simultaneous equations can be rewritten as:

$$z_1 s_1^2 + z_2 s_{12} = (\bar{R}_1 - r_f) \tag{6.15}$$

$$z_1 s_{12} + z_2 s_2^2 = (\bar{R}_2 - r_f) \quad (\text{note: } s_{12} = s_{21}) \tag{6.16}$$

The solution of this simultaneous equation model can be achieved in Lotus (the control data and input requirements for the `MARKOW.WK3` spreadsheet are illustrated in Tables 6.1 and 6.2) by making use of the matrix inverse and multiplication operations which it offers:

$$\begin{vmatrix} s_1^2 & s_{12} \\ s_{12} & s_2^2 \end{vmatrix}^{-1} \begin{vmatrix} \bar{R}_1 - r_f \\ \bar{R}_2 - r_f \end{vmatrix} = \begin{vmatrix} z_1 \\ z_2 \end{vmatrix} \tag{6.17}$$

So that

$$z_1 = \frac{s_2^2(\bar{R}_1 - r_f) - s_{12}(\bar{R}_2 - r_f)}{(s_1^2 s_2^2 - s_{12}^2)} \tag{6.18}$$

$$z_2 = \frac{s_1^2(\bar{R}_2 - r_f) - s_{12}(\bar{R}_1 - r_f)}{(s_1^2 s_2^2 - s_{12}^2)} \tag{6.19}$$

Using data in respect of British Telecom plc (range: TWO) and Welsh Water (range: FOUR) from the `TEXT_DAT.WK3` spreadsheet the relevant computations can be performed to obtain values for z_1 and z_2. The actual numbers calculated for z_1 and z_2, using equations (6.18) and (6.19) are approximately 0.006 in BT plc and 0.0338 in Welsh Water plc, respectively, and using the data on returns, variances, covariance and the risk-free rate shown in Table 6.3 (see page 154) rounding to two decimal places provides the 0.01 and 0.03 which appear in the z_i (levered position) column in Table 6.4 (see page 155).

An interpretation of these figures can proceed as follows. A total budget of £1 is available for investment in risky asset 1, risky asset 2 and the risk-free asset, the levered solution (z_i) permits proportions that are calculated to sum to a figure which falls short of, or exceeds, the £1 budget available. In other words if the risk-free rate is relatively high compared to the returns available on risky assets the investor may well decide to place a portion of the budget on deposit and be certain of a return equal to the risk-free rate. On the other hand if the risk-free rate is relatively low compared to the returns available on the risky assets, then it is worth while for the investor to borrow funds and invest them in the risky assets. In this case the returns on risky assets are low compared to those that can be achieved by investing in the risk-free asset so that, in the levered portfolio solution, approximately 0.04 (0.01 in BT + 0.03 in Welsh Water) of the budget is invested in risky assets while 0.96 goes into the risk-free asset. The corresponding unlevered position where the £1 must be invested in the two risky assets and no borrowing is allowed yields the x_i proportions which are 0.15 of the £1 invested in BT plc and 0.85 of the £1 in Welsh Water plc (refer to Table 6.4 on page 155). These proportions for the unlevered portfolio can be obtained by using the formulae below:

$$x_1 = \frac{z_1}{z_1 + z_2} \tag{6.20}$$

and

$$x_2 = \frac{z_2}{z_1 + z_2} \tag{6.21}$$

Notice that the λs used in Equations (6.13) and (6.14) will cancel when used to obtain the x_i proportions in Equations (6.20) and (6.21).[1]

Lotus demo: `MARKOW.WK3`

Spreadsheet `MARKOW.WK3` has been constructed as a means of automating the process of calculating the optimal levered and unlevered portfolio proportions. The spreadsheets draws on the `TEXT_DAT.WK3` data where a range of log returns has been created that can be combined with the `MARKOW.WK3` spreadsheet. Five ranges have been defined to enable the calculation of the returns, variances and covariance terms needed to estimate the proportions for a two risky asset case. These ranges are given in Table 6.1.

To operate this spreadsheet press the Alt + A keys. This will activate a special offering the choices shown in Table 6.2.

The control data for the companies listed in Table 6.1 is already in place for the operation of this spreadsheet and is illustrated in Tables

Table 6.1. Five ranges for calculations

COMPANY	RANGE NAME
Abbey National	ONE
BT	TWO
Hanson	THREE
Welsh Water	FOUR
Sainsbury	FIVE

Table 6.2. Menu for `MARKOW.WK3`

Input	Input data
Covariances	Calculate covariances for 2 selected assets
Markowitz	Levered and unlevered solution for the optimal proportions
Quit	Exit Macro

6.3 (inputs) and 6.4 (solution). The user may choose to incorporate updated or modified observations but will then have to alter the dates in column A of the spreadsheet, accordingly.

The initial solution in respect of BT and Welsh Water can be viewed by selecting M (m) and is shown below in Table 6.4.

To run a *new* example, say Abbey National and Hanson (data ranges, ONE and THREE, respectively), select C (c). This will perform a regression that will enable the covariance term for these two data sets to be calculated. While running the regression the user will be prompted to confirm or enter *X* and *Y* ranges. Since the term required is a covariance term the order of input is not a problem. In this example type ONE in response to the *X*-range prompt and THREE at the *Y*-range prompt. The appropriate data will then be selected, the regression performed and the covariance term carried down to the Markowitz input table.

When the special menu reappears type M (m) to input the returns, variances and the risk-free rate. The covariance term will automatically be included in the matrix computations that will be performed later. To assist the user a table of variances and returns is displayed at the foot of the Markowitz input table (Table 6.3), in this Abbey National and Hanson example the required inputs would be as displayed in Table 6.5.

This spreadsheet automatically performs the matrix computations and moves to the results area of the sheet where the levered and unlevered solutions are displayed.

The results for the Abbey National and Hanson example are shown in Table 6.6. Note that in this case the methodology suggests that no investment be made in Hanson plc in either the levered or unlevered

Table 6.3.   Inputs

```
Input the following data:
Variance Asset 1: 380.22
                              Covariance:    214.4468
Variance Asset 2: 876.85
Return Asset 1:    20.56
Return Asset 2:    41.97
Risk-Free Rate    11.00
```

Range	ONE ABNAT	TWO BT	THREE HANSON	FOUR WELSHWAT	FIVE SAINSBRY	FTSE
Variance	895.84	380.22	547.68	876.85	505.73	243.59
Returns	27.79	20.56	15.49	41.97	40.28	13.26

Table 6.4. Solution

```
MARKOWITZ Portfolio optimization
     VCM
    380.22     214.4468
   214.4468     876.85
VCM_inverse              Ri — rf          zi
   0.003051   −0.00075        9.56           0.01 levered
  −0.00075     0.001323      30.97           0.03 position
                                          xi
                                             0.15 unlevered
                                             0.85 position
```

Table 6.5. Inputs

INPUT REQUIRED	VALUE
Variance Asset 1	895.84
Variance Asset 2	547.68
Return Asset 1	27.79
Return Asset 2	15.49
Risk-Free Rate	11.00

portfolios. The investment is concentrated in the Abbey National plc equity.

Extending this methodology to the 'n' risky asset case is quite straightforward. In longhand notation the general model will appear as:

$$s_p^2 = x_1^2 s_1^2 + x_2^2 s_2^2 + \ldots + x_n^2 S_n^2 + 2\,x_1 x_2 s_{12} + \ldots + 2x_{n-1}x_n s_{(n-1)(n)} \tag{6.22}$$

This represents the portfolio's variance which must be minimized subject to:

Table 6.6. Results

```
MARKOWITZ Portfolio optimization
     VCM
    895.84     335.7912
   335.7912     547.68
VCM_inverse              Ri — rf          zi
   0.001449   −0.00089       16.79           0.02 levered
  −0.00089     0.002371       4.49           0.00 position
                                          xi
                                             1.00 unlevered
                                             0.00 position
```

$$\bar{R}_p = x_1\bar{R}_1 + x_2\bar{R}_2 + x_n\bar{R}_n + (1 - x_1 - x_2 - \ldots - x_n)r_f \tag{6.23}$$

the return on the portfolio if investment in the risk-free asset is allowed.

These cumbersome expressions can be easily summarized by making use of the summation notation (Σ) from statistics, into:

$$s_p^2 = \sum_{i=1}^{n} x_i^2 s_i^2 + 2\sum_{i=1}^{n}\sum_{\substack{j=1\\i<j}}^{n} x_i x_j s_{ij} \tag{6.24}$$

for the portfolio's variance, and

$$\bar{R}_p = \sum_{i=1}^{n} x_i\bar{R}_i + (1 - \sum_{i=1}^{n} x_i)r_f \tag{6.25}$$

for the portfolio's return.

The solution proceeds exactly as described in the two asset case above but the dimensions of the matrices involved are now of course much larger.

$$\begin{bmatrix} s_1^2 & s_{12} & \ldots & s_{1n} \\ s_{21} & s_2^2 & \ldots & s_{2n} \\ \cdot & & & \cdot \\ \cdot & & & \cdot \\ \cdot & & & \cdot \\ s_{n1} & s_{n2} & \ldots & s_n^2 \end{bmatrix}^{-1} \begin{bmatrix} \bar{R}_1 - r_f \\ \bar{R}_2 - r_f \\ \cdot \\ \cdot \\ \cdot \\ \bar{R}_n - r_f \end{bmatrix} = \begin{bmatrix} z_1 \\ z_2 \\ \cdot \\ \cdot \\ \cdot \\ z_n \end{bmatrix} \tag{6.26}$$

and

$$x_i = \frac{z_i}{\sum_{i=1}^{n} z_i} \quad \text{for } i = 1, 2, \ldots, n$$

One practical difficulty with this approach is that the number of covariance terms required to construct the variance–covariance matrix (Equation (6.26)) increases very rapidly as additional risky assets are introduced.

Example 6.1
Two risky assets require the calculation of one covariance: s_{12}.
Three risky assets require the calculation of three covariances: s_{12}, s_{13}, s_{23}.
Four risky assets require the calculation of six covariances: $s_{12}, s_{13}, s_{14}, s_{23}, s_{24}, s_{34}$.
Five risky assets require the calculation of ten covariances: $s_{12}, s_{13}, s_{14}, s_{15}, s_{23}, s_{24}, s_{25}, s_{34}, s_{35}, s_{45}$.
etc.

Obtaining a figure for each covariance amounts to a tedious computational exercise. In the MARKOW.WK3 spreadsheet the single necessary covariance term was calculated using the formula:

$$s_{ij} = \sqrt{s_i^2 s_j^2 r_{ij}^2} \tag{6.27}$$

following the procedure described in Chapter 1. Since this covariance term could be negative and, again from Chapter 1, a negative relationship is very desirable in terms of the gains from diversification, the sign of the slope coefficient (β) in a regression between the two sets of logarithmic returns is checked in the spreadsheet for negativity. Should this coefficient, when tested, be shown to be negative then the covariance term is set equal to $-s_{ij}$.

Another practical difficulty lies in the accurate inversion of the variance–covariance matrix. Lotus can handle up to a (10×10) matrix, for example, but a 'real-world' situation may require far more risky assets to be taken into consideration.

6.2 Specific risk—the single index model approach

To overcome the computational problems involved in obtaining estimates of many covariance terms and matrix inversion, Sharpe proposed an alternative methodology—which can be described as the single index model (SIM). The approach can be used to estimate the covariance terms and also to establish the proportions in which the risky assets should be held in order to set up a minimum risk portfolio. The basis of the approach is a bivariate regression analysis carried out on a model of the form:

$$R_{it} = \alpha_i + \beta_i I_t + \epsilon_{it} \tag{6.28}$$

where:

R_{it} represents the return on the ith risky asset at time period t;
I_t represents some index at time period t^2;
α_i and β_i represent unknown parameters;
ϵ_{it} represents the error term for the ith risky asset at time period t.

This error term takes account of the fact that the relationship between any R and the index[2] is unlikely to be exact and, for the regression results to be statistically sound, a number of assumptions about the behaviour of the error term need to be satisfied. They are:

$E(\epsilon_{it}) = 0$ (assumption 1)
$E(\epsilon_{it}\epsilon_{is}) = 0$ for $t \neq s$ (assumption2)
$E(\epsilon_{it}^2) = \sigma^2$ (assumption 3)
$E(I_t\epsilon_{it}) = 0$ (assumption 4)

where E represents the expectation operator.

- Assumption 1 states that the mean of the error term is zero.
- Assumption 2 states that on average there is no time relationship between the error terms—in other words knowledge of the value of yesterday's error does not help in predicting where it will be today.
- Assumption 3 states that the variance of the error term is constant and equal to a value σ^2.

- Assumption 4 states that, again on average, the relationship between the error term and the index is equal to zero.

In addition to these standard regression assumptions the methodology also makes the assumption that the error term generated by the equation for the ith risky asset is on average unrelated to the error term generated by the jth risky asset. Formally this can be represented by:

$$E(\epsilon_{it}\epsilon_{jt}) = 0 \qquad \text{(assumption 5)}$$

The choice of an appropriate equity index against which the R_{it} could be regressed might prove to be the source for some philosophical debate. In practice the index of an appropriate share market is normally adopted; for example the construction of an equity portfolio based around shares of large UK companies might use the FT-SE 100 Index as the right-hand-side variable in the equation; a portfolio built around shares in large US companies might use the S&P 500; a portfolio of blue chip German shares might have the DAX (Deutsche Aktien Index) as the right-hand-side variable, etc. Using this type of approach gives rise to a whole set of equations where the return for each risky asset in the analysis is made a function of the same index—see Equation (6.29). Immediately, though, one problem becomes evident: the choice of index to use in the model is not unique and the estimated beta coefficient will differ depending upon which index is chosen.

$$R_{1t} = \alpha_1 + \beta_1 R_{mt} + \epsilon_{1t}$$
$$R_{2t} = \alpha_2 + \beta_2 R_{mt} + \epsilon_{2t}$$
$$\dots\dots\dots\dots\dots \qquad (6.29)$$
$$\dots\dots\dots\dots\dots$$
$$R_{nt} = \alpha_n + \beta_n R_{nt} + \epsilon_{nt}$$

Although it is relatively straightforward to state the formal 'n' risky asset model in the form above, it will be useful to revert to the two asset case in order to get an insight into how methodology works. Note that the expected return on a typical asset can be expressed as:

$$E(R_{it}) = \alpha_i + \beta_i E(R_{mt}) \qquad (6.30)$$

and that the variance of a typical risky asset can be written as:

$$\text{Var}(R_{it}) = E[(\alpha_i + \beta_i R_{mt} + \epsilon_{it}) - (\alpha_i + \beta_i E[R_{mt}])]^2$$
$$= E(\beta_i(R_{mt} - E[R_{mt}] + \epsilon_{it})^2 \qquad (6.31)$$

By using the binominal expansion, making use of assumption 1 above and the fact that statistically the variance of a random variable can be defined as: $\text{Var}(X) = E(X - E[X])^2$ the variance of the return on a typical risky asset can be expressed as:

$$\text{Var}(R_{it}) = \beta_i^2\sigma_m^2 + \sigma_{\epsilon_{it}}^2 \qquad (6.32)$$

This is an extremely useful expression. It introduces the idea that risk can be divided into two components. One component is defined as systematic (market) risk ($\beta_i^2\sigma_m^2$) while the other is defined as being non-systematic risk (σ_{eit}^2). These types of risk are also known as non-diversifiable and diversifiable risk, respectively. The systematic risk is the risk that the market index will move down as a whole. Even a well-diversified portfolio will tend to move as a market moves, so if the market falls this fall will, to a greater or lesser extent, be reflected in the value of the portfolio—hence the label non-diversifiable risk. Non-systematic risk on the other hand is that risk embodied in that particular risk asset. By creating a portfolio from several risky assets this type of risk can be reduced—hence the label diversifiable risk.

Considering now the problematic covariance terms, a similar approach to that adopted in the development of Equation (6.32) can be used. In this case the starting expression is:

$$\text{Cov}(R_{it}R_{jt}) = \text{E}[(\alpha_i + \beta_i R_{mt} + \epsilon_{it}) - (\alpha_i + \beta_i \text{E}[R_{mt}]) \\ \times (\alpha_j + \beta_j R_{mt} + \epsilon_{jt}) - (\alpha_j + \beta_j \text{E}[R_{mt}])] \tag{6.33}$$

Recall assumption 5, $\text{E}(\epsilon_{it}\epsilon_{jt}) = 0$, and that by making use of this together with assumption 1, and by performing some algebra, Equation (6.33) can be reduced to:

$$\text{Cov}(R_{it}R_{jt}) = \text{E}[(\beta_i(R_m - \text{E}[R_m]))(\beta_j(R_m - \text{E}[R_m]))] \tag{6.34}$$

This in turn can be rearranged to form:

$$\text{Cov}(R_{it}R_{jt}) = \text{E}[\beta_i\beta_j(R_m - \text{E}[R_m])^2] \tag{6.35}$$

where $\text{E}(R_m - \text{E}[R_m]) = \sigma_m^2$ and hence the covariance term can be rewritten as:

$$\text{Cov}(R_{it}R_{jt}) = \beta_i\beta_j\sigma_m^2 \tag{6.36}$$

which states that the estimates of the beta coefficients from the ith and jth regressions multiplied by the variance of the market will provide an estimate of the covariance between those two assets. Bear in mind, however that in arriving at this formula an assumption has been made about the average relationship between ϵ_i and ϵ_j and that in practice this assumption may not be valid.[3] Note that in this expression the non-systematic component of risk does not appear.

The algebra used above can be adapted quite simply to link the Markowitz and Sharpe approaches to the constructing of efficient portfolios.

Recall that the average return on a portfolio consisting of 'n' risky assets only can be expressed as:

$$R_p = x_1 R_1 + x_2 R_2 + \ldots + x_n R_n \tag{6.37}$$

This can now be expressed as:

$$R_p = x_1(\alpha_1 + \beta_1 R_m + \epsilon_1) + \ldots + x_n(\alpha_n + \beta_n R_m + \epsilon_n) \tag{6.38}$$

when the SIM regression method is incorporated as a means of estimating the return on the ith asset. This in turn can be separated out into three sections: one section in which the constant terms (α) are collected, one in which the slope coefficients (β) are collected, and one where the errors are collected together.

$$R_p = (x_1\alpha_1 + x_2\alpha_2 + \ldots + x_n\alpha_n)$$
$$+ (x_1\beta_1 + x_2\beta_2 + \ldots + x_n\beta_n)R_m$$
$$+ (x_1\epsilon_1 + x_2\epsilon_2 + \ldots + x_n\epsilon_n)$$

So that the returns on the portfolio can be written as:

$$R_p = \alpha_p + \beta_p R_m + \epsilon_p \tag{6.39}$$

where:

$$\alpha_p = \Sigma\, x_i\, \alpha_i$$
$$\beta_p = \Sigma\, x_i\, \beta_i$$
$$\epsilon_p = \Sigma\, x_i\, \epsilon_i$$

If the expected value of the portfolio can be defined as:

$$R_p = \alpha_p + \beta_p E[R_m] \tag{6.40}$$

the the total risk of the portfolio can be expressed as:

$$Var_p = E(R_p - E[R_p])^2$$
$$= E[(\alpha_p + \beta_p R_m + \epsilon_p) - (\alpha_p + \beta_p E[R_m])]^2 = E(\beta_p(R_m - E[R_m]) + \epsilon_p)^2 \tag{6.41}$$

Expanding this last equation, and making use of some of the statistical assumptions used earlier, provides an expression for the total risk of the portfolio in terms of beta, the risk of the market and the risk attaching to this particular portfolio:

$$Var_p = \beta_p^2\sigma_m^2 + \sigma_{ep}^2 \tag{6.42}$$

where:

$$\sigma_{ep}^2 = \sum_{i=1}^{n} x_i^2\sigma_{ei}^2$$

The interpretation of this equation runs along similar lines to that used when discussing equation (6.32) above. The first term on the right-hand side of equation (6.42) captures the risk due to the market while the second term measures the risk involved with this particular portfolio. The first term is thus non-diversifiable risk, while the second term represents diversifiable risk. Theoretically, the second term in Equation (6.42) should tend to zero in a well-diversified portfolio.

The methodology used in finding the optimal proportions for a portfolio on the basis of beta and non-systematic risk calculations appears different to that adopted for the Markowitz solution although the approaches are related (for a proof of this see Levy and Sarnat, 1984). The optimal levered proportions can be found using the formula:

$$z_i = \frac{\beta_i}{\sigma_{ei}^2}\left[\frac{(\bar{R}_i - r_f)}{\beta_i} - C^*\right] \tag{6.43}$$

where C* is found using:

$$
C^* = \frac{\sigma_m^2 \left(\sum_{j=1}^{n} \left[\dfrac{\bar{R}_j - r_f}{\sigma_{ej}^2} \right] \beta_j \right)}{\left(1 + \sigma_m^2 \sum_{j=1}^{n} \dfrac{\beta_j^2}{\sigma_{ej}^2} \right)}
\tag{6.44}
$$

Once the levered proportions have been found the unlevered position can be established by summing the z_i and then dividing the figure obtained into each individual z_i as follows:

$$
x_i = \frac{z_i}{\sum z_i}
\tag{6.45}
$$

The sum of the x_is will be unity by construction and will thus ensure that the budget constraint is satisfied. This particular approach is the one used in spreadsheet SIM.WK3 and allows for short sales to appear in the solution for both the levered and the unlevered portfolios.

Lotus demo   SIM.WK3

This spreadsheet enables the user to read in a set of observations on the logarithmic returns for four shares and an index set up previously on a separate data file. (For this demo the data is stored in the TEXT_DAT.WK3 file.) The control spreadsheet has this data on Allied-Lyons, Boots, BT and ICI for the share return data and the FT-SE for the index. Users can set up their own data to read into this sheet using the Lotus /FCN [name of range] [ENTER] F [name of file storing the data] [ENTER], i.e. the /File Combine Name File, commands.

The special menu is activated using the Alt + A keys and this will call up the menu shown in Table 6.7.

- Selecting D (d) brings the data into the file from the previously established database.
- R (r) will perform the regressions and gather together the results

Table 6.7.   Special menu for SIM.WK3

Data	Input Data
Regressions	Perform regressions for optimization routine
Table_of_Results	Optimal portfolio with short sales allowed
Quit	Exit

into a table showing raw betas, and weighted betas, systematic risk (market risk—due on the index), unsystematic risk (the risk due to this portfolio), and the return on the portfolio.

- T (t) moves the cursor to the `Table_of_Results` area of the spreadsheet where the computations performed under R (r) are displayed.
- The optimal proportions and other results for the set of control data are shown in Table 6.9.
- Q (q) exits the special menu.
- *External database:* the user is advised to follow the instructions below when setting up an external database for use in this spreadsheet.
- Using an empty spreadsheet import the data so that the first *date* observation appears in cell A4 and the $\log_e$ returns for the shares and the index appear as shown in Table 6.8.

Each set of data will then need to be named in order to combine it later into the `SIM.WK3` spreadsheet. The `SIM.WK3` spreadsheet requires that the date column in the external database commences three cells above the first date entry, as mentioned above, using the `/R N C` commands type `DATES` as the name of the range housing the date values. Since the cursor is already at the start of the range simply press arrow ↓ three times and press [END] followed by [DOWN] and [ENTER] to define the size of the range. Next move the cursor to cell B1 and again using the `/R N C` commands type `SHARES` to create the name of the range housing the $\log_e$ returns on the shares. The size of the range in this case will be larger than the date range since there are observations on four sets of returns.

To define the range type · , press arrow ↓ three times followed by [END] [DOWN], then arrow → three times followed by [ENTER]. The share return range is now named.

Now place the cursor on cell F1 and use `/R N C INDEX` to name the range with the FT-SE $\log_e$ returns. To define the size of this range since the cursor is already at the start of the range type · press arrow ↓

Table 6.8.   Setting up a database

Cell A1	Cell B1	Cell C1	Cell D1	Cell E1	Cell F1
Cell A2					
Cell A3	ALL-LYONS	BOOTS	BT	ICI	FTSE-100
31/12/90	Cell B4				
02/01/91	0.004149	−0.03822	−0.01418	−0.00928	−0.00712
03/01/91	0.002068	0.012903	0.005343	−0.00467	−0.00495
04/01/91	0.01232	0.00639	0.001775	0.012798	0.003912

three times followed by [END] [DOWN] and [ENTER] and the range will be saved.

Save the file using /F S [filename]. Whatever filename is chosen here is the name in the SIM.WK3 spreadsheet that will need to be typed in at the prompt, or selected using the F3 key and highlighting the appropriate file with the cursor, after selecting D (d).

Table 6.9 displays the table-of-results for the spreadsheet's control data, the optimal unlevered solution appears in the column on the far right-hand side and, on the basis of this methodology together with the historic data, informs the investor to create a portfolio comprising 15 per cent in Allied-Lyons plc shares, 61 per cent in Boots plc, 62 per cent in ICI plc. These positions are all long in the underlying security. The negative sign in front of the BT plc proportion of (39 per cent) suggests that the investor should hold short positions in this particular share.[4]

Other useful information provided by the spreadsheet is the portfolio β (0.88), the annualized diversifiable risk (2.30 per cent), the annualized return on the portfolio 13.28 per cent and the market risk (133.92 per cent) reported as a variance. It is the hedging of the market (non-diversifiable) risk that must now be examined.

6.3 Managing market risk

Once the specific risk of a portfolio has been diversified the major element of risk that remains is the systematic (market) risk. In the example used in Sec. 6.2 the diversifiable risk was reduced to 2.30 per cent, the market risk that remains, as measured by variance, is 133.92 per cent. It is this risk that now needs to be managed. To consider how this might be achieved take the case where a portfolio has been painstakingly constructed to track an index. It will be assumed that the index being tracked is the FT-SE 100 Index, and that the portfolio beta is equal to 1 ($\beta_p = 1$). In this case there are then two fundamental ways in which the portfolio can be hedged against adverse market movements using exchange-based derivatives: the FT-SE 100 futures contract and options on the future spot rate of the FT-SE index both of which are products of LIFFE LTOM.

6.3.1 Using futures

Initially attention will be focused on the use of the LIFFE futures contract the specification of which appears in Table 6.10. Note that the contract has a cycle of four delivery dates the three nearest of which will be traded at any time. Each index point is valued at £25 so that the cost of a contract will be £25 times the index quote at any time. For example, on 10 March 1993 the March 1993 FT-SE 100 future closed at 2958 making the cost of one contract £73,950 which, recall from

Table 6.9. Results

MARKET RISK 0.017346 FTSE-100
Start Date: 02/10/91 risk-free rate 11
End Date: 31/12/91

Company	Beta	N-S.Risk	Return	Numerator	Denominator	Ratio	Reward/Volatility Proportions	
							z_i	X
ALL-LYONS	0.97	0.0335886	0.2522	4.0921	27.800	0.147	1.11399	0.16
BOOTS	0.87	0.0202881	0.2931	7.8890	37.648	0.210	4.35399	0.61
BT	0.97	0.0251753	0.1456	1.3637	37.019	0.037	-2.74703	-0.39
ICI	0.92	0.0284797	0.3345	7.2148	29.417	0.245	4.39625	0.62
				0.356626		3.288	7.117	1.000

$C* =$ 0.108

Levered Unlevered

*Portfolio
Beta 0.88
Market Risk 133.92%
Non-systematic Risk 2.30% Expected
Total Risk 136.22% Annualized Return % 13.28

Table 6.10. FT-SE 100 Index futures contract

Unit of Trading	Valued at £25 per index point (e.g. value £67,500 at 2700.0)
Delivery Months	March, June, September, December (nearest 3 available for trading)
Delivery Day	First business day after the Last Trading Day
Last Trading Day	10.30 Third Friday in delivery month*
Quotation	Index points
Minimum Price Movement	0.5
(Tick Size & Value)	(£12.50)
Trading Hours	08.35–16.10
APT Trading Hours	16.32–17.30

Source: LIFFE. Reproduced with permission.

FT-SE 100 Index Future

Contract Standard   Cash settlement based on the Exchange Delivery Settlement Price.

Exchange Delivery Settlement Price (EDSP)   The EDSP is based on the average level of the FT-SE 100 Index between 10.10 and 10.30 on the Last Trading Day.

*In the event of the third Friday not being a business day, the Last Trading Day shall normally be the last business day preceding the third Friday.

Chapter 3, will be bought or sold on margin. The question immediately arises: how many contracts will need to be shorted in order to hedge the long index tracking portfolio described above? To determine this four inputs are required:

1   The current quote for the futures contract of interest.
2   The current value of the portfolio.
3   The beta of the portfolio (β_p).
4   The value of one contract tick.

Once these inputs are known the number of contracts required can be found using the formula:

$$\text{Number of contracts} = \frac{\text{Current value of portfolio}}{\text{Current futures quote} \times \text{Value of one tick}} \times \beta_p \qquad (6.46)$$

This format for finding an appropriate number of contracts to hedge a given portfolio is encountered often in hedging literature. Intuitively it takes the cash value of the portfolio and divides that value by the value of the instrument being used, to obtain a rough estimate of the number of contracts that should be bought or sold. Since a portfolio's beta contains information about the structure of the portfolio, beta can be used to adjust the initial number of contracts obtained to get a better match between the cash portfolio and the hedge instrument. It will be noted below that delta may be introduced as an additional adjustment parameter, and in the next chapter relative volatility will be introduced.

In the case of a portfolio currently valued at £1,000,000, a March futures quote of 2958, a portfolio beta of 1, and a defined tick value of £25, the formula provides a figure for the number of contracts required to set up a hedge of 13.5227. Since the contract is not to be traded in fractions of a unit, the portfolio manager seeking to put on a hedge must decide whether to short 13 or 14 contracts. Had the portfolio's beta been calculated at 0.9 fewer contracts would be required to hedge the position: a minimum of 12 contracts would be adequate to put on a hedge. On the other hand, had the portfolio's beta been estimated at 1.1 more contracts would be needed: at least 14 and possibly 15 could be used. A spreadsheet entitled HED_FUT.WK3 has been constructed to consider the potential outcome of putting on a short futures hedge in an equity index framework.

Lotus demo   HED_FUT.WK3

This spreadsheet can be used to demonstrate how short stock index futures contracts can be used to hedge a long portfolio of shares. It requires some inputs from the user, namely the future date for which the hedge is being put in place, the futures quotes for each of the relevant months, the current value of the portfolio, the estimated portfolio beta, the value of one tick, and *the projected future level of the spot index*.

The special menu for this spreadsheet is activated using the Alt+A keys and appears as shown in Table 6.11.

Selecting I (i) will allow the user to enter the data needed to carry out the computations for this spreadsheet. When inputting the data the user is reminded not to steer the cursor through the requested inputs with the arrow keys but to type in the requested value and press the [ENTER] key. The sequence of requests will run as follows:

- Future date of interest: to which a date must be entered in the form DD-MMM-YY (e.g.' 22-Jun-93—remember to type an apostrophe as the first character otherwise the 2 will be treated as a numeric input rather than the desired label).
- Futures prices: input the *current quotes for the futures contracts*.

Table 6.11.   Special Menu for HED_FUT.WK3

Input_Data	Input operational data
Contracts	Suggested number of contracts
Near_Contract	Table of outcomes for the next maturing contract
Middle_Contract	Table of outcomes for the middle maturity contract
Far_Contract	Table of outcomes for the longest traded contract
Quit	Exit special menu

- Spot: input the corresponding *current quote for the spot index.*
- Current value of the portfolio: input a numerical value—this will be shown as a currency input.
- Portfolio beta: input the estimated value of the beta coefficient.
- Value of one tick: input the value of a contract tick (£25 for the FT-SE 100 contract).
- Projected future level of index: input your *forecast/guess of the value of the spot index on the future date that you have selected.* It is against this figure that movements in the cash and futures markets will be measured.

The control spreadsheet inputs are displayed in Table 6.12. They are based on closing prices on 10 March 1993, the futures quotes are: 2958 for the March contract, 2976 for the June contract, 2993.5 for the September contract, with the spot index at 2949.9. Assuming a current portfolio value of £1,000,000, a portfolio beta of 1 and an expectation that the index will fall to 2800 on 21 June 1993 the spreadsheet can calculate the number of contracts required to hedge the portfolio until the June contract matures on 21 June. This figure can be established using C (c) from the special menu, and reading off for the June contract either 13 or 14, shown in Table 6.13. In this example the next step is selecting M (m) to see the results of the short, matching-dates hedge: these are displayed in Table 6.14. In view of the dynamic nature of this spreadsheet the user must input a new contract maturity date and then select either N (n), M (m) or F (f) to see updated results.

On the cash market side of Table 6.14 the starting value of the portfolio is reported as £1,000,000. By the 21 June the portfolio manager's fears have been realized and the index has fallen to 2800

Table 6.12.   Control spreadsheet inputs

Today	11-Mar-93		
Future date of interest	21-Jun-93		
Contract Prices	MARCH	JUNE	SEPT
Future	2958	2976	2993.5
Spot	2949.9		
Basis	8.1	26.1	43.6
Current Portfolio Value (£s)	£1,000,000	Current Portfolio Beta:	1
Value of One tick:	£25.00		
Projected Future Level of Index:		2800 on	21-Jun-93

Table 6.13. Number of contracts required

	RECOMMENDED		Rounding	
			Down	Up
MARCH	22-Mar-93	No. of Futures contracts		
CONTRACT		to buy/sell:	13.00	14.00
JUNE	21-Jun-93	No. of Futures contracts		
CONTRACT		to buy/sell	13.00	14.00
SEPT	21-Sep-93	No. of Futures contracts		
CONTRACT		to buy/sell:	13.00	14.00

with the consequent effect that the value of the portfolio is now £949,185, a loss of £50,815. The futures side of the transaction shows a decision to sell 13 contracts for £967,200 on 11 March, subsequently closing down the position on 21 June by purchasing 13 futures contracts for a sum of £910,000. The resulting profit in the futures market is £57,200. On the face of it the portfolio manager has made a small profit on the transaction (£57,200−£50,815 = £6,385), however, it must be remembered that a margin account has been in operation throughout the time that the portfolio manager has been maintaining the futures position which implies, potentially, some loss of interest income from the funds deposited which, in conjunction with other costs involved, could well result in the profit and loss figures from the two sides of the transaction being much closer together.

In the example above the horizon of the hedge exactly matched the maturity of an exchange-based instrument. Although the spot and the future market indexes will converge to be equal on maturity of the contract, at any time prior to delivery day there will be a difference between the price of the future and the price of the spot (i.e. basis):

Table 6.14. Results of short matching-dates hedge

Short Hedge Results		JUNE	CONTRACT
	Cash	Futures	
Dates	Market	Market	
	Portfolio	Sell	13
11-Mar-93	Value	Futures contracts	
	£1,000,000	£967,200	
	Portfolio	Buy	13
21-Jun-93	Value	Futures contracts	
	£949,185	£910,000	
	Profit/Loss:	(£50,815) Profit/Loss:	£57,200

Basis = Future price − Spot price   (6.47)

If the horizon for a hedge is required in respect of a date not matching the maturity date of a specific contract then the portfolio manager must take this basis difference into account; movements in basis constitute a real risk—*basis risk*. Forecasting basis accurately is not a trivial exercise and at times the future − spot basis can widen dramatically, an example of this would be the gap between the spot index in New York and future stock indexes in Chicago that opened up on 'Black Monday' in October 1987. A simple, but not necessarily accurate, approach would be to make the assumption that the basis erodes linearly over time. That is to say that if the basis for the June futures contract on 11 March 1993 is 26.1 (see Table 6.15) and there are 101 days until 21 June 1993, the basis will decrease at a rate of 0.2584 points per day. Using this approach it is possible to project the results for a hedge that falls between exchange-based maturity dates.

Lotus demo   HED_FUT.WK3
Using this spreadsheet again, it is possible to examine a short hedge for non-matching dates. To see these results type N (n), M (m), F (f) when the special menu has been activated. An example of this situation is illustrated in Tables 6.15 and 6.16.

In this example the date of interest is *1 June 1993* when the index is expected to be at 2870. Table 6.16 shows, under the assumption that the projected fall proves to be accurate, that the value of the portfolio will have fallen to £972,914, a loss of £27,086. On the other side of the transaction the futures contracts shorted on 11 March can be bought back cheaper, realizing a profit of £32,683. Once again the hedge is imperfect in that the loss on the cash side of the transaction is not exactly offset by the profit from the futures side, moreover, it must be remembered that transactions costs, dividend receipts, movements in margin account and other costs have not been brought into the picture.

The menu displayed in Table 6.11 allows the user to choose which contract he or she wishes to use. Should the user select an inappropriate contract for the hedge— for example, trying to hedge a 1 June horizon with a March contract—the selected table will report that the contract is inappropriate. However, 1 June could still be hedged using the June or September contracts. It must also be stressed that there is unfortunately no guarantee that basis will ever behave in the linear manner suggested above. Should the basis widen or shrink in some other way the hedge will not be as efficient as intended. To some extent this problem can be handled and the methodology for putting an *interpolative hedge* will be discussed below.

A word of caution is required in using this spreadsheet. In an attempt to automate the process of demonstrating the short futures hedge, a set of dates for the contract has been set up. This list will be checked for contracts which have expired and will automatically update the list of live contracts. The list currently

Table 6.15. June futures contract basis on 11 March 1993

```
Today          11-Mar-93
Future Date
of Interest 1-Jun-93
Contracts    MARCH        JUNE        SEPT
Prices
Futures              2958        2976      2993.5
Spot             2949.9
Basis               8.1          26.1        43.6
Current                      Current
Portfolio                    Portfolio
Value(£s)    £1,000,000      Beta            1
Value of
One tick:        £25.00
Projected Future Level of Index:    2870    on    1-Jun-93
```

has dates up to December 1998. The user should augment this list as 1998 approaches otherwise the spreadsheet will cease to function. The dates start in cell I2 and are listed as a column.

Lotus demo NON_MAT.WK3
This spreadsheet has been designed to demonstrate the use of a short stock index futures contract position to set up an interpolative hedge on a long portfolio of shares for horizons which do not match the expiry dates of exchange-based contracts. It requires some inputs from the user:

Portfolio
– Scenario   Market falls or market rises.
– Horizon   Future date of interest (*Note*: this should be a date before the date on which the middle contract expires).

Table 6.16. Short hedge for non-matching dates

```
Short Hedge Results              JUNE                    CONTRACT
              Cash               Futures
Dates         Market             Market
              Portfolio          Sell                          13
11-Mar-93     Value              Futures contracts
              £1,000,000         £967,200
              Portfolio          Buy                           13
1-Jun-93      Value              Futures contracts
              £972,914           £934,517
              Profit/Loss:       (£27,086)Profit/Loss:  £32,683
```

– Value of portfolio   Current value of the portfolio.

– Portfolio's beta.

Scenarios   The *assumed* future values for the middle and far contract values, and future spot indexes.

Middle contract expiry date   The expiry date of the contract which is the middle contract at the time that the hedge is put in to place.

Contracts   The split between the near and middle contracts that have to be shorted to put on the hedge. These are calculated on the *middle contract expiry date* and the *portfolio details* dates have been entered. The value of one tick is assumed to be £25.

The special menu for this spreadsheet is activated using the Alt + A keys and appears as shown in Table 6.17.

- Selecting D (d) enables the user to input the date on which the contracts are to be closed out—the *horizon*.
- Selecting N (n) allow the user to enter the current futures quotes for the nearest contract, and *current spot index*. Note that [ENTER] must be pressed after each quote has been typed in.
- Selecting M (m) allows the user to enter the current futures quotes for the middle contract, and the *projected spot index at the expiry of the near contract*. Note that [ENTER] must be pressed after each quote has been typed in.

Table 6.17.   Special menu for NON_MAT.WK3

Dates	Month in which the contract expires
NEAR	Input quoted Spot and Future quotes for the NEAR contract
MIDDLE	Input quoted Spot and Future quotes for the MIDDLE contract
FAR	Input quoted Spot and Future quotes for the FAR contract
Contracts	Number of contracts to buy/sell
Portfolio	Inputs to the Portfolio, value, beta etc.
Results	Results of Hedge: Gain and Loss Table
Quit	Exit Macro

- Selecting F (f) allows the user to enter the current futures quotes for the far contract, and the *projected spot index at the horizon.* Note that [ENTER] must be pressed after each quote has been typed in.
- C (c) Once the portfolio's profile has been entered (P or p, see below) the number of contracts that need to be shorted in the near and middle contracts can be calculated. To achieve this the user must enter the expiry date of the middle contract and press [ENTER].
- P (p) enable the entry of the current portfolio's profile. The sequence of inputs will be:
  - Scenario: type in market fall or market rises.
  - Horizon: type in *a date between the expiry of the near contract and the expiry of the middle contract.*
  - Value: type in the current value of the portfolio. This will be shown as a currency value.
  - Beta: type in the portfolio's beta.
    Note that [ENTER] must be pressed after each quote has been typed in.

The control spreadsheet inputs are displayed in Tables 6.18, 6.19 and 6.20, and are based on closing prices on 10 March 1993.

Table 6.18.   Control spreadsheet inputs

11-Mar-93	Futures Contracts	Quote	STRATEGY & PAYOFFS	
	March	2958	Sell	12 March
	June	2976	Sell	2 June
	September	2993.5		
	Spot Index	2949.9		
March Contract Matures EDSP	Futures Contracts	Quote		
	March	2925	Buy	12 March
	June	2951	Sell	12 June
	September	2979		
			Sell	14 June
	Spot		Buy	14 September
	Index	2925		
1-Jun-93	Futures Contracts	Price		
	June	2825	Buy	2 June
	September	2854	Buy	26 June
	December	2877	Sell	14 September
	Spot Index	2800		

Table 6.19. Control spreadsheet inputs

Scenario:	Market falls	
Horizon:	1-Jun-93	
Portfolio		
Value:	£1,000,000	(LONG)
beta:	1	

Table 6.20. Control spreadsheet inputs

CONTRACT SPLIT

Middle Contract expires	17-Jun-93	
	March	12
	June	2

- R (r) provides the user with the results of the interpolative hedge. These are displayed in Table 6.21.
- Selecting Q (q) exits the special menu and returns.

The current futures quotes are: 2958 for the March contract, 2976 for the June contract, 2993.5 for the September contract, with the spot index at 2949.9.

The projected value on expiry of the near contract are: EDSP March contract, 2925, for the June contract, 2951, and for the September contract, 2979. The projected level of the spot index on that date is equal to the EDSP of the near contract and is thus 2925.

At the horizon of interest the projected values are: June contract, 2825, September contract, 2854, and 2877 for the December contract. The projected spot index at that date is 2800.

Assuming a current portfolio value of £1,000,000 a portfolio beta of 1

Table 6.21. Results of interpolative hedge

Interpolative Short Hedge Results

	Profit/Loss	
	£9,900	on March
	£7,550	on June
	£81,900	on June
	(£43,750)	on September
		contracts
Total (Futures):	£55,600	
Profit/Loss (Portfolio):	(£50,815)	
Net Profit/Loss:	£4,785	

and an expectation that the index will fall to 2800 on 1 June 1993 the
spreadsheet can calculate the number of contracts required to put on a
start-up hedge. From Table 6.20 it can be seen that 12 March and 2 June
contracts should be sold. This figure can be established using C (c) from
the special menu.

In this example the results of the interpolative short hedge show that
the strategy adopted in Table 6.18 would result in a gain of £55,600
from the futures leg of the strategy, a loss of £50,815 on the value of the
underlying portfolio, resulting in a net gain of £4785:

- 11 March 93: Sell 12 March contracts   (*initial hedge*).
                Sell 2 June contracts.
- March contract expires:
  - Buy 12 March (to close the short March position) *(spot hedge)*.
  - Sell 12 June (to replace the closed out March position—
    a total of 14 contracts are required to cover the portfolio's
    market risk).
  - Sell 14 June contracts *(basis risk hedge)*.
    Buy 14 December contracts.
- 1 June 93:   Buy a total of 28 June contracts to close the 28 short
                positions entered into on 11 March 93 and at expiry of
                the March contract, and sell 14 December contracts to
                close the long December position.

Once again it must be remembered that transactions' costs, dividend
receipts, movements in margin account and other costs, which would
play a real-life role in the hedge, have not been brought into the picture.

6.3.2 Using stock index options

As an alternative to the short futures hedge discussed in Sec. 6.3.1 an option hedge
could have been put in place. In the case of a long equity portfolio a hedge is
required to protect the portfolio's downside risk when the benchmark index falls
or is expected to fall. From Chapter 4 it will be recalled that there are many
profit/loss profiles that can be constructed using options—two basic possibilities
are considered here:

1 Buy put options on the index.
2 Buy put and write call options on the index, with the same strike, to create a
   synthetic short position.

LIFFE LTOM has two types of options available on the FT-SE 100 Index: the
American-style option and the European-style option. The contract specifications
for these instruments appear in Table 6.22(a) and (b).

To develop the first of these two strategies a profile can be obtained by using the

Table 6.22(a). FT-SE 100 Index option (American style exercise)

Unit of Trading	Valued at £10 per index point
Expiry Months	June and December plus such additional months that the nearest 4 calendar months are always available for trading.
Exercise/ Settlement Day	Exercise by 16.31 on any business day, extended to 18.00 for expiring series on the Last Trading Day. Settlement Day is the first business day after the day of exercise/Last Trading Day.
Last Trading Day	10.30 Third Friday of expiry month*
Quotation	Index points
Minimum Price Movement (Tick Size & Value)	0.5 (£5.00)
Trading Hours	08.35–16.10

Source: LIFFE. Reproduced with permission.

FT-SE 100 Index Options

Contract Standard Cash settlement based on a Daily Settlement Price for non-expiring series of the Exchange Delivery Settlement Price for expiring series.

Daily Settlement Price The Daily Settlement Price is the equivalent of FT-SE 100 Index level at 16.10.

Exchange Delivery Settlement Price (EDSP) The EDSP is based on the average level of the FT-SE 100 Index between 10.10 and 10.30 on the Last Trading Day.

Option Premium Option is payable in full by the buyer on the business day following a transaction.

Exercise Price and Exercise Price Intervals The interval between exercise price is determined by the time to maturity of a particular expiry month and is either 50 or 100 index points.

Introduction of New Exercise Prices Additional exercise prices will be introduced on the business day after the underlying index level has exceeded the second highest or fallen below the second lowest, available exercise price.

*In the event of the third Friday not being a business day, the Last Trading Day shall normally be the last business day preceding the third Friday.

OPT_STR1.WK3 spreadsheet encountered in Chapter 4. Taking the index information used in Sec. 6.3.1 (see Table 6.15) together with the call and put premiums shown in Table 6.23, the pay-off profiles presented in Figs. 6.1(a), (b) and (c) reveal profit/loss profiles that result from different strikes. Although the profiles appear similar they differ substantially in terms of the cost of the hedge.

Case 6.1(a)

A June put with a strike of 2750 is purchased at a premium of 28 per contract. Figure 6.1(a) illustrates that the cost of portfolio insurance will be 228 units if the index declines by 20 per cent to 2360. However, if the index rises from its current level (2950) by only 28 points or more the portfolio moves back into overall profit.

Case 6.1(b)

A June put with a strike of 2950 is purchased at a premium of 84 per contract. Figure 6.1(b) illustrates that the cost of portfolio insurance will be 84 units if the index declines by 20 per cent to 2360. However, the index will now have to

Table 6.22(b).   FT-SE 100 Index option (European style exercise)

Unit of Trading	Valued at £10 per index point
Expiry Months	March, June, September and December plus such additional months that the 3 nearest calendar months are always available for trading
Exercise/ Settlement Day	Exercise by 18.00 for expiring series on the Last Trading Day Settlement Day is the first business day after the Last Trading Day. (An option can only be exercised on the Last Trading Day.)
Last Trading Day	10.30 Third Friday of expiry month*
Quotation	Index point
Minimum Price Movement (Tick Size & Value)	0.5 (£5.00)
Trading Hours	08.35–16.10

Source: LIFFE. Reproduced with permission.

FT-SE 100 Index Options

Contract Standard   Cash settlement based on the Exchange Delivery Settlement Price.

Exchange Delivery Settlement Price (EDSP)   The EDSP is based on the average level of the FT-SE 100 Index between 10.10 and 10.30 on the Last Trading Day.

Option Premium   Option Premium is payable in full by the buyer on the business day following a transaction.

Exercise Price and Exercise Price Intervals   The interval between exercise prices is determined by the time to maturity of a particular expiry month and is either 50 or 100 index points.

Introduction of New Exercise Prices   Additional exercise prices will be introduced on the business day after the underlying index level has exceeded the second highest or fallen below the second lowest, available exercise price.

*In the event of the third Friday not being a business day, the Last Trading Day shall normally be the last business day preceding the third Friday.

rise by 84 points or more from it current 2950 level before the portfolio moves back into overall profit.

Case 6.1(c)

A June put with a strike of 3100 is purchased at a premium of 175 per contract. Figure 6.1(c) illustrates that the cost portfolio insurance will be 25 units if the index declines by 20 per cent to 2360. However, in this situation the index will have to rise by 175 points or more from its current 2950 level before the portfolio moves back into overall profit.

Table 6.23.   Call and put premiums

```
Input the following information:
Current Price of the underlying security:     2949.9
                                 Premiums
Strike Prices:              CALLS         PUTS
Low              2750       251.00        28.00
Middle           2950       108.00        84.00
High             3100        46.00       175.00
```

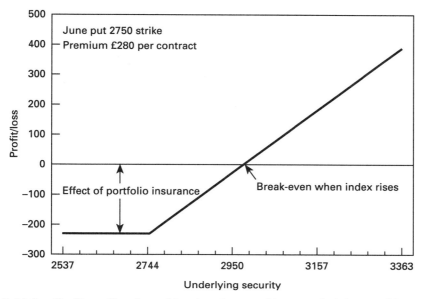

Fig. 6.1(a).   Profit profile of combined options and long underlying position

Clearly each of the cases outlined provides a different type of insurance, however, the stronger the indications that the index will suffer a bad decline the greater the incentive for portfolio managers to adopt the strategy of buying a put with a high strike (Case 6.1(c)).

Figure 6.2 displays the profile of the combined synthetic short position and the

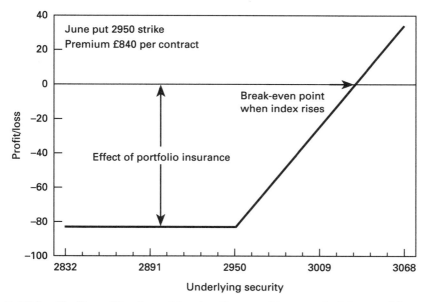

Fig. 6.1(b).   Profit profile of combined options and long underlying position

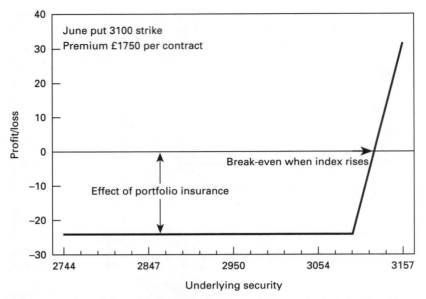

Fig. 6.1(c).   Profit profile of combined options and long underlying position

long, underlying index tracking portfolio position.

In this case the position, at least in theory, is that whatever happens to the market the total combined position—long equity, short call, long put—leaves the position flat. This is the same sort of profile that would have been achieved using a short futures contract.

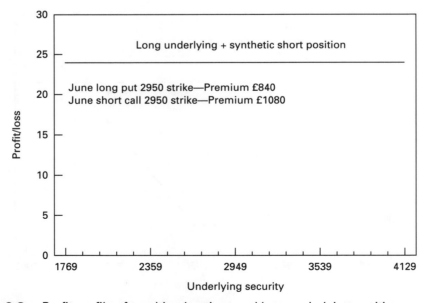

Fig. 6.2.   Profit profile of combined options and long underlying position

Of course these profiles are only illustrative. To get a more realistic idea of pay-offs involved more information is needed concerning the structural characteristics of the portfolio being hedged. If the portfolio structure used in Sec. 6.3.1 is adopted, then the relevant data required in order to establish the number of contracts needed to put on a *fixed* options hedge is:

1 The option strike price
2 The current value of the portfolio
3 The portfolio's beta (β_p)
4 The value of one index point.

Fixed hedge

$$\text{No. of contracts} = \frac{\text{Current value of portfolio}}{\text{Selected strike price} \times \text{Value of one index point}} \times \beta_p \qquad (6.48)$$

Note that in this formula the futures quote of Equation (6.46) is replaced by the selected strike price and that the value of one futures tick (£25 from the LIFFE LTOM contract specification) will be replaced by the value of one index point (£10 from the LIFFE LTOM contract specification).

In the case of a portfolio currently valued at £1,000,000, a spot index quote of 2949.5, a portfolio beta of 1, and a defined contract index point value of £10 the formula provides a figure for the number of contracts required to set up a hedge of 33.9041. Since the contract will not be sold in fractions of a unit the portfolio manager seeking to put on a fixed hedge must decide whether to buy 33 or 34 puts. Had the portfolio's beta been calculated at 0.9, fewer contracts would be required to hedge the position: a minimum of 30 contracts would be adequate to put on a fixed hedge. On the other hand, had the portfolio's beta been estimated at 1.1, more contracts would be required: at least 37 and possibly 38 puts could be used.

This type of fixed hedge could also be described as a static hedge. The put options are purchased as a form of insurance policy against adverse movements in the underlying market index, the hedge is set up and is then left untouched, being exercised on expiration only if the option has an intrinsic value. However, a more dynamic hedging approach could be adopted by making use of the option's delta (see Chapter 5). The number of contracts needed to put on a delta-neutral hedge—also known as a ratio hedge—can be found by employing the formula shown in Equation (6.49).

Delta-neutral hedge formula

$$\text{No. of contracts} = \frac{\text{Current value of portfolio}}{\text{Selected strike price} \times \text{Value of one tick}} \times \frac{\beta_p}{\delta} \qquad (6.49)$$

To demonstrate how this formula might be used take the example above where, say, 34 put contracts are needed to hedge a portfolio with a beta of 1, and a delta calculated as 0.5. The modified number of contracts required to initiate a delta-neutral position would be given by 34/0.5 = 68 contracts.

A spreadsheet entitled HED_OPT.WK3 has been constructed to consider the potential outcomes of setting up option-based hedges.

Lotus demo   HED_OPT.WK3
This spreadsheet enables the user to examine long put or short call hedging strategies for user-defined expiration dates, projected future index value at user-specified dates—date must be less than or equal to the expiration date of the contract. The spreadsheet is driven by a special menu that can be activated using the Alt+A keys and which offers the facilities shown in Table 6.24.

Selecting D (d) enables the user to input the data necessary to carry out the valuation of the position. The sequence of inputs that are required is as follows:

- Expiration date: type a date or modify the existing entry using the F2 key. Press [ENTER].
- Strike price: type in a valid strike price. Press [ENTER].
- Volatility: type in the annualized volatility of the index. Press [ENTER].
- Dividend yield: type in an annualized percentage figure. Press [ENTER].
- Future date: type in the date at the horizon of interest—this date must not be greater than the expiration date selected as the first entry. Press [ENTER].

Table 6.24.   Special menu for HED_OPT.WK3

Data_Input	Input basic data
Option_Table	Option Pricing for Stock Indexes (FT-SE100, S&P500, etc.)
Synthetic	Long Put and Short Call combined
Put_Hedge	Table of Results for Profit and Loss using Long Puts
Call_Hedge	Written call position
Valuation	Valuation of the Option 'x' days from expiration
Quit	Exit Macro

- Value of one index point: type in the tick value, e.g. FT-SE options £10. Press [ENTER].
- Portfolio value: type in the current value of the portfolio. Press [ENTER].
- Portfolio Beta: type in the value of the portfolio's beta. Press [ENTER].
- Projected future level of index: input a guess of where the index will be at the chosen time horizon. Press [ENTER].
- The user is reminded *not* to steer the cursor through these inputs. The macro will automatically move to the next input cell once the [ENTER] key has been pressed.
- The original control data for this problem is shown in Table 6.25.

The projected future level of the index is 2870 which matches the level used in the futures example and other data shown in Table 6.15. Having input the data for the case that the user wishes to examine, the special menu reappears at the top of the screen waiting for the next choice to be made:

- Selecting O (o) takes the user to the option pricing table. This table provides information on the option's call/put premium, associated deltas and gammas.
- Selecting S (s) enables the user to view the table of results for a combined short call plus long put position which is a synthetic short forward position.
- Selecting P (p) displays the profit and loss table that would result from a long put only position being used to hedge the downside risk of the portfolio. When viewing this option on a special menu the user is invited to input the number of contracts that are to be used to hedge the position. Recommended numbers of contracts for a fixed or a delta-neutral hedge are displayed at the bottom of the table. Once the number of contracts has been typed in press [ENTER] to reactivate the special menu at the top of the screen.
- Selecting C (c) displays the profit and loss table that would result from a short call only position being used to hedge the downside risk of the portfolio. (The maximum benefit that will be derived from this type of hedge is the premium received for the calls. If the market moves up, the calls will pick up an intrinsic value and the upside potential of the portfolio will be negatively affected.) When viewing this option on the special menu the user is prompted to input the number of contracts that are to be used to hedge the position. Recommended numbers of contracts for a fixed or a delta-neutral hedge are displayed at the bottom of the table. Once the number of contracts has been typed in press [ENTER] to reactivate the special menu at the top of the screen.
- Selecting V (v) will allow the user to see a valuation of the option's premiums and associated deltas at the specified date in the future.

Table 6.25. Control data

INPUT DATA	Today:	11-Mar-93		
Input the following values:				
			Put	Call
Expiration Date	16-Jun-93			
Days to Expiration	98.00			
Strike Price	2950	Option Premium	85.00	108.00
%Volatility p.a.	15.89			
Current Underlying Price	2949.9	Current	Current	
Rate of Interest (%) p.a.	6	Portfolio	Portfolio	
		Value (£s) £1,000,000	Beta:	1
Approx. dividend yield (%) p.a.	3			
(Required for pricing Stock		Value of	£10.00	
index options)		One Index point:		
		Project Future		
Future Date of Interest	1-Jun-93	Level of Index:	2870 on	1-Jun-93

182

Remember that the horizon date must be less than or equal to the expiration date of the option.

- Selecting Q (q) exits the special menu and returns Lotus to normal mode.

With this spreadsheet it is possible to compare the option-based hedge with outcome for the futures-based hedge of similar if not identical maturity.

Lotus demo   `HED_OPT.WK3`
Consider the control data for this spreadsheet displayed in Table 6.25. The dateline now is 11 March, the current index stands at 2949.9, the future date of interest is 1 June when the index is expected to be at 2870. The portfolio manager decides on a strategy of buying a put option with a strike of 2950 to hedge the index tracking £1,000,000 portfolio. The put is priced at 85 which translates to £850 per contract given the LIFFE LTOM contract specification. The results of this hedge can be seen by examining Table 6.26. The figures in that table indicate that if a fixed hedge had been put on, 33 contracts would have been needed at an initial cost on 11 March of £28,050.

If, on 1 June, the market has fallen by 80 points the portfolio's value will have shrunk to £972,914. The option will have an intrinsic and time value and the position is valued at £28,783 (the option's value has been eroded with the elapse of time hence the low valuation given the index's 80 point fall). Note that although there is a net gain on the option side of the transaction, overall the position is showing a loss of

Table 6.26.   Results of hedge

Long Put Hedge Results

Dates	Cash Market	Options Market				
11-Mar-93	Portfolio Value £1,000,000	Buy Put Contracts £28,050	33			
1-Jun-93	Portfolio Value £972,914	Valuation of Put contracts £28,783	33			
				Net Profit/Loss		
Profit/Loss: (27,086)		Profit/Loss: £733		(£26,352)		

RECOMMENDED NUMBER OF CONTRACTS
FOR   LONG PUTS

	Rounding		Delta Neutral	Rounding	
Fixed hedge	Down	Up	hedge	Down	Up
Contracts	33	34	Contracts:	76	77

£26,352. A delta hedge might have been selected which would have required 76 or 77 contracts but this position would have required a dynamic hedging policy frequently reviewing the position and adjusting the number of contracts used to hedge the portfolio.

An alternative strategy would have been to use written calls to hedge the position, or at least provide some income to compensate for a market fall. Adopting the same scenario as in the previous paragraphs the outcome here would be as depicted in Table 6.27. In this case the written calls have no intrinsic value (index 2870 < strike 2950) and the remaining time value only amounts to £3614. The difference between the call option's current value and the premium paid on 11 March represents a profit to the writer. This leaves the position with a small overall profit of £4940.

Yet another strategy would be to replicate the short futures position by combining written calls with long puts. The outcome of this strategy is presented in Table 6.28 and demonstrates the idea that movements on the long side of the position are offset by almost equal but opposite movements on the short side of the position. The user is referred back to Fig. 6.2 which shows the flat nature of this strategy.

Now consider the opposite scenario, that is, the index rises rather than falls. Tables 6.29, 6.30, 6.31 and 6.32, demonstrate the outcome under the assumption that the index rises to 3100 for the long put, short call and synthetic short strategies, respectively. The input data for this situation appears as Table 6.29. In each case the net pay-off is positive. However, one thing must be borne in mind, namely, that getting the forecast wrong and taking out a counter position has resulted in the

Table 6.27.   Written calls to hedge position

```
Short Call Hedge Results
            Cash        Options
Dates       Market      Market
            Portfolio   Sell            33
11-Mar-93 Value         Call Contracts
            £1,000,000     £35,640
            Portfolio   Valuation of  33
1-Jun-93  Value         Call contracts
            £972,914       £3,614
                                        Net Profit/Loss
Profit/Loss:(£27,086)Profit/Loss: £32,026     £4,940
RECOMMENDED NUMBER OF CONTRACTS FOR SHORT PUTS
                  Rounding        Delta Neutral      Rounding
Fixed hedge   Down        Up      hedge           Down        Up
Contracts      33         34      Contracts:       61         62
```

Table 6.28.   Combining written calls and long puts

```
Combined Long Put and Short Call Hedge Results
                Cash          Options
Dates          Market        Market
               Portfolio    Net Cost
11-Mar-93 Value            of contracts
               £1,000,000    £7,590
               Portfolio    Valuation of
1-Jun-93  Value            of contracts
               £972,914      £25,169
                                             Net Profit/Loss
Profit/Loss:(£27,086)Profit/Loss: £32,759        £5,674
CONTRACTS USED:     CALLS          PUTS          STRIKE
                      33            33             2950
Future date of interest:      1-Jun-93
```

gain that accrues to the long position being reduced.

The user of this spreadsheet is encouraged to try the effects of using different strikes and differing numbers of call and put contracts to hedge the portfolio.

Sections 6.3.1 and 6.3.2 focused on the use of derivatives to protect the value of the long equity portfolio against *market risk*. The earlier sections of this chapter considered diversification as a means of reducing the *specific risk* of holding equity. In closing it must be mentioned that, if the holder of the portfolio of shares suspects that share prices for one of the constituent members of the portfolio is likely to fall, *individual stock options* could be used to protect the portfolio's value against a fall in the price of that one security. Several theoretical strategies relating to individual shares were discussed in Chapter 4.

6.4 Spreadsheets

There are five demonstration spreadsheets used in this chapter:

1   MARKOW.WK3 which is described in Sec. 6.1 and whose special menu is illustrated in Table 6.2.
2   SIM.WK3 which is discussed in Sec. 6.2 and whose special menu appears as Table 6.7.
3   HED_FUT.WK3 which is described in Sec. 6.3.1 and whose special menu appears as Table 6.11.
4   NON_MAT.WK3 which is also described in Sec. 6.3.1 and whose special menu appears as Table 6.17.

Table 6.29. Input data

INPUT DATA	Today:	11-Mar-93		
Input the following values:				
			Put	Call
Expiration Date	16-Jun-93			
Days to Expiration	98.00			
Strike Price	2950	Option Premium	85.00	108.00
% Volatility p.a.	15.89			
Current Underlying Price	2949.9	Current		Current
Rate of Interest (%) p.a.	6	Portfolio		Portfolio
		Value (£s) £1,000,000		Beta: 1
Approx. dividend yield (%) p.a.	3	Value of	£10.00	
(Required for pricing Stock		One Index point:		
index options)		Project Future		
		Level of Index:	3100 on	1-Jun-93
Future Date of Interest	1-Jun-93			

186

Table 6.30. Long put hedge results

```
Long Put Hedge Results
               Cash         Options
Dates          Market       Market
               Portfolio    Buy              33
11-Mar-93 Value             Put Contracts
                £1,000,000     £28,050
               Portfolio    Valuation of  33
1-Jun-93  Value             Put contracts
                £1,050883      £784
                                        Net  Profit/Loss
Profit/Loss:(£50,883)Profit/Loss: (£27,266)    £23,618
RECOMMENDED NUMBER OF CONTRACTS
FOR        LONG PUTS
                    Rounding          Delta Neutral      Rounding
Fixed hedge    Down         Up       hedge            Down        Up
Contracts       33          34       Contracts:        76         77
```

5   HED_OPT.WK3 which is described in Sec. 6.3.2 and whose special menu appears as Table 6.24.

6.4.1 MARKOW.WK3

The special menu, which appears as Table 6.2, provides users with an opportunity of inputting the variances and returns of two risky assets, and the appropriate risk-

Table 6.31. Short call hedge results

```
Short Call Hedge Results
               Cash         Options
Dates          Market       Market
               Portfolio    Sell             33
11-Mar-93 Value             Call Contracts
                £1,000,000     £35,640
               Portfolio    Valuation of  33
1-Jun-93  Value             Call contracts
                £1,050,883     £51,421
                                        Net  Profit/Loss
Profit/Loss: £50,883 Profit/Loss: (£15,781)    £35,102
RECOMMENDED NUMBER OF CONTRACTS FOR SHORT CALLS
                    Rounding          Delta Neutral      Rounding
Fixed hedge    Down         Up       hedge            Down        Up
Contracts       33          34       Contracts:        61         62
```

Table 6.32.   Combined Long Put and Short Call Hedge Results

```
Combined Long Put and Short Call Hedge Results
              Cash        Options
Dates         Market       Market
          Portfolio   Net Cost
11-Mar-93 Value        of contracts
           £1,000,000    £7,590
          Portfolio   Valuation of
1-Jun-93  Value         contracts
           £1,050,883     (£50,637)
                                            Net Profit/Loss
Profit/Loss:£50,883 Profit/Loss:  (£43,047)       £7,836
CONTRACTS USED:     CALLS          PUTS              STRIKE
                     33             33                 2950
Future date of interest:       1-Jun-93
```

free rate of interest:

(Input);

estimates the covariance for two, user-selected assets:

(Covariances);

calculates the optimal levered and unlevered portfolio proportions:

(Markowitz);

a final macro exits the special menu returning the spreadsheet back to normal Lotus operating mode:

(Quit).

6.4.2 SIM.WK3

The special menu, which appears as Table 6.7, provides users with an opportunity of inputting a date range, $\log_e$ returns and an index over that date range, on a semi-automatic basis as described in the text:

(Data);

performing the regressions required for the optimization routine:

(Regressions);

viewing the optimized portfolio:

(Table_of_Results);

a fourth macro exits the special menu returning the spreadsheet back to normal Lotus operating mode:

(Quit).

6.4.3 HED_FUT.WK3

The special menu, which appears as Table 6.11, provides users with an opportunity of inputting up-to-date futures quotes, the current spot quote, a portfolio valuation, a portfolio beta and a future horizon:

(Input_Data);

it provides a suggested number of contracts to use to hedge the position:

(Contracts);

and tables of hedge outcomes at the specified horizon for the:

(Near_Contract), (Middle_Contract) and (Far_Contract);

a final macro exits the special menu returning the spreadsheet back to normal Lotus operating mode:

(Quit).

6.4.4 NON_MAT.WK3

The special menu, which appears as Table 6.17, provides users with an opportunity of inputting the horizon of interest, current spot quote, projected spot at the expiry of the near contract, the projected spot at the horizon date:

(Dates);

inputting spot and futures quotes for the:

(NEAR), (MIDDLE), and (FAR) contracts;

it also provides a suggested number of contracts to use to hedge the position:

(Contracts);

the opportunity to input portfolio details (current valuation and beta):

(Portfolio);

to obtain tables of hedge outcomes at the special horizon:

(Results);

a final macro exits the special menu returning the spreadsheet back to normal

Lotus operating mode:

`(Quit).`

6.4.5 `HED_OPT.WK3`

The special menu, which appears as Table 6.24, provides users with an opportunity of inputting the index option's expiration date, its strike price, the associated volatility of the underlying index, the dividend yield of the index, the future horizon, the tick value of the contract, the current valuation of the portfolio, the portfolio's beta, and a prediction of the level of the index at the horizon:

`(Data_Input)`

calculates the current call and put option premiums:

`(Option_Table);`

provides hedge results for long puts and written calls combined, long puts only, short calls only:

`(Synthetic), (Put_Hedge), (Call_Hedge);`

provides a valuation of the options at the horizon (which need not be the expiration of the option):

`(Valuation);`

and a final macro exits the special menu returning the spreadsheet back to normal Lotus operating mode.

`(Quit).`

Questions

6.1 Use the `MARKOW.WK3` spreadsheet to find the optimal portfolio proportions for the BT plc and Sainsbury plc shares, assuming a risk-free rate of interest of 12 per cent. Interpret the levered and unlevered solutions.

6.2 Use the `MARKOW.WK3` spreadsheet to find the optimal portfolio proportions for the Welsh Water plc and Abbey National plc shares, assuming a risk-free rate of interest of 6 per cent. Interpret the levered and unlevered solutions.

6.3 Use `SIM.WK3` and the control data it contains to obtain the optimal levered and unlevered portfolio proportions assuming a risk-free rate of:

(a) 10 per cent   (b) 8 per cent   (c) 6 per cent
Comment on your solutions.

6.4   If DATASTREAM, or similar data source, is available construct an up-to-date $\log_e$ returns database for Allied-Lyons plc, Boots plc, BT plc, ICI plc, and the FT-SE 100 Index for a period of one year, and using the appropriate, current risk-free rate of interest, calculate the optimal portfolio proportions. Compare your results with those obtained in Table 6.9 of the text.

6.5   Explain what is meant by an 'interpolative' hedge.

6.6   Extract the current futures quote for the FT-SE 100 Index from the financial pages of one of today's newspapers and, using HED_FUT.WK3 or NON_MAT.WK3 as appropriate, hedge a £1,500,000 portfolio against a projected 20 per cent fall in the level of the index in 60 days' time. Assume that the beta of the portfolio is 1.2.

(a) What would have been the outcome of the hedge had the index risen by 10 per cent by the specified horizon?

(b) Apart from using futures contracts what other actions could have been taken to hedge the portfolio?

Notes

1

$$x_1 = \frac{\frac{\lambda}{2}z_1}{\left(\frac{\lambda}{2}z_1 + \frac{\lambda}{2}z_2\right)}$$

The $\lambda/2$ terms cancel, leaving the unlevered proportions expressed in terms of the levered proportions alone.

$$x_1 = \frac{z_1}{(z_1 + z_2)}$$

[2] This text will concentrate on the method as applied to a share and an equity index. It should however, be mentioned that many non-equity indexes are also available. An index of commodity prices or bond prices could also be used. If such an index were to be used the relationship between a share and the non-equity index would, in general, be much weaker but would still provide a vehicle for making the allocations of equity to a portfolio.

[3] This problem is not insurmountable. Several statistical/econometric computer software packages enable users to perform seemingly unrelated regression estimation (SURE) which is designed to take account of this type of across equation error term linkage.

[4] If short sales are not permitted then an alternative technique for estimating the optimal proportions can be used. That approach would still use a C^* value the formula of which would be identical to that presented as Equation (6.44) but the construction of C^* and the value it takes would be based on the introduction of securities one at a time until

$$\frac{(\bar{R}_i - r_f)}{\beta_i} - C^* < 0$$

This procedure will then define the number of securities to be included in the portfolio.

References and further reading

Blake, D. (1990), *Financial Market Analysis*, McGraw-Hill, London.

Dubofsky, D. (1992), *Options and Financial Futures: Valuation and Use,* McGraw-Hill, New York.

Elton, E.J. and Gruber, M.J. (1991), *Modern Portfolio Theory and Investment Analysis* (4th edn), Wiley, New York.

Hull, J. (1993), *Options, Futures and other Derivative Securities* (2nd edn), Prentice-Hall, Englewood Cliffs, NJ.

Levy, H. and Sarnat, M. (1984), *Portfolio and Investment Selection: Theory and Practice,* Prentice-Hall, Englewood Cliffs, N.J.

7 Managing Bond Risk

7.1 Bonds—market conventions and yields

The very real problem of interest rate risk was identified and introduced in Chapter 1, where Cases 1.1 and 1.2 highlighted the risk faced by parties with long and short positions in an underlying security that would be affected by interest rate movements. There are, however, many other scenarios that can be imagined in terms of interest rate risk and these risks are a problem not only for large corporations, banks or other financial institutions, but also for everyone in the community from pensioners and children with savings deposited on building society accounts to home buyers paying off mortgages.

In capital markets another concept is referred to in addition to interest rates—yields. Yields play a crucial role in these markets: yields on debt securities indicate the cost of money to borrowers and the return on funds to investors; yields enable comparison of cash flows between different investments; and yields provide a framework for understanding and analysing capital market products.

The shape of government securities par[1] yield curve provides a picture of what investors can earn on 'risk-free' paper of different maturities. The shape that this curve takes, on those curves which can be derived from it by adding risk premiums, is by no means fixed and considerable specialist literature in economic and financial journals has discussed theories, which might determine the *term structure of interest rates*, for many years. Sometimes the yield curve is positively sloped, sometimes negatively sloped and frequently these days displays a hump somewhere along its maturity span (see Blake, 1990).

The government securities par yield curve offers a basis from which other securities (e.g. local government, corporates, etc.) can be priced. In the United States, for example, Treasury+basis points (bps) will be the amount paid for funds raised by a corporate body. The higher the number of bps above Treasury the greater the risk as perceived by the market. This also provides a mechanism for identifying comparative advantage of participants in different markets. Comparative advantage is a useful indicator of the benefit likely to be derived from interest rate swaps—a topic which will be discussed in Chapter 8—and yield differences (spreads) can be used to identify switching (sometimes also referred to as substitution swaps) possibilities between different types of paper.

193

Example 7.1

Based on calculations of mean and standard deviations, comparison of the differences between yields on 10 year German bank paper (low risk, high quality bonds issued by German regional banks) and 10 year German government paper (Bunds) may reveal opportunities for switching out of one type of paper and into the other in order to take advantage of potential under- or over-pricing of one of the instruments. Assume that yields shown in Table 7.1 have been observed over a period of time.

Estimation of the mean and two standard deviation limits for this sample are 35 and 1.3, respectively.[2] If the next period shows bank paper offering 8.46 per cent and Bunds at 8.08 per cent the 38 bp spread would be taken as indicative of a switching possibility. An appropriate strategy in this case would be to move out of (sell) and (over-priced) Bunds and switch into (buy) and (under-priced) bank paper picking up a few bps profit in the process. The rationale behind this strategy is simply that the price of Bunds has fallen by less than bank paper so that switching into the relatively cheaper bank sector presents an opportunity to buy cheap and sell high if and when the mean spread is re-attained.

There are, of course, many types of possibilities that exist for this type of comparison that would permit the type of trading strategy described. It is a strategy not without risk. In many cases past history will provide evidence that the spread between the instruments being compared does tend to behave in a regular way; drifting apart, drawing back together and then drifting apart again. Some market participants will look to the interest rate behaviour displayed between countries and will trade on movements in those spreads. For example they may measure the three-month Euro-rate spread between Eurodollar and other Eurocurrency time deposits and trade on departures from a (somehow) calculated norm. One danger is that however strong the evidence supporting some average, stable spread, rates sometimes move apart and do not revert back to the historically established norm spread. This may have been one of the motivating factors for the CME's introduction of the DIFF futures contract in 1989 (trading in this contract has now been suspended). Three figures contracts were in fact introduced:

1   The Eurodollar–EuroDeutschmark;
2   The Eurodollar–Euro Yen;
3   The Eurodollar–Euro Sterling contracts.

The example above presupposes that the yields on Bunds and bank paper were

Table 7.1. Yields (%) obtained from German bank and government paper

Bank	8.35	8.36	8.34	8.37	8.34	8.38	8.39	8.40	8.40	8.43
Bund	8.00	8.01	8.00	8.02	7.99	8.02	8.04	8.06	8.05	8.07
Spread (bps)	35	35	34	35	35	36	35	34	35	36

directly comparable. Generally, unless some preliminary arithmetic has been performed, direct comparison of yields is not possible. The definition of yield can be written as:

Yield = (Earnings/Outlay) × Day count convention/Days to maturity

Example 7.2

Assume that £1,000,000 is invested for 90 days in Treasury bills, which have a 360-day year, day count convention, and earn £16,250, what is the yield on the investment?

Yield = £16,250/£1,000,000 × 360/90
$\qquad$ = 0.01625 × 4
$\qquad$ = 0.065 or 6.5 per cent

Different markets have different interpretations that can be placed on the inputs required to solve for yield using the above formula. For example, there are discounts as well as interest-bearing instruments; interest can be paid annually or semi-annually, quarterly, etc., and day counts for calculating interest payable vary between different markets (money markets typically adopt a 360-day year as used in the example above). More will be said on this topic later in the chapter.

It is worth mentioning here, however, that in a technical sense discounts are not yields. The discount rate is based on another formula:

Discount rate =
(Earnings/Value at maturity) × Day count convention/Days to maturity

Example 7.3

Assume that £16,250 is earned on a £1,000,000 investment in a 90 day discount instrument. The discount rate on the instrument can be found by applying the formula once again using a 360 day, day count convention.

Discount rate = £16,250/£1,000,000 × 360/90
$\qquad$ = 0.065 or 6.5 per cent

This does not mean that the money market yield obtained in Example 7.2 is at the same time a discount rate. To turn the discount rate into a money market yield it is necessary to establish the *outlay* for the yield formula.

Outlay = Value at maturity − Earnings
Outlay = £1,000,000 − £16,250
$\qquad$ = £983,750

so that the money market yield can be found using:

Yield = £16,250/£983,750 × 60/90
$\qquad$ = 0.0660474 = 6.6074 per cent

Clearly, interpreting the meaning of the variable inputs in these two equations depends crucially on the operational framework in which the formula is being used.

Earnings for instance, can be discount on discount instruments, end-of-period interest rates on certificates of deposit (CDs), bank loans, etc., semi-annual interest (coupons) on US, Japanese and UK bonds, annual interest payments made on Eurobonds, German and French bonds.

Outlay can be face value or discount on a discount instrument, or market price paid for new issue or secondary market bonds (new issue and secondary market bonds may be priced at par, premium or discount depending on issue coupon, and current interest rates).

Moreover, price quoting conventions differ between issuers. The UK gilts and US notes and bonds, for example, quote prices in 1/32nds, US corporates quote in 1/8ths, while US Treasury bills quote in 1/64ths. Eurobonds, German and Japanese issues are quoted in pure decimals.

Day count varies between types of securities. Short-term instruments are usually worked on a 360-day year. Long-term instruments are usually worked with the actual number of days in a year (365 or 366 as appropriate).

These different conventions naturally lead to various types of yield quote. When dealing with yields it is important to know how a quoted yield has been calculated so that the investment potential of inter-market as well as intra-market instruments can be compared.

7.1.1 Types of yield

1   Money market yield (MMY). This is appropriate for all short-term, interest-bearing securities. It is a nominal yield based on a 360-day year and does not include compound interest.
2   Bond equivalent yield (BEY), also known as yield to maturity (YTM), is the yield quoted for securities with maturities greater than one year. It is a nominal yield quoted on a 365 basis (366 in leap years) and does not include compounding interest.
3   Association of International Bond Dealers (AIBD) is the yield quoted for Eurobonds and German paper among others. Interest is calculated on a 365-day count basis and is paid annually. The rate is an annual effective rate.

There are of course formulae available for transforming yields and discounts to make them comparable. For example conversion from BEY to AIBD is achieved through the formula:

$$AIBD = (1 + BEY/2)^2 - 1$$

where:

> AIBD represents Association of International Bond Dealers yield as a decimal;
> BEY represents bond equivalent yield as a decimal.

This formula simply states that to calculate the AIBD yield, recognition has to be made of the fact that BEY makes semi-annual coupon payments, hence the BEY yield needs to be halved, added to one and then squared to take account of the compounding process.

Reversing the order of calculation in order to find BEY given AIBD requires:

$BEY = ((1 + AIBD)^{0.5} - 1) \times 2$

where the labels of the variables are as described in the AIBD formula.

Example 7.4   Conversion of yields

What is the annual effective (AIBD) rate on a $1,000,000 CD (certificate of deposit) which earns $25,000 for a single period of 90 days?

$MMY = (25,000/1,000,000) \times (360/90) = 10$ per cent

where MMY represents money market yield on a nominal annual basis.

The conversion of this yield to BEY still requires a number of steps. First establish the effective period yield (Y_1):

$Y_1 = $ (MMY nominal annual yield)$\times$(Days to maturity/360) $= 2.5$ per cent

This rate, however, is based on a 360-day year. The effective[3] period yield calculated on a 365-day regime (Y_2) can be found by using the following conversion formula:

365-day yield = 360-day yield $\times$ 365/360

Thus

$Y_2 = Y_1 \times 365/360 = 2.5 \times 365/360 = 2.5347$ per cent

Now convert (Y_2) to semi-annual, nominal BEY:

$[(1 + Y_2)^{180/(DM.MMI)} - 1] \times N.BEY$

where:

DM.MMI represents days to maturity of the money market instrument; N.BEY represents the number of coupon payments on the bond market instrument.

$((1 + 0.025347)^{180/90} - 1) \times 2 = 10.2673$ per cent

This, however, is still only a nominal rate.

To convert this nominal rate, which does not take account of compounding, to an annual effective (AIBD) rate the following conversion is needed:

$AIBD = (1 + BEY/2)^2 - 1$
$(1 + 0.102673/2)^2 - 1 = 10.5308$ per cent

This is now an AIBD annual effective rate.

Some examples of the different conventions appear in Table 7.2.

7.1.2 UK gilt yields

In the British Funds section of the London Share Service in *The Financial Times* two types of yields are quoted:

Table 7.2.   Examples of conventions
(a) US capital market instruments

Instruments	Maturity years	Interest payments	Yield quote	Price quote	Accrued interest
Treas. notes	2–10 Years	Semi-annual	BEY	32nds	A/A
Treas. bonds	15, 20, 30 Years	Semi-annual	BEY	32nds	A/A
Corp. notes	2–10 Years	Semi-annual	BEY	8ths	A/A
Corp. bonds	10–30 Years	Semi-annual	BEY	8ths	A/A
Eurodollar	2–10 Years	Annual	AIBD	Decimal	30/360

(b) Government debt outside the United States

Instruments	Maturity years	Interest payments	Yield quote	Price quote	Accrued interest
UK Gilts	5–20 years	Semi-annual	BEY	32nds	A/A
French OATs					
Treas. bills	90 Days–5 Years	1 Payment at Maturity	Discount	Discount	A/360
Treas. bonds	2–7 Years	Annual	AIBD	Decimal	A/A
German gvnt					
Bills	90 Days–5 Years	1 Payment at Maturity	Discount	Discount	30/360
Bonds	10–15 Years	Annual	AIBD	Decimal	30/360
Notes	2–5 Years	Annual	AIBD	Decimal	30/360

1   *Current (running or interest) yield*   This appears in the first 'yield' column and is calculated as:
(Redemption value/clean price × Coupon) × 100
where:
> redemption value represents the face value of the bond to be repaid at maturity; clean price represents the current price of the bond excluding accrued interest (see below for more on accrued interest). Note that UK gilts are quoted on a 32nd basis hence a quote of 99–24 implies a price of 99²⁴⁄₃₂nds, which is 99.75 as a decimal.

Example   Treasury 10 per cent   Conversion 91 : 100 × (100/99.75 × 10/100) = 10.3 per cent

2   *Yield to maturity (YTM) (also known as redemption yield)*   This is an important concept and plays a pivotal role in the analysis of interest-bearing securities and is usually presented as a problem of calculating interest rate, r, that satisfies the expression:

$$P_0 = \frac{C}{(1 + r)^1} + \frac{C}{(1 + r)^2} + \ldots + \frac{C}{(1 + r)^T} + \frac{RV}{(1 + r)^T} \tag{7.1}$$

or using statistical shorthand notation:

$$P_0 = \Sigma \frac{C}{(1 + r)^t} + \frac{RV}{(1 + r)^T} \tag{7.2}$$

where:

P_0 represents the clean price of the bond (i.e. interest accruing to the holder of a bond is not quoted in the price;
C represents the bond's face coupon as a percentage;
RV represents the bond's redemption value as a proportion;
r represents the interest rate that ensures that the equality in Equation (7.2) holds;
t represents a typical time period ($t = 1, 2, 3, \ldots, T$);
T represents the final time period when the bond will be redeemed.

Example 7.5

A UK Treasury gilt-edged stock, due to be redeemed in exactly two years' time with a face coupon of 10 per cent pays interest on a semi-annual basis. It has just paid a coupon and is now priced at £108. What is the YTM of this bond?

Employing Equation (7.2) the expression becomes:

$$£108 = \frac{(10/2)}{\left(1 + \frac{r}{2}\right)^1} + \frac{(10/2)}{\left(1 + \frac{r}{2}\right)^2} + \frac{(10/2)}{\left(1 + \frac{r}{2}\right)^3} + \frac{(10/2)}{\left(1 + \frac{r}{2}\right)^4} + \frac{(100)}{\left(1 + \frac{r}{2}\right)^4} \qquad (7.3)$$

for which a value of r needs to be found that will ensure that the left- and right-hand sides of the equation are equal. In this example the YTM (r) is 5.7105 per cent.

Lotus demo   YTM.WK3
This spreadsheet enables the user to find the YTM of a bond paying semi-annual coupons for a period of greater than one year and up to 10 years. Table 7.3 illustrates the special menu, while Table 7.4 displays the input framework for this spreadsheet. The easiest way to operate this calculator is to enter the required dates, coupon and *clean* price before entering the macro which is activated by pressing the Alt+A keys. *Note:* the YTM for any new problem will *only* be calculated using the macro.

Selecting D (d) places the cursor on the cell requiring the purchase (settlement) date (19-Mar-93) from Table 7.4.

Once this has been typed—with ` as the first character indicating a label—press [ENTER]. The sequence of inputs then runs:

Table 7.3.   Special menu

Data	Input bond settlement, coupon, maturity dates and clean price
CF	Calculates the CF for this bond
Quit	Exit special menu

Table 7.4.   Input framework for `YTM.WK3`

Bond's maturity horizon > 1 year	(Face Value £100)
	(Max. 20Yr Bond)
Purchase Date: 19-Mar-93	
	Accrued Interest
Date of next	to be paid on
Coupon: 19-Mar-93	Purchase of Bond
	£0.00
Maturity	for each £100 of
Date: 19-Mar-95	nominal stock.
Coupon: 10	
Clean Purchase	YTM
Price: £108.00	5.71%
Dirty Purchase	Running Yield
Price: £108.00	9.26%
(with accrued interest)	

- *Date of next coupon:* this input must start with ` to indicate a label and will appear as, e.g. `19-Mar-93`. After the data has been typed in press [ENTER].
- *Maturity date:* this input must start with ' to indicate a label and will appear as, e.g. `19-Mar-95`. After the data has been typed in press [ENTER].
- *Coupon:* entered as a number—10 in Table 7.4 to indicate a 10 per cent coupon. After the coupon has been typed in press [ENTER].
- *Clean price:* entered as a number. After the data has been typed in press [ENTER].
- *Accrued interest, dirty price, yield to maturity (YTM), and running yield* are then calculated and reported automatically.
- Selecting C (c) from the special menu allows the user to obtain an approximate conversion factor value for this bond for use in the gilt futures contract. This will be discussed more fully later in this chapter.
- Q (q) exist the special menu and returns the user to normal Lotus operating mode.

The results for the example introduced above are also displayed in Table 7.4. The YTM is 5.71 per cent and the running yield is calculated as 9.26 per cent. Notice that the clean price—by convention this is the price quoted in the columns of the financial press—is in this case equal to the dirty price. There is no accrued interest to be added on to the clean price since a coupon has just been paid.

This would not be the case, however, if a bond were to be purchased between coupon dates. In that case the purchaser would pay the clean price plus any interest that has accrued since the payment of the last coupon. An example of this, much more common, situation than the one covered above, is given below and is based on a 'real-world' example.

Example 7.6

The UK 9½ per cent Treasury Stock, 1999, pays interest on a semi-annual basis on 15 January and 15 July, it is due to be redeemed on 15 January 1999. Today's date is 10 March 1993 and the current clean price of the bond is £112¹³⁄₃₂. What is the YTM of this bond?

The results for this example are shown in Table 7.5. The YTM is calculated as 6.94 per cent and the running yield at 8.45 per cent. Notice that the price that the investor will have to pay for this bond will be £112.41 (the bond's clean price) plus £1.44 (the accrued interest) which equals £113.85. Accrued interest is calculated on the basis of the number of days that the bond has been held since the last coupon payment multiplied by the coupon divided by 365.

Table 7.5. Calculation of YTM

Bond's maturity horizon > 1 year	(Face Value £100)	
	(Max. 20Yr Bond)	
Purchase Date: 10-Mar-93		
	Accrued Interest	
Date of next	to be paid on	
Coupon: 15-Jul-93	Purchase of Bond	
	£1.44	
Maturity	for each £100 of	
Date: 15-Jan-99	nominal stock	
Coupon: 9.5		
Clean Purchase	YTM	
Price: £112.41	6.94%	
Dirty Purchase	Running Yield	
Price: £113.85	8.45%	
(with accrued interest)		

7.1.3 Zero coupon bonds

At this point some mention should be made of the notion of a pure discount or zero coupon bond. This is a bond which, as its name suggests, pays no coupon during its life span which implies that $C = 0$ in Equation (7.2). The formula for calculating the price of the bond will then be given by:

$$P_0 = \frac{RV}{(1 + r)^T}$$

(7.4)

where P_0, RV, r and T are as defined for Equation (7.2). The YTM can be found using:

$$r = \left\langle \frac{RV}{P_0} \right\rangle^{1/T} - 1$$

Example 7.7

A five year zero coupon bond with a redemption value of £100, currently priced at £78, will have a YTM of:

$$r = \left(\frac{100}{78} \right)^{0.2} - 1 = 0.0509$$

which multiplied by 100 gives 5.09 per cent.

7.2 Bonds with special features

Recent years have seen an explosion of hybrid debt issues. In the government sector there are dual-dated bonds and index-linked bonds while in the Eurobond and corporate sector there are callable bonds, puttable bonds, bonds with warrants attached, convertible bonds, dual currency bonds, floating rate notes (FRNs; bonds whose coupon can be adjusted at intervals to reflect current market rates), etc. Pricing of these instruments is more complex than the pricing mechanisms described in Sec. 7.1. One basic reason lies behind the issue of these hybrids: to fund debt at the cheapest cost. There are, however, dangers for both holders and issuers in using these less transparent instruments but a discussion of them is outside the scope of this text (see Urry, 1991).

Example 7.8   Callable bond

Assume a bond with a five year life span. The issuer offers a coupon slightly higher than that currently available in the market. Why?

The answer probably lies in the background scenario perceived to exist by the issue. In this case the issuer expects interest rates to fall in the future and is therefore buying a call option by offering the higher coupon. Assume the issue appeared in 1989 priced at par with a 15 per cent coupon, maturing in five years callable in 1992. If in 1992 the rate on corporate paper with this credit rating is 11 per cent, it is then in the interests of the issuer to call the issue and arrange new funding at the currently lower market rates.

Example 7.9   Puttable bond

Consider a ten year bond issued in 1991 at par with a coupon of, say 10 per cent, with the embedded option to put the bond back to the issuer in 1994.

If interest rates do rise, and by 1994 stand at, say 16 per cent it is in the interests of the investor to exercise the put option.

In this case the bond will have been issued at a lower coupon than the current market rate because the investor has in effect purchased a put option on the bond. The investor believes that interest rates will be high when the time comes to exercise the put. The investor will then be in a position to put the bond back to the issuer and invest the funds in the market at the prevailing higher rates.

The examples above raise the question: How are interest rates expected to move over a specified time period?

This is no easy question to answer. In Chapter 2 forecasting techniques were reviewed and the conclusion was reached that while accurate predictions about the actual value that a variable may take or even the direction in which it may move may not be possible, some attempt should be made to get an idea of the variable's direction in order to make best use of the risk management instruments that are available. The techniques outlined in Chapter 2 can all be applied to the task of forecasting interest rate movements. But successful use of those methods probably depends as much on the skills and intuitive judgement of the forecaster as on the technique itself (for a good discussion of this topic see Antl, 1988).

It also raises the question: Which interest rates are to be forecast?

7.3 Yield curves

A very important branch of fixed interest security analysis is devoted to the study of yield curves (see Blake, 1990, Ch. 5).

The following data are intended to give an intuitive guide as to the structure of a yield curve. In practice, setting up a yield curve is by no means trivial, predicting how yield curves will react to changes in central bank base rate changes with any degree of accuracy is virtually impossible.

The yields below relate to 25 January 1993 and are based on data published in *The Financial Times*. They are plotted in Fig. 7.1.

6 month money	6.375%	LIMEAN (LIMID)[4]
1 year	6.500%	LIMEAN(LIMID)
2 year	6.520%	YTM
3 year	7.060%	YTM
4 year	7.250%	YTM
5 year	7.600%	YTM
10 year	8.270%	YTM
>15 years	8.810%	YTM

In drawing out these figures a number of questions can be raised:

1 Is there any government bond which is due to be redeemed in exactly one year's time, two years' time, etc.?

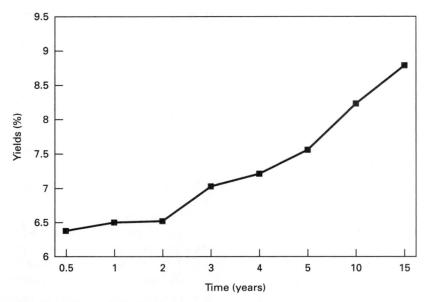

Fig. 7.1. Hypothetical yield curve

2 If there is more than one bond that will mature on that date, one, two, etc., years in the future, the YTM of which bond should be taken for purposes of constructing the yield curve? If a selection of bonds are used how will they be weighted to provide a representative YTM?
3 Which collection of bonds will be taken to provide a YTM for the >15 year maturity range? If a selection of bonds are used how will they be weighted to provide a representative YTM?
4 At the shorter end of the time scale which bank's or financial institution's rate should be taken as being representative of short-term money? If a selection of bonds are used how will they be weighted to provide a representative YTM?
5 Will the type of yield curve constructed like this really be useful?

In practice there are several types of yield curves that are employed by those analysing interest-related instruments. Three types of curve will be considered in this chapter: the *spot zero yield curve*, the *par yield curve*, and the *forward yield curve*, all of which are related. In constructing these curves a point will be established for each six months up to five years. No consideration will be given to differences in day counts or other potentially differing conventions, or to the problems raised in points 1 to 4 and bid–offer spreads will be ignored.

The spot zero yield curve
In order to demonstrate how this yield curve can be constructed, Equation (7.4) can be used to find the current prices of, so-called, zeros and solving for their YTMs over different maturities. Assume that such computations have been performed and have resulted in the outcomes shown in Table 7.6.

Table 7.6.   Spot zero and forward rates

Monthly periods	Spot rate labels	Current spot rates %	Forward rate labels	Forward rates %
6	0.R.6	7.167		
12	0.R.12	7.234	6.R.12	7.301
18	0.R.18	7.340	12.R.18	7.552
24	0.R.24	7.500	18.R.24	7.981
30	0.R.30	7.670	24.R.30	8.353
36	0.R.36	7.560	30.R.36	7.012
42	0.R.42	7.589	36.R.42	7.763
48	0.R.48	7.778	42.R.48	9.110
54	0.R.54	7.800	48.R.54	7.976
60	0.R.60	7.821	54.R.60	8.010

The par yield curve
Armed with the yields presented in Table 7.6 it is now possible to calculate par yields over the same maturities. This is achieved by employing a slightly modified version of Equation (7.2).

$$P_0 = \frac{C}{(1 + {_0}r_1)^1} + \frac{C}{(1 + {_0}r_2)^2} + \ldots + \frac{C}{(1 + {_0}r_T)^T} + \frac{RV}{(1 + {_0}r_T)^T} \tag{7.5}$$

where P_0, C, r, RV are as defined for Equation (7.2) and T is the final time period when the bond will be redeemed.

Since the bond is trading at par it will be reasonable to assume an RV of £100. So that to find a C in Equation (7.5) that will be equivalent to the yield on a zero bond maturing in, say, one year's time, the equation becomes:

$$100 = \frac{C/2}{(1 + 0.07167)^{0.5}} + \frac{C/2}{(1 + 0.07234)^1} + \frac{100}{(1 + 0.07234)^1} \tag{7.6}$$

Solving this expression for C gives the solution for the YTM associated with a semi-annual coupon paying bond with one year to redemption which will be equal to the yield obtainable from a zero coupon bond maturing in one year. The arithmetic provides a solution of 7.1066 per cent.

Moving the problem one period forward would give an equation of the form:

$$100 = \frac{C/2}{(1 + 0.07167)^{0.5}} + \frac{C/2}{(1 + 0.07234)^1} + \frac{C/2}{(1 + 0.0734)^{1.5}} + \frac{100}{(1 + 0.0734)^{1.5}} \tag{7.7}$$

On solving, this gives a yield of 7.2056 per cent.

This method clearly becomes more laborious and tedious as the time to maturity increases. As spreadsheet SPOT_PAR.WK3 has been constructed which will perform these calculations for six monthly intervals up to a five year period. The results from that spreadsheet are reproduced on Table 7.7.

The forward yield curve
Forward rates for periods of up to one year were discussed in Chapter 3 and a

Table 7.7.   Calculations of par yield curves

Years	Par
0.50	7.04299
1.00	7.10657
1.50	7.20566
2.00	7.35273
2.50	7.50671
3.00	7.41361
3.50	7.43967
4.00	7.59938
4.50	7.62095
5.00	7.64058

general formula was presented. A modification of that formula—but based on the same logic—will allow forward rates to be calculated for periods of greater than one year. Equation (7.8) provides a general formula for obtaining the forward rates and was used to calculate the rates which appear in Table 7.6:

$$_tr_T = \{(1 + {_0r_T})^T/(1 + {_0r_t})^t\}^{1/(T - t)} - 1 \tag{7.8}$$

where:

$_tr_T$ represents the estimated forward rate as a proportion from t to T;
$_0r_T$ is the spot rate as a proportion from now until the far time horizon T;
$_0r_t$ is the spot rate as a proportion from now until the near time horizon t;

note that time is measured in years.

By way of illustration the forward rate for $T = 1$, $t = 0.5$ is given by:

$$\{[(1 + 0.07234)^1/(1 + 0.07167)^{0.5}]^2-1\} \times 100 = 7.301 \text{ per cent;}$$

and for $T = 5$, $t = 4.5$ is given by:

$$\{[(1 + 0.07821)^5/(1 + 0.0780)^{4.5}]^2-1\} \times 100 = 8.0102 \text{ per cent.}$$

Once again the spreadsheet SPOT_PAR.WK3 calculates these rates automatically and they can be accessed by selecting F on the special menu.

Lotus demo   SPOT_PAR.WK3
This spreadsheet enable the user to calculate spot, par and forward yield curves once either the spot or par rates have been entered. A special menu is available to drive the macros and this can be obtained by pressing Alt + A keys. The menu appears as shown in Table 7.8.

- Selecting S (s) permits the user to enter the *spot rates* necessary to perform the par and forward yield curve computations. In all 10 rates are expected, press [ENTER] after each rate has been typed in.
- Selecting P (p) permits the user to enter the *par rates* necessary to perform the spot and forward yield curve computations. In all 10 rates are expected, press [ENTER] after each rate has been typed in.

- Selecting F (f) performs the *forward rate calculations* and copies the latest, entered spot rates to the forward yield curve table in order to perform update calculations. The cursor moves to the forward table to allow the user to view the forward rates.
- Selecting T (t) enables the user to change the length of time gap between measurements. For example typing T (t) moves the cursor to the cell containing 0.5 (in the control spreadsheet). If the user wishes to use one year gaps simply type 1 and press [ENTER]—the entries in the time period column will now be adjusted to show a one year gap.
- Selecting C (c) copies the par rates that were calculated on entry of the spot rate to the par rate table. *This is essential in order to view the latest par rates—their calculation is not automatic.*
- Selecting G (g) permits the user to select graphs to view. The named graphs are ZERO, PAR, FORWARD, or ALL_THREE. When the names menu appears at the top of the screen make a choice by highlighting the graph name with the cursor and press [ENTER].
- Q (q) exits the special menu and puts the user back in normal Lotus operating mode.

Table 7.8.   Menu for SPOT_PAR.WK3

Spot-Zero	Input Spot Zero rates
Par	Input Par Rates
Forward	Copy Spot Zero Rates to Forward Rates Table
Time_Period	Change length of time period for calculations
Copy	Move Calculated Par Rates to Par Rates Table
Graph	Graphs of the Yield Curves
Quit	Exit

Although the rates in each one of these sets of calculations look different do not forget that they are based on different market conventions and computational rules; once the spot or zero yield curve is known the par curve can be calculated or, vice versa, if the par yield curve is known the spot yield curve can be calculated. Were big differences in yields to exist in reality between markets they would not do so for long. Money would flow to the best yield, and given that these yields are all based on 'risk-free' rates of interest there would be no risk differential to distort investment possibilities, demand would drive up the price of the instrument lowering the yield and bringing it back in line with other risk-free rates.

7.4 Bond price behaviour

Unlike shares, bonds do have predictable behaviour patterns and several rules have been established that can assist a fixed income security analyst/portfolio manager when deciding which bonds to hold in a portfolio given a future interest rate scenario and the goal of the portfolio. At the lowest level of predictability there is a fundamental negative relationship between the price of a bond and its yield. As yield rises the bond's price must fall and vice versa (see Fig. 7.2). There is, however much more that can be said about this negative relationship. To illustrate the price/yield relationship take the case of a straightforward bond: no options attached, non-convertible, no warrants associated with the bond, a fixed coupon, non-index-linked, and a defined redemption date. From this list of restrictive assumptions there are still two features that can be allowed to vary:

1   The bond's coupon
2   The bond's fixed redemption date.

The interplay between these two variables provides a clue to some simple risk

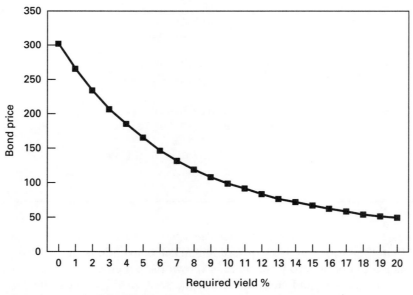

Fig. 7.2.   Effect of a change in yield on the price of a 20 year 10 per cent coupon bond

management strategies assuming a given background interest rate scenario.

Example 7.10

Consider the case where a portfolio manager suspects that interest rates are about to rise and by as much as 1 per cent. Further assume that currently the portfolio contains only a 20 year, 5 per cent coupon bond priced at £57.10. A rise in interest rates from 10 to 11 per cent will, if reflected exactly in the yield change that takes place, result in a fall in the bond's price to £51.86, a drop of 9.17 per cent. A simple but effective strategy in this case would be to switch the portfolio holding to a bond with both a shorter time to maturity and a higher coupon. If the bond selected were to be a five year bond with a coupon of 20 per cent the relative fall in the bond's price would be limited to 3.38 per cent.

The logic behind this outcome is that the coupons which will be paid at regular intervals throughout the bond's life can now be reinvested at the higher interest rates prevailing in the market place. The higher proceeds from this investment will help to offset the fall in the bond's price brought about by the increase in yield.

On the other hand, if interest rates were expected to fall, switching to long-dated, low coupon bonds—or zero coupon bonds—would be a way of benefiting most from the rise in the bond's price that must follow.

Figure 7.3 shows very clearly the price responses for three 20 year bonds offering 15 per cent, 10 per cent and zero coupon payments. One feature worth noting is that the curvilinear, price-yield relationship is not constant. It varies at different points on the curve for each type of bond. Figure 7.4 displays the percentage change in a bond's price brought about by the change in yield. Clearly when interest rates are rising—or are expected to rise—zero coupon bonds are the bonds to avoid; each 1 per cent change in yield from 0 per cent up to 19 per cent brings about a fall in price of between 15 and 20 per cent. If there is no alternative to holding bonds in a portfolio—for example, cashing in the bonds and depositing the proceeds at short-term rates until the interest rate picture has been resolved—then switching to higher coupon bonds, of comparable maturities to those already held in the portfolio, would present a simple and effective strategy.

To develop further the ideas outlined above there are a number of formal rules that can be defined and which will help establish a more scientific approach to the study of bond price–yield behaviour.

1   If a bond's market price increases, its yield decreases and vice versa.

Example 7.11

On Thursday 4 October 1990 the closing price of the 10.25 per cent Exchequer 1995 stood at 93-30 at a quoted 11.91 YTM. (Recall that price quotes for UK gilts are in 32nds hence a quote of 90-30 is read as $90^{30}\!/_{32}$ which is 90.9375 as a decimal.) At 16.04 on Friday 5 October 1990 the Chancellor of the Exchequer

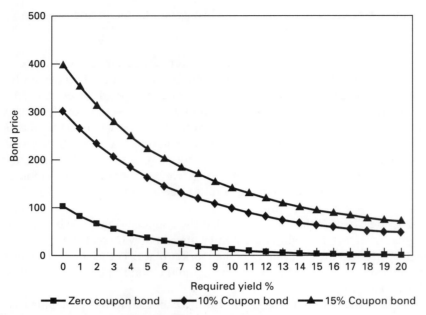

Fig. 7.3.   Price–yield relationships for three 20 year bonds

announced Britain's entry into the Exchange Rate Mechanism (ERM) and, simultaneously, a 1 per cent cut in interest rates. The theoretical price of this gilt, assuming a 1 per cent drop in yield, would lead to a price of approximately 97-17. The actual price in the market at close on Monday was 96-23, the high

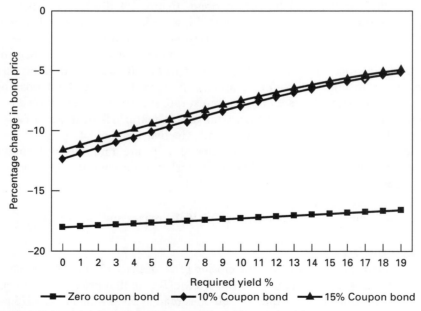

Fig. 7.4.   Price–yield relationships for three 20 year bonds

for the day was 97-5 with a 11.19 per cent YTM (*Source: The Financial Times*, Tuesday 9 October 1990).

2   As the maturity date of a bond approaches the size of the bond's discount/premium decreases.

Example 7.12

Consider the 10.5 per cent Treasury (UK) 1992, the FT quoted price for this bond was 97-1, compare this to the 10.5 per cent Exchequer 1997 quoted at 93-10. (*Source: The Financial Times*, 9 October 1990).

3   As the maturity data of a bond approaches the size of its discount/premium will decrease at an increasing rate.
4   A fall in the bond's yield will raise the bond's price by more than the fall in the bond's price that would result from an equivalent increase in the bond's yield.

Example 7.13

Taking as a base the example in rule 1 above the theoretical increase in the bond's price is approximately 3.8 per cent ($\{[97\text{-}17/93\text{-}30] - 1\}\times100$) assuming a YTM of 10.91 per cent. If, on the other hand, the bond's yield were to rise 100 bps to 12.91 per cent the accompanying fall in the bond's price would be 3.5 per cent. This is due to the non-linear relationship that exists between a bond's price and its yield.

5   For high coupon bonds with a quoted maturity date greater than one year, the percentage change in a price will be smaller than for low coupon bonds with the same maturity.

Example 7.14

Treasury 13 per cent maturing 3 March 2000 was quoted at 104-28 on Friday 5 October, Monday's close was quoted at 107-31, a rise of 2.9 per cent. The 14 July 2000 9 per cent Conversion stock had quotes respectively of 84-20 and 87-16, a rise of 3.4 per cent. (*Source: The Financial Times*, Tuesday 9 October 1990). The implication of this is as discussed above: if interest rates are expected to fall and medium- to long-term bonds are to be the investment instruments held in a portfolio, then lower coupon issues should be used.

Clearly some of these rules can easily be verified by considering the price/yield behaviour of a real or fictitious bond under a variety of maturity and interest rate scenarios as demonstrated above (see Table 7.9).

Interest rate fluctuations are the driving force behind the volatility of interest rates. Expectations concerning the magnitude and direction of future movements in interest rates provide the rationale behind a multitude of bond portfolio strategies. To undertake a more thorough discussion of some of these approaches attention must now be given to duration and convexity: two vital tools in bond portfolio and risk management analysis.

7.5 Duration and convexity

Duration is an extremely important concept in bond analysis and provides a useful measure for a number of strategies. The framework for duration was first developed by F. Macaulay in a paper published by the National Bureau of Economic Research (USA) in 1938. The work suggested a measure that would take account of a bond's maturity, coupon and yield. One of the key assumptions underpinning the formula he proposed is that the spot or par yield curve is flat. Many researchers have since challenged this assumption and have suggested alternatives (see, especially, Bierwag *et al.*, 1988) but Macaulay's approach, together with a slight modification, have proved to be very robust and will be used here to provide an understanding of the methodology and use of duration.

In essence, duration can be defined as a measure of the average maturity stream of cash flows. In view of the fact that the calculated figure is in terms of years, it can also be thought of as the (weighted) average amount of time taken for the cash flows to be received by the investor.

The calculation of Macaulay duration is a straightforward but tedious procedure the formula for which is shown as Equation 7.9.

$$\text{Mac}_\text{D} = \sum \frac{(PV(\text{Cash flow})_t \times t)}{P_0} \tag{7.9}$$

where:

$PV(\text{Cash flow})_t$ represents the present value of the cash flow to be received at time t calculated using a discount rate equal to the bond's YTM;
P_0 represents the current market price of the bond;
Mac_D represents Macaulay duration.

Example 7.15
A certain bond with a face value of £100 and currently priced at par, has just paid a coupon, it has exactly two years remaining to maturity, it has a yield to maturity of 10 per cent, the bond's coupon is 8 per cent, interest is paid semi-annually and accrued interest is calculated on an A/A basis. Calculate the bond's Macaulay duration.

Table 7.9.   Interest rate sensitivity of hypothetical bonds

Time period	Cash flow	Present value factor	Present value of cash flow	Time weighted present value of cash flow
1	4.00	0.9524	3.809	3.809
2	4.00	0.9070	3.628	7.256
3	4.00	0.8638	3.455	10.366
4	104.00	0.8227	85.561	342.243
Totals			96.453	363.674

Macaulay duration = 363.674/96.453 = 3.7705(half-years) or approximately 1.885 years.

Example 7.16   Macaulay duration of a zero bond
Weights for $t = 1, 2, 3, \ldots, T-1 = 0$, therefore,
Macaulay duration is given by:

$$\text{Mac}_D = \sum \frac{(PV(\text{Cash flow})_t \times t}{P_0}$$

but since P_0 is nothing other than the PV of the cash flow Macaulay duration
reduces to T, the number of time periods to maturity.

In the example used above if the 8 per cent coupon is set to 0 per cent then
the Macaulay duration measured in half-years is 4. The Macaulay duration
measured in years is of course 2.

Duration can be, and is, used in many ways by different sections of the financial
community:

1   It can be used as an index of price risk (bond price volatility), and as such
    facilitates comparison between bonds when deciding on an investment strategy.
    The lower the value calculated for duration, the less sensitive will be the bond's
    price to changes in yields brought about by changes in interest rates.
2   It can be used to predict the approximate change in price that will result in a
    fixed rate instrument given a change in yield.
3   It serves as an input for the construction of hedges for portfolios of bonds.
4   It can be used to construct a portfolio that will meet a future liability.
5   It can be used to help swappers measure the risk associated with swap
    portfolios.

Like bonds, duration has a number of properties which both help to justify its
application to problems and define the limits in which it might be expected to
operate successfully:

● Duration increases as the risk associated with an instrument increases.
● Duration is proportional to risk.
● The duration figures calculated from different instruments are additive.
● Duration can be multiplied by yield changes to determine price change.

Macaulay duration as a measure of bond price volatility can be examined as
follows:

The current price of a bond (P_0) can be expressed as:

$$P_0 = \frac{C}{(1 + r)^1} + \frac{C}{(1 + r)^2} + \ldots + \frac{C}{(1 + r)^T} + \frac{RV}{(1 + r)^T}$$

where:

   C represents the coupon paid at t ($t = 1, 2, \ldots, T$);
   r represents the YTM;
   RV represents the redemption value or maturity value of the bond.

In order to consider the impact of a change in r on a change in P_0 (dP_0/dr) the first
derivative of the price equation is required.

$$\frac{dP_0}{dr} = \frac{(-1 \times C)}{(1+r)^2} + \frac{(-2 \times C)}{(1+r)^3} + \ldots + \frac{(-T \times C)}{(1+r)^{T+1}} + \frac{(-T \times RV)}{(1+r)^{T+1}}$$

This expression can be rearranged to obtain:

$$\frac{dP_0}{dr} = \frac{-1}{(1+r)} \times \left[\frac{C}{(1+r)^1} + \frac{2C}{(1+r)^2} + \ldots + \frac{T \times C}{(1+r)^T} + \frac{T \times RV}{(1+r)^T} \right]$$

The term in brackets demonstrates clearly where the notion of a set of weighted cash flows comes from in the Macaulay duration formula.

Now taking the ratio:

$$\frac{dP_0}{dr}\frac{1}{P_0} = \frac{-\dfrac{1}{(1+r)} \times \left(\sum \dfrac{Ct}{(1+r)^t} + \dfrac{T \times RV}{(1+r)^T} \right)}{P_0}$$

The expression:

$$\frac{\left(\sum \dfrac{Ct}{(1+r)^t} + \dfrac{T \times RV}{(1+r)^T} \right)}{P_0}$$

or

$$\sum \frac{(PV(\text{Cash flow})_t \times t)}{P_0}$$

is the formula for calculating Macaulay duration as described in Equation (7.9).

Another tool can be constructed from this result, namely *modified duration*. This is simply a ratio of Macaulay duration to the term $(1 + r)$:

$$\text{Mod}_D = \frac{\text{Mac}_D}{(1+r)} = -1 \times \frac{dP_0}{dr}\frac{1}{P_0}$$

It can be employed to provide an approximation of the percentage change in price brought about by a change in yield. Like Macaulay duration, when calculated it gives a figure in years or some fraction of years. For example, in the case of the UK Treasury stock paying semi-annual coupons, the initial calculations will result in a duration figure reported in half-years. This follows since the present value of the cash flows will be discounted every six months when the coupons are paid. To convert the duration figure obtained to years divide by two.

Another handy concept is that of *dollar duration* which can be expressed as:

$$\frac{dP_0}{dr} = (-1) \times \text{Mod}_D \times P_0 \tag{7.10}$$

and gives an indication of the change in the price of a bond brought about by a change in yield.

Example 7.17

In the example introduced at the start of this section Macaulay duration was measured as 1.88 years. By applying the formula for modified duration, and performing the arithmetic transformation just described, the modified duration figure is found to be:

$$\text{Mod}_D = 1.885/(1 + r/2) = 1.885/1.05 = 1.7952$$

The dollar duration enable the calculation of the change in the price of a bond which for this example works out as follows:

$$dP/dr = \text{dollar duration} = -(1.7952)(96.453) = -173.1561$$

In order to calculate the value of a 10 bp change in r (i.e. 0.001) a small rearrangement of the dP/dr formula yields:

$$dP = -(173.1561) \times (0.001) = -0.1732$$

Given a 10 bp increase in yield the revised bond price will be:

Old price + Dollar duration × Change in yield

   $96.453 - 0.1732 = 96.2798$ (approximately). For this example see also Table 7.10 which was obtained from the Lotus spreadsheet DURA.WK3 designed to calculate duration and will be developed more fully later in this section.

   This figure is only an approximation to the actual change in price that will occur. The reason why this is so is due to the curvilinear nature of the price/yield

Table 7.10.   Bond duration

BOND DURATION	(Face Value 100)	
(use ALT+A to activate)	(Max. 20Yr Bond)	Macaulay Duration in Years 1.88525
Purchase Date:23-Mar-93		
Date of first Coupon:	23-Mar-93	Modified Duration in Years 1.795476
Maturity Date:	23-Mar-95	Relative price change −0.01795
Coupon	8	
Purchase Price:	£96.45	Input Yield as a decimal 10.00%
Change in yield: (in bps)	10.00	

relationship allied to the fact that duration is making use of the rate of change (dP_0/dr) which will only hold for very small changes in yield (r). To get a more accurate approximation it is necessary to take into account a concept called convexity which introduces a correction factor that can be used alongside duration when the change in yield is large. Appendix 7.A shows more formally where the convexity formula comes from and its relationship to delta and gamma hedging in options theory. A figure here will provide an intuitive idea of why convexity is important for larger changes in yield.

Figure 7.5 makes use of the price/yield profile of the bond depicted in Fig. 7.2 to examine how the price of the bond will change given changes in yield. Suppose initially that the price of the bond is P_0 with YTM of r_0. Now suppose that the YTM rises to r_1, the change in price that this brings about can be approximated by constructing a straight line $(A–B)$ tangent to the price/yield curve at (P_0, r_0), then drawing a vertical line from the new YTM (r_1) to touch the $(A–B)$ line at C, and a horizontal line from C to the vertical axis at P_1. In this way the bond's revised price can be established.

In terms of algebra the ratio:

$$(P_0 - P_1)/(r_0 - r_1) = \Delta P_0/\Delta r$$

measures the slope of the bond price/yield curve at (P_0, r_0). For very small Δ this approximation will be quite good and can be taken as dP_0/dr, however, from Fig. 7.5 it becomes clear that for larger yield changes this approximation becomes inaccurate. To illustrate this point consider a rise in yield from r_0 to r_2, using the methodology just outlined this would imply a fall in the bond's price to P_2. The

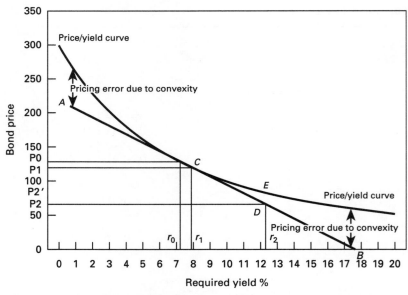

Fig. 7.5.   Effect of a change in yield on the price of a 20 year 10 per cent coupon bond

bond's price/yield curve, however, does not follow the same track as the (*A–B*) line with the result that the bond's price falls to P_2' and not to P_2. The distance (*D–E*) on the figure illustrates the pricing error that results when ignoring the curvilinear nature of the price/yield curve: the bond's *convexity*.

The formula for convexity is:

$$\text{Convexity} = \frac{1}{2} \frac{\text{d}^2 P_0}{\text{d}r^2} \frac{1}{P_0}$$

where:

$$\frac{\text{d}^2 P}{\text{d}r^2} = \sum \frac{t(t+1)(C)}{(1+r)^{t+2}} + \frac{(T)(T+1)(RV)}{(1+r)^{T+2}}$$

Convexity is a sought-after feature in bond analysis. The greater the convexity of a bond the more desirable the bond: its price will rise faster when yields fall, but its price will fall more slowly when yields rise. Convexity has to be paid for.

Lotus demo   `DURA.WK3`

This spreadsheet enables the user to input the characteristics of a bond in order to calculate that bond's Macaulay duration, modified duration, convexity and the changes in price that are to be expected when the YTM of the bond changes. Alt+A brings up a special menu from which the user can make the selections shown in Table 7.11.

Selecting I (i) calls up the data input screen as shown in Table 7.12. (*Note*: 200 bp change in yield.) The sequential inputs required are:

- Purchase (settlement) date: `DD-MMM-YY` [ENTER]
  Note: `DD` must be numbers representing a day of the month, `MMM` a literal entry for the month, e.g. Dec for December, `YY` must be a number representing the last two digits of the year in question, e.g. 1993 requires 93.
- Date of next coupon: enter as for Purchase date [ENTER].
- Date of maturity: enter as for Purchase date [ENTER].
  Note: For maturity dates beyond 1999 type in the full year, e.g. 2009.
- Coupon: enter as a number, e.g. 11 for 11 per cent [ENTER].

Table 7.11.   Menu for spreadsheet `DURA.WK3`

`Data_Input`	`Input data frame and duration calculations`
`Prices`	`Changes in Bond Price using Duration and Convexity`
`Quit`	`Exit special menu`

Table 7.12.   Data input screen

BOND DURATION	(Face Value 100)	
(use ALT+A to activate)	(Max. 20Yr Bond)	Macaulay Duration in Years
Purchase Date:23-Mar-93		1.885309
Date of first		Modified
Coupon: 23-Mar-93		Duration in Years
		1.795532
Maturity		
Date: 23-Mar-95		Relative price change −0.35911
Coupon 8		
		Input Yield as
Purchase		a decimal
Price: £96.45		10.00%
Change in yield: 200.00 (in bps)		

- Purchase price: [ENTER].
- Basis point change: e.g. entering 1 will be taken as a one basis point (bp) change 0.0001 [ENTER].
- YTM: entered as a decimal [ENTER].
- After YTM has been input the calculations for Macaulay and modified duration will be performed and will appear on the top right-hand side of the screen.
- Selecting P (p) will take the user to the price change section of the spreadsheet (see Table 7.13). (*Note*: typing [ENTER] at each prompt in I will generate Table 7.13, the control output, typing new values will alter the results and a different table of price changes will be obtained.)
- Selecting Q (q) exits the special menu and puts the user back in normal Lotus operating mode.

It was suggested earlier that duration could also be used to construct a portfolio that would meet a future cash outflow or liability. In the case of meeting a single period future liability this procedure is known as *immunization*. If more than one future payment is to be made the procedure is known as *multi-period immunization* or cash flow matching. There are several duration-based strategies that can be used in this context. One strategy would be to find a zero coupon bond, or a *strip* of zero coupon bonds, with a maturity date matching the cash flow(s). Alternatively, for coupon paying bonds, two often applied strategies, and the ones which will be described here, are known as the *bullet* and the *barbell* strategies.

Table 7.13. Price change section of spreadsheet

Price Change in Bond due to DURATION ONLY	−3.46358
Price Change in Bond due to CONVEXITY ONLY	0.08082
New Price = £92.99	
DURATION	
Old Price = £96.45	
New Price = £93.07	
DURATION & CONVEXITY	
Old Price = £96.45	

These names give a pointer to the type of structure being put in place:

1 The bullet strategy sets out to create a portfolio of bonds which have durations equal to, or as close as possible to, the date that the sum is required in the future and which will deliver a sum of money that will satisfy the amount required by the future liability on that date.

2 The barbell strategy sets out to create a portfolio which has bond durations some time distance before and some time difference after the required date, but whose weighted average is equal to the future date on which the cash outflow falls due.

Example 7.18 Maturity matching

Assume that an investor has £35,000 to invest and requires £42,500 in exactly two years' time.

The best building society/bank two-year, fixed interest deposit rate of interest is currently 9.75 per cent paid semi-annually which will generate a sum of £42,340 in two years: a shortfall of £160. Using bonds one intuitive approach that might be adopted to achieve the required principal is to buy a 12 per cent coupon bond which matures in exactly two years' time. So for example if the YTM of the bond in question is 10 per cent, assuming that: (i) a coupon has just been paid; (ii) the current price is £103.50 (at which the investor can purchase £33,816 of nominal stock); (iii) no change to the interest rates occur during the time that the bond is held; and (iv) the coupons received semi-annually can be invested at the building society rate of 9.75 per cent. The future value that will be generated by the bond can be found on Lotus by using the @FV function: @FV(future payments of equal amounts:pmt, the periodic interest rate:int, number of payment periods:term). The inputs in this case will be £33,816 × 0.06 (the nominal stock held multiplied by the coupon received annually: 0.12/2 = 0.06), the semi-annual reinvestment rate: 0.0975/2, and 4: the number of semi-annual periods involved. The outcome of £42,545, which matches the required £42,500 with a small over-shoot of £45, is shown in Table 7.14:

Table 7.14.   Maturity matching

```
Building Society Deposit:
        £42,340 @FV((35000*0.0975/2),0.0975/2,4)+35000

Maturity matched bond (no interest rate changes):
          £42,545 @FV(33816*0.06,0.0975/2,4)+33816

Maturity matched bond (one interest rate change):
          £42,432 @FV(33816*0.06,0.08/2,4)+33816

Duration matched bond (no interest rate changes):
        £42,709 @FV(33692*0.06,0.0975/2,4)+(33692*1.0095)

Duration matched bond (one interest rate change):
        £42,923 @FV(33692*0.06,0.08/2,4)+(33692*1.0192)
```

Coupon + interest-on-interest	£ 8,729
Redemption value of bond	£33,816
Total	£42,545

Now reconsider this case under the assumption that immediately after the bond has been purchased, because of a reduction in interest rates, the reinvestment rate falls to 8 per cent and that 8 per cent is the best rate achievable for reinvesting the coupons as they are received. Table 7.14 reveals that the outcome under this scenario results in a pay-off of £42,432, a shortfall of £68 on the required £42,500. The breakdown in this case will be:

Coupon + interest-on-interest	£ 8,616
Redemption value of bond	£33,816
Total	£42,432

Bullet strategy

Using the same scenario as the one above, the problem can be regarded as one where a bond (or bonds) needs to be found such that it has a weighted average Macaulay duration equal to (or close to) the date on which the cash flow is required. Assume that such a bond can be found and that it has a Macaulay duration of approximately two years. Let the profile of that bond be as follows: purchase price £103,88, coupon 12 per cent and YTM 10 per cent. With £35,000 available £33,692 of nominal stock can be purchased. The cash flows that will be generated by the bond will now be:

Coupon + interest-on-interest	£ 8,697
Cash-in value of bond	£34,012
Total	£42,709

Note: being a coupon-paying bond the investor can expect to get a price

somewhat higher than the par value since there is still some time to its
maturity. For the bond used in this example the market valuation of the bond
will be £100.95 for each £100 of nominal stock, hence the figure of
33692*1.0095 in the Lotus formula in Table 7.14.

Again adopting the assumption that immediately after purchasing the bond
interest rates fall to 8 per cent, the cash flows that would be generated are:

Coupon + interest-on-interest	£ 8,584
Cash-in value of bond	£34,340
Total	£42,924

The fall in yield affects the potential reinvestment income but at the same
time will increase the price of the bond on the market. With some time still
remaining to maturity, the bond's valuation will be £101,92 which when
multiplied by the amount of nominal stock held gives a cash-in figure of
£34,340 and the required sum can be met from the proceeds of the investment
with a £424 overshoot despite the fall in interest rates (see Table 7.14).

Although this example has only used one bond with duration very close to
the liability date it would have been possible to match the duration with two or
more bonds whose weighted average Macaulay duration matched the liability
date. If the bonds chosen to create this type of portfolio all have durations
close to liability date the strategy is still known as a bullet strategy.

Barbell strategy
Using the same scenario as the one above, the problem can be regarded as one
where two (or more) bonds need to be found that have weighted average
Macaulay duration equal to (or close to) the date on which the cash flow is
required but which themselves have Macaulay durations some distance away
from the date of the future liability.

Whether for a bullet or a barbell strategy once two or more bonds are used
to construct a cash flow matching portfolio the added problem arises of how
many of each type of bond to hold. A straight 50–50 split could be assumed but
a better pay-off might be obtained by holding the appropriate bonds in some
other proportion providing that the sum of the weights (w_i) equals one. If the
optimal weights are to be found then mathematical programming methods can
be employed to find them. The problem revolves around defining an objective
function based on weights and yields of the bonds (r_i) and a set of constraints:
such a model might for example, have a goal of maximizing the yield of the
portfolio (r_p) subject to the sum of the unknown weights being equal to one,
the sum of the unknown weights multiplied by their associated duration (d_i)
being equal to the duration required to meet the liability (d_p), and that on
solution all the weights have values greater than or equal to zero. A simple
example might appear as:

Maximize:
$r_p = w_1 r_1 + w_2 r_2$

Subject to:
$$w_1 + w_2 = 1$$
$$w_1 d_1 + w_2 d_2 = d_p$$
$$w_1, w_2 \geq 0$$

Obviously the Example 7.18 developed above is hypothetical (for a profile of the bonds used in this example see Appendix 7B). Yields fluctuate on a daily basis and, as was highlighted in Chapter 3, interest rates, and through them yields, have changed dramatically over relatively short periods of time in recent years. To imagine a state where only one change takes place over a two year period is unrealistic. The example does demonstrate, however, that the Macaulay duration approach can help to match a future liability better than a bond which matures at exactly the time when the cash is required.

Rebalancing of the duration of a liability matching portfolio, however, will be needed. For, as time passes and interest rates change, the duration of the bonds held in the portfolio will change: a bond with a five year duration today will, in six months' time, have a duration of less than five years. Convexity provides an indication of the frequency of rebalancing which is required, and Appendix 7A draws a comparison between the delta, gamma hedges of Chapter 5 and duration, convexity terms encountered in this chapter.

7.6   Hedging with futures and options

As well as the risk management methods discussed in the previous sections there are also exchange-based instruments available to the bond portfolio manager. LIFFE, for example, has futures contracts available on the long UK gilt, the US Treasury bond, the German government long- and medium-term bonds: the Bund (Bundesanleihen) and Bobl (Bundesobligation or Bundesschatzanweisung) the Italian government bond, the Japanese government bond, and on 10 March 1993 introduced a contract on the long-term Spanish government bond. Most of these futures contracts also have associated options contracts—one notable exception being the Japanese government bond. The future and option contracts for the UK gilt are reproduced in Table 7.15 for information.

The contract specification for a bond future introduces a concept which has not been encountered in the context of any other futures contract. The concept is of a *notional* bond. For the UK gilt the description of a bond which may be delivered in the contract is: *a notional gilt with a 9 per cent coupon;* for the Bund future it is: *a notional German government bond with a 6 per cent coupon,* etc. In other words the 9 per cent gilt, or the 6 per cent Bund, around which the contracts are built do not exist: a bond deliverable into the contract on maturity has to be created. Reading deeper into the list of deliverable gilts it is apparent that there are other restrictions which are imposed in order to identify those bonds which can actually

Table 7.15. Future and option contracts for UK gilt

	Long Gilt Future	Option on Long Gilt Future
Unit of Trading	£50,000 nominal value notional gilt with 9% coupon	1 Long Gilt futures contract
Delivery Months	March, June, September, December	
Delivery/Expiry Month		March, June, September, December
Delivery Day	Any business day in delivery month (at seller's choice)	Exercise by 17.00 on any business day, extended to 18.30 on Last Trading Day. Delivery on the first business day after the
Exercise Day/		exercise day. Expiry at 18.30 on Last Trading Day.
Last Trading Day	11.00 Two business days prior to last business day in delivery month	
Expiry Day		16.15 Six business days prior to first day of delivery month
Quotation	Per £100 nominal	
Minimum Price Movement (Tick Size & Value)	£1/32 (£15.625)	Multiples of 1/64 £1/64 (£7.8125)
Trading Hours	08.30–16.15	08.32–16.15
APT Trading Hours	16.30–18.00	

Long Gilt Future

Contract Standard   Delivery may be made of any Gilts on the List of Deliverable Gilts in respect of a delivery month, as published by the Exchange on or before the tenth business day prior to the First Notice Day of such delivery month. All gilt issues included in the List will have the following characteristics:-
a) having terms as to redemption such as provide for redemption of the entire gilt issue in a single instalment on the maturity date falling not earlier than 10 years from, and not later than 15 years from, the first day of the relevant delivery month;
b) having no terms permitting or requiring early redemption;
c) bearing interest at a single fixed rate throughout the term of the issue payable in arrears semi-annually (except in the case of the first interest payment period which may be more or less than six months);
d) being denominated and payable as to the principal and interest only in Pounds and pence;
e) being fully paid or, in the event that the gilt issue is in its first period and is partly paid, being anticipated by the Board to be fully paid on or before the Last Notice Day of the relevant delivery month;
f) not being convertible;
g) having been admitted to the Official List of the London Stock Exchange; and
i) being anticipated by the Board to have on one or more days in the delivery month an aggregate principal amount outstanding of not less than £500 million which, by its terms and conditions, if issued in more than one tranche or tap issue, is fungible.

Exchange Delivery Settlement Price (EDSP)   The LIFFE market price at 11.00 a.m. on the second business day prior to Settlement Day. The invoicing amount in respect of each Deliverable Gilt is to be calculated by the price factor system. Adjustment will be made for full coupon interest accruing as at Settlement Day.

Option on Long Gilt Future

Contract Standard   Assignment of 1 Long Gilt futures contract for the delivery month at the exercise price.

Exercise Price Intervals   £1 e.g. £106–00, £107–00 etc.

Introduction of New Exercise Prices   13 exercise prices will be listed for new series. Additional exercise prices will be introduced on the business day after the Long Gilt futures contract settlement price is within £16/32 of the sixth highest or lowest existing exercise price.

Option Price   The contract price is *not* paid at the time of purchase. Option positions, as with futures positions, are marked-to-market daily giving rise to positive or negative variation margin flows. If an option is exercised by the Buyer, the Buyer is required to pay the original contract price to the Clearing House and the Clearing House will pay the original option price to the Seller on the following business day. Such payments will be netted against the variation margin balances of Buyer and Seller by the Clearing House.

Source: LIFFE. Reproduced with permission.

223

be used as *physicals* to deliver into the contract. It is important to note that the bond that will eventually be delivered into the contract, and the date on which it will be delivered, will be decided by the seller of the futures contract. This flexibility on the part of the seller allows him or her to select a bond which from a personal point of view will be the *cheapest-to-deliver* (CTD).

A rough idea of which bond will be the CTD can be obtained by using the *raw basis*, that is the current offer price of a bond (S) minus the current futures (F) quotes multiplied by that bond's conversion factor (CF).

Raw Basis = S − F×CF

From the set of bonds which meet the regulations regarding deliverability, that bonds which has the smallest absolute value will be the CTD. Having established a rule that will facilitate the identification of the CTD there is one component of the formula which needs to be found, namely CF, the conversion factor. As was mentioned above, the future is based on a fictitious bond but delivery will be in the form of a real bond. The real bond, therefore, will have to be converted in order to meet the contract specification and determine how much will have to be delivered into the contract to satisfy the £50,000 nominal contract size. The CF can be thought of as the price of the deliverable bond were it to be priced with a YTM of 9 per cent, the specified contract yield.

Example 7.19

Using a June 1993 UK long gilts futures contract and assuming delivery on 1 June 1993 the theoretical price for the 9½ per cent Conversion Stock maturing on 18 April 2005 will be £103.50. The conversion factor will then be quoted as 1.035. A reasonable approximation can be obtained quite easily on Lotus by using the @NPV function: @NPV(periodic fixed interest rate: int, spreadsheet range of cash flows:range). For the current example this can be expressed as:

$$P_0 = \frac{4.75}{(1 + 0.045)} + \frac{4.75}{(1 + 0.045)^2} + \ldots + \frac{104.75}{(1 + 0.045)^{2T}}$$

where 4.75 represents the 9 per cent coupon paid on a semi-annual basis, 0.045 represents the semi-annual discount factor based on the 9 per cent notional coupon of the future, and $2T$ represents the number of semi-annual cash flows between now and maturity of the deliverable bond which will generate a price of (P_0) of £103.50.

Note: Lotus demo   YTM.WK3 has a macro that will calculate the conversion factor for input bonds. The macro is activated by using the Alt+A key and selecting CF on the special menu. The cursor will automatically move to the CF section of the spreadsheet where the CF is reported.

For the bonds used in Table 7.16 the estimated CFs are 1.0362939, 1.035369, 1.067024, respectively. They have been calculated as described above, but with fewer cash flows in the case of the Conversion Stock of 2004, and fewer cash flows and 5 per cent as the semi-annual coupon received in the case of the Treasury Stock of 2003.

Once the CFs for the deliverable bonds are known, using raw basis to find the CTD becomes a matter of arithmetic.

Example 7.20

Assuming today's date is 15 March 1993, that the bonds shown in Table 7.16 are deliverable into the June contract on 1 June and that the June future stands at 107-5 the raw bases are as shown in Table 7.16.

Recall that the UK and US quote bond prices in 32nds thus 112-3 is 112 $\frac{3}{32}$ which as a decimal is 112.0938. From the deliverable bonds used in this example the 9½ per cent Conversion Stock of 18 April 2005 will be the CTD into the June contract. A word of caution is in order here: the method used for this demonstration takes no account of accrued interest. When calculating conversion factors an exchange will make a number of additional assumptions which have not been made here. The exchange-based CFs for the bonds used in the above example are 1.0357, 1.0349 and 1.0655, respectively. There is, of course, a more rigorous way of identifying the CTD bond. The method calculates an *implied repo rate* which takes into account accrued interest up to a target delivery date (see Dubofsky, 1992, for good coverage of this topic).

The bond which is eventually delivered may, or may not, be the CTD. There are many reasons which impinge upon the decision of which bond to deliver and when to deliver. It must also be pointed out that the CTD identified at any moment in time does not necessarily remain so for the entire period of a contract. Market forces may interact to chase up the price of a bond currently regarded as the CTD to a point where some other bond becomes more attractive in terms of the implied repo rate or raw basis. There may be in-house reasons why the seller of a futures contract decides to deliver another bond; tax reasons may enter the picture; as may the composition of the portfolio being managed, particularly if options on the future are involved. Nevertheless, statistics do seem to indicate that players in this market do look to the CTD as a benchmark of the futures contract, and the bond identified as the CTD is the most popular bond delivered into the contract.

Table 7.16. Deliverable bonds

Deliverable Stock	S	CF*F	Raw Basis
9½% Conv 2005	112-3	110.9817	1.0484
9½% Conv 2004	112-3	110.8960	1.0850
10% Treas 2003	115-31	114.1750	1.6305

7.6.1 Using a futures contract to hedge a portfolio of bonds

In hedging portfolios of bonds modified duration plays an important role in establishing a relationship between a bond (or several bonds) and the CTD. The basic number of contracts required to hedge a portfolio of bond(s) is given by the formula:

$$\text{No. of contracts} = \frac{\text{Nominal value of the portfolio}}{\text{Nominal value of contract}} \text{ Conversion factor}_{\text{CTD}}$$

This indicates that the basic number of contracts required to hedge the portfolio is given by the ratio:

$$\frac{\text{Nominal value of the portfolio}}{\text{Nominal value of contracts}}$$

which will need to be adjusted to take account of the fact that the CTD has to be converted to match the futures contract specification.

This formula is fine if the bond to hedge is the CTD. If, however, the bond(s) is not the CTD then finding a further adjustment factor can help the hedger to establish a more appropriate number of contracts—to buy or sell—in order to hedge the exposed position. An adjustment factor can be estimated in a number of ways and is known as *relative volatility*. Equation (7.11) shows how duration may be used to find a value for this term:

$$\text{Rel.vol.} = \frac{P_b}{P_{\text{CTD}}} \times \frac{\text{Mod}_{\text{dur.b}}}{\text{Mod}_{\text{dur.CTD}}} \times \frac{\text{ACT}\Delta r_b}{\text{ACT}\Delta r_{\text{CTD}}} \qquad (7.11)$$

where:

> Rel.vol. represents relative volatility:
> P_b represents the price of bond(s) to be hedged;
> P_{CTD} represents the price of the cheapest-to-deliver instrument;
> $\text{Mod}_{\text{dur.b}}$ represents the modified duration of the bond(s) position;
> $\text{Mod}_{\text{dur.CTD}}$ represents the modified duration of the CTD instrument;
> $\text{ACT}\Delta r_b$ represents actual change in yield of the bond(s) position;
> $\text{ACT}\Delta r_{\text{CTD}}$ represents actual change in yield of the CTD instrument.

This somewhat fearsome looking formula is in fact quite simple to use. Referring back to the way in which duration can help predict the effect of small changes in yield on the price of a bond the formula below was developed:

$$dP = (-1) \times \text{Mod}_d \times P_0 \times dr$$

Now assume that the value of the portfolio position in bonds can be expressed as:

$$V_p = V_b + h \times V_f$$

> V_p represents the current value of the portfolio;

V_b represents the current valuation of the bond(s) held in the portfolio;
V_f represents the value of a futures contract held in the portfolio;
h represents the number of futures contracts held.

Intuitively, if the value of the portfolio is hedged then a long position in bonds would need to be set against a short position in the futures contract. A negative value for h indicates the number of contracts that will need to be shorted.

Any change in the value of the portfolio can be explained by the expression:

$$\Delta V_p = \Delta V_b + h \times \Delta V_f$$

where Δ represents a finite change in the value of a variable. To maintain a neutral position $\Delta V_p = 0$ so that any gain on the bond side of the portfolio will be offset by a loss on the futures side and vice versa. If that is the case then:

$$0 = \Delta V_b + h \times \Delta V_f$$

which in turn implies that:

$$h = (-1) \times \frac{\Delta V_b}{\Delta V_f}$$

If only one bond is held in the portfolio then from the price change formula, assuming small changes in yield, ΔV_b can be written as dP while ΔV_f can be written as dP_{CTD}. If more than one bond is held in the portfolio then, given that duration is additive, ΔV_b will be found by adding together the changes in each bond's price that have occurred, estimated in the same way as for the one bond case but additionally taking into account the proportions of each bond's holding in the portfolio. Note that ΔV_f will still be given by dP_{CTD}.

The effect of any change in yield ($ACT\Delta r_b$ and $ACT\Delta r_{CTD}$) is often assumed to be the same for the bond(s) to be hedged and the CTD which allows the change in yield terms in the numerator and the denominator to cancel.

Example 7.21

(a) Hedging the CTD
Assume a portfolio with a current valuation of £10,000,000 which contains only one bond–the 9½% Conversion Stock of 2005. The current price of the bond is £112-3, its conversion factor is 1.0362939 and it is also the CTD. The basic number of shorted futures contracts needed to hedge this long portfolio will be given by:

Number of contracts = Nominal value of portfolio/Nominal value of contract

$$= £10,000,000/£50,000$$

$$= 200 \text{ contracts}$$

But from the discussion of the nature of the futures contract this figure needs to be modified to take account of the bond that may eventually be delivered into the futures contract at maturity, and the relation of that bond to the CTD.

The first of these modifications involves using the CF of the CTD so that the revised number of contracts will be given by:

$$200 \times 1.0362939 = 207.2588$$

A decision needs to be made whether to short 207 or 208 contracts, since fractions of contracts are not available.

Note: no further adjustment is required in this case since the bond to be hedged is the CTD.

(b) Hedging a non-CTD bond

If the bond to be hedged is not the CTD then a further adjustment needs to be made to the number of contracts shorted. This is the case where the relationship—known as *relative volatility*—between the CTD and the bond to be hedged plays an important role. For this example assume that the bond to be hedged is the 10 per cent Treasury Stock of 2003, priced at £115-31. From the formula above it is evident that to be able to perform the necessary calculations the modified durations of the two bonds need to be established. This exercise can be performed using the DURA.WK3 spreadsheet described earlier in this chapter. For the two bonds in question the modified durations are: 7.375714 CTD and 6.761665 non-CTD calculated from the DURA.WK3 spreadsheet. Using the data available on the bonds in conjunction with Equation (7.11) (see page 226) the formula appears as:

$$\text{Relative volatility} = (115\text{-}31 \times 6.761665)/(112\text{-}3 \times 7.375714) = 0.948438$$

So a further adjustment to the extent of 0.948438 is required using this duration measure of relative volatility. The number of contracts required will then be:

$$\text{Adjusted no. of contracts} = 0.948438 \times 207.2588 = 196 \text{ or } 197$$

(c) Hedging two non-CTD bonds

To examine the case where there are two bonds included in the portfolio consider the following example: bond 1 is the 9½ per cent Conversion Stock of 2004, the second is the 10 per cent Treasury Stock of 2003, used in (b). The profile of the CTD is assumed to be as stated in Example (a) and (b), and the modified duration of the first bond is 7.194419 (refer to Table 7.16). The valuation of the holding in bond 1 is £4,000,000 and in bond 2 is £6,000,000. A straightforward alteration to Equation (7.11) gives:

$$\text{Rel.vol.} = \frac{(w_1)(P_{b1})(\text{Mod}_{dur.b1}) + (w_2)(P_{b2}) \times (\text{Mod}_{dur.b2})}{(P_{CTD})(\text{Mod}_{dur.CTD})}$$

where:

w_i represents the proportion of the ith bond held in the portfolio ($i = 1, 2$ in this example);
P_{bi} represents the price of the ith bond ($i = 1, 2$ in this example);
$\text{Mod}_{\text{dur.b}i}$ represents the modified duration of the ith bond ($i = 1, 2$ in this example).

which yields:

$$\text{Rel.vol.} = \frac{[(0.4)(£112.0313)(7.194419) + (0.6)(£115.9688)(6.761665)]}{(£112.0938)(7.375714)}$$
$$= 792.8885 / 826.7718 = 0.9590$$

An adjustment to the extent of 0.9590 is required in this case, again using the duration measure of relative volatility. The number of contracts required will then be:

Adjusted no. of contracts = $0.9590 \times 207.2588 = 198$ or 199

Note: this type of hedge will need further modification if large movements in interest rates occur.

Using duration is by no means the only way of establishing a relationship between the CTD and the bonds to be hedged. Other methods such as *regression analysis* could be used in which case a relationship could be expressed as:

$\text{Bond}_t = a + b \, \text{Future}_t + e_t$

where:

Bond_t represents the price of the bond to be hedged (or the $\log_e$ returns of the bond to be hedged) at time t;
Future_t represents the price (quote) of the future (or $\log_e$ returns of the future), at time t;
e_t represents the error term (the relationship between the bond and the future will not be exact; the behaviour of the error term was outlined in Chapter 6), at time t;
a and b are coefficients to be estimated.

There are problems with this approach: one is that the CTD does not remain constant throughout the life of the futures contract so that the right-hand-side variable in the expression may change; additionally, deciding over what time period to estimate the relationship is not immediately apparent and the values of a and b will change for different T.

Yet another approach to estimate relative volatility could involve the use of both duration and convexity. The method is known as *perturbation analysis* and uses the money value of 1 per cent change in yield per amount of nominal stock. For example, assuming the gilt held in the portfolio is the 10 per cent Conversion Stock described above together with the CTD from above. The formula below suggests how many contracts would be needed to hedge a £10,000,000 portfolio of the non-CTD bond.

$$\text{No. of contracts} = \frac{\text{Portfolio value}}{\text{Nominal contract value}} \times \frac{\Delta P_{\text{b}}}{\Delta P_{\text{CTD}}} \times \text{CF}_{\text{CTD}}$$

where:

ΔP_{b} represents the price change in the bond that would occur when yield falls by 1 per cent (100 bps);

ΔP_{CTD} represents the price change in the CTD that would occur when yield falls by 1 per cent (100 bps);

CF_{CTD} represents the conversion factor of the CTD.

Note: the price changes employed in the formula below were calculated using DURA.WK3 and selecting *Prices* from the special menu.

$$\text{No. of contracts} = \frac{£10,000,000}{£50,000} \times \frac{8.19}{8.69} \times 1.0362939 = 195.3336$$

In this example 195 or 196 long gilt contracts would be needed to hedge the portfolio compared to the 196/197 found using the duration measure above.

In all of these examples it must be remembered that if the position to be hedged has a time horizon different to the defined exchange maturity dates then a basis risk exists and this would need to be taken into consideration when putting the hedge in place. Moreover, in the formulae used to calculate the duration and perturbation effects it was assumed that the change in yield (dr) that occurred affected both bonds in exactly the same way. This may not be the case in reality as market forces and shifts in the yield curve could result in quite different yield changes (dr) for each bond. In view of this and given that the measurement of the relative volatility between any two bonds, by whatever means, is only an estimate, putting on a hedge will probably be more effective in a well-diversified bond portfolio context than in the case of portfolio comprising only one bond.

7.6.2   Using options to hedge a portfolio of bonds

The basic pay-off strategies that can be put in place using options alone or in conjunction with a long or short position in an underlying security have been discussed at length in Chapter 4. Diagrams for these strategies can be obtained using the OPT_STR1.WK3 worksheet—remember to convert the futures and options premiums for the UK long gilt contract to decimals, the premiums are quoted in 32nds for the futures contract and 64ths for options.

The pricing of options together with the calculation of Δ and Γ ratios can be obtained from the B&S.WK3 spreadsheet. The method used to calculate the information is the Black formula as shown in Equation (5.13) for calls and (5.14) for puts. By selecting F (f), after inputting the basic data, move the cursor to the Futures Premium screen, there are two tables of information reported. At the top of the screen options premiums are reported as decimals and are suitable for options on the Bund future, the Italian government bond and the Spanish government bond. The lower part of the screen reports prices in 64ths for the UK and US long bonds.

Chapter 8 returns to the use of options and futures in the context of interest rates instruments in more detail.

7.7   Spreadsheets

There are three demonstration spreadsheets used in this chapter:

1   YTM.WK3 which is described in Sec. 7.12 and whose special menu is illustrated in Table 7.3;
2   SPOT_PAR.WK3   which is discussed in Sec. 7.3 and whose special menu appears in Table 7.8;
3   DURA.WK3 which is described in Sec. 7.5 and whose special menu appears as Table 7.11.

7.7.1   YTM.WK3

The special menu, which appears as Table 7.3, provides users with an opportunity of inputting a bond's settlement date, its coupon, maturity date and clean price:

(Data);

it automatically calculates and reports the YTM in the input frame. The spreadsheet also calculates the bond's conversion factor for use in hedging with a futures contract:

(CF);

a final macro exits the special menu returning the spreadsheet back to normal Lotus operating mode:

(Quit).

7.7.2   SPOT_PAR.WK3

The special menu, which appears as Table 7.8, provides users with an opportunity of inputting up-to-date spot interest rates:

(Spot_Zero);

or par interest rates:

(Par);

and calculates forward rates on the basis of input spot or par rates:

(Forward).

The frequency of the yield observations can be altered by the user from the initial six month frequency using:

(Time_Period);

Par rates calculated from spot rates must be copied to the appropriate section of the spreadsheet in order to keep it up to date:

(Copy).

The spreadsheet also provides the user with graphs of the yield curves either individually or on one graph as described in the text:

(Graphs);

a final macro exits the special menu returning the spreadsheet back to normal Lotus operating mode:

(Quit).

7.7.3 DURA.WK3

The special menu, which appears as Table 7.11, provides users with an opportunity of inputting a bond's settlement date, the date of its next coupon, its clean price and its current YTM:

(Data_Input);

it calculates durations and convexity as output and applied those values to the bond's original price:

(Prices);

a final macro exits the special menu returning the spreadsheet back to normal Lotus operating mode:

(Quit).

Questions

7.1 Use the YTM.WK3 spreadsheet to find the yield to maturity (YTM) of the following bonds. Assume that each bond pays semi-annual coupons, accrued interest is calculated on a A/A basis:

(a)   10.0 per cent Conversion 1996

(b)   13.25 per cent Treasury Stock 1997

(c)   10.5 per cent Exchequer Stock 2005.

7.2   Explain the differences between the clean and dirty price of a bond.

7.3   Calculate the modified duration for each of the following hypothetical 10-year bonds, settled today and maturing on 14/10/2000:

		Price	YTM
(a)	10 per cent coupon	149.05	4%
		129.75	6%
		113.59	8%
		100	10%
(a)	0 per cent coupon	67.30	4%
		55.37	6%
		45.64	8%
		37.69	10%

7.4   Plot the (a) and (b) data on a graph (using the graph facility on Lotus). What implications do your findings have for investment strategies?

7.5   Making use of the results obtained in Question 7.3 find the money (dollar) price change that occurs and the new price that obtains when:

(a)   The yield on a 10 per cent coupon bond drops from 8 to 7.9 per cent.

(b)   The yield on a 10 per cent bond rises from 6 to 6.05 per cent.

(c)   Under what circumstances might the money price change formula give a poor approximation?

7.6   What is meant by duration hedging? Why might the standard duration measures (Macaulay and Modified) lead to less than perfect hedges in the real world?

7.7   Derive the formula for calculating the following:

(a)   Modified duration of a bond

(b)   Convexity of a bond.

State any assumptions you make in order to facilitate the derivation of the formulae.

7.8   Discuss ways in which duration can be helpful to bond analysts. Pay particular attention to the following:

(a)   Bond price sensitivity

(b)   Hedging

(c)   Achieving a target portfolio value.

7.9   Explain what is meant by the expression, 'an immunized bond portfolio'. Why might an immunized portfolio fail to achieve a target yield?

7.10   Discuss ways in which the relative volatility between the cheapest-to-deliver (CTD) and another bond may be estimated.

7.11 A bond portfolio manager has a holding of £1,000,000 of deliverable gilt in his or her portfolio which is being held on a long-term basis. The portfolio manager wishes to hedge the portfolio using the LIFFE gilt futures contract.

The gilt in question has the following characteristics:

UK Treasury 8 per cent, 25/9/2009, at 75-04 clean, YTM 11.154 per cent, CF 0.9086422 and modified duration 8.37 years.

The CTD has the following profile:

UK Treasury 11.75 per cent, 22/1/2007, at 99-08 clean, YTM 11.855 per cent, CF 1.2055878 and modified duration 7.18 years.

(a) Calculate the relative volatility required to estimate the number of contracts needed to hedge the gilt.

(b) Estimate the number of contracts required to set up a hedge for delivery on exchange-based dates.

7.12 A bond portfolio manager has two deliverable gilts in his or her £100,000,000 gilt portfolio which he or she wishes to hedge using the long gilt contract on LIFFE.

The profile of the CTD is as in Equation (7.11) (see page 226).

The two deliverable gilts are as follows:

(a) £6,000,000 in UK Treasury 9.5 per cent, 25/10/2004, at 85-07 clean, YTM 11.633 per cent, CF 1.0396210 and modified duration 7.13 years;

(b) £4,000,000 in UK Treasury 13.5 per cent, 26/3/2008, at 111-13 clean, YTM 11.796 per cent, CF 1.3509974 and modified duration 7.25 years.

Estimate the number of contracts needed to hedge the portfolio.

7.13 How might a bond portfolio manager seek to cover a perceived yield risk whose horizon does not match an exchange-based contract?

Appendix 7A

Using a Taylor series expansion it is possible to draw a comparison between the delta and gamma hedge parameters encountered in Chapter 5 and the duration and convexity terms used in Chapter 7.

For simplicity assuming that a variable Y is a function of a variable X then the total change that occurs in Y as a result of a change in the variable X can be expressed as:

$$\Delta Y = \frac{dY}{dX}\Delta X + \frac{1}{2}\frac{d^2 Y}{dX^2}\Delta X^2 + \Phi \tag{7A.1}$$

where Φ captures terms in ΔX^3 and less.

The first term on the right-hand side of Equation (7A.1) incorporates the delta from option pricing theory if C is substituted for Y and S is substituted for X—$\partial C/\partial S$; while the second term incorporates gamma—$\partial^2 C/\partial S^2$.

Returning to Equation (7A.1) and moving to bonds by setting Y equal to the price of a bond (P) and X equal to yield (r), the change in the price of a bond can be expressed as:

$$\Delta P = \frac{dP}{dr}\Delta r + \frac{1}{2}\frac{d^2P}{dr^2}\Delta r^2 + \Phi \tag{7A.2}$$

using a Taylor series expansion, where Φ captures terms in ΔX^3 and less.

Dividing both sides of Equation (7A.2) by P gives:

$$\frac{\Delta P}{P} = \frac{dP}{dr}\frac{1}{P}\Delta r + \frac{1}{2}\frac{d^2P}{dr^2}\frac{1}{P}\Delta r^2 + \Phi \tag{7A.3}$$

where Φ captures terms in ΔX^3 and less, and of which the term:

$$\frac{dP}{dr}\frac{1}{P} = -\text{Modified duration}$$

contains the first derivative term dP/dr which is comparable to the delta ($\partial C/\partial S$) term from the options formula and

$$\frac{1}{2}\frac{d^2P}{dr^2}\frac{1}{P} = \text{Convexity}$$

which contains the second derivative term which is comparable to the gamma ($\partial^2 C/\partial S^2$) term.

This comparison can also be put in the context of a portfolio. Again for simplicity assume that the value of the portfolio (Π) is determined by the price of the asset it contains (P) and time (t). Then using a Taylor series expansion the change in the value of the portfolio can be expressed as:

$$\Delta\Pi = \frac{\partial\Pi}{\partial P}\Delta P + \frac{\partial\Pi}{\partial t}\Delta t + \frac{1}{2}\frac{\partial^2\Pi}{\partial P^2}\Delta P^2 + \frac{1}{2}\frac{\partial^2\Pi}{\partial P^2}\Delta t^2 + \frac{\partial^2\Pi}{\partial P\partial t} + \Phi$$

where Φ captures terms in ΔX^3 and less.

Chapter 5 demonstrates how a portfolio can be made delta neutral which in practice means that the first term on the right-hand side of Equation (7A.2) is equal to zero. By the same token a portfolio can be made gamma neutral by ensuring that $\partial^2\Pi/\partial P^2$ is equal to zero.

When considering a portfolio of bonds small changes in yields can be protected against by putting on a duration hedge, which would set the first term on the right-hand side of the equation to zero, while larger changes could be handled by taking convexity into account and setting the third term equal to zero. Note, however, that the value of the portfolio is not immune to the passage of time.

Appendix 7B

The profile of the bond in the maturity matching case is:

Settlement date: 23 March 1993
Maturity date: 23 March 1995
Coupons paid: 23 March and 23 September
Coupon 12 per cent
YTM 10 per cent
Price: £103.50.

The profile of the bond in the duration matching case is:

Settlement date: 23 March 1993
Maturity date: 23 September 1995
Coupons paid: 23 March and 23 September
Coupon 12 per cent
YTM 10 per cent
Price: £103.875
Macaulay duration: 2.25 years.

Notes

[1] A bond trading at par implies that the price paid by the buyer will be £1 for each £1 of nominal stock—ignoring bid–offer spreads—in consequence the yield on the bond will be equal to the bond's coupon, i.e. the interest paid to the holder of the bond at regular intervals.
[2] Note that the mean and standard deviation calculations can be performed easily on Lotus using the @AVG and @STD functions on a range of data.
[3] The yields on two instruments are *effective yields* if they relate to the same period of time. Thus if a bond pays semi-annual coupons a money market instrument must have a six month life span for the day count conversion formula to be appropriate. Otherwise further conversions will be required to place the quotes on a comparable basis.
[4] The mid-point between the London Interbank bid–offer rate spread.

References and further reading

Antl, B. (1988), *Management of Interest Rate Risk*, Euromoney Publications, London.
Bierwag, G.O., Kaufman, G.G and Latta, C.M. (1988), Duration models a taxonomy, *Journal of Portfolio Management*, Autumn, pp. 50–54, New York.
Blake, D. (1990), *Financial Market Analysis*, McGraw-Hill, London.
Dubofsky, D. (1992), *Options and Financial Futures: Valuation and Use*, McGraw-Hill, New York.

Eckl, S., Robinson, J.N. and Thomas, D.C. (1991), *Financial Engineering: A Handbook of Derivative Products*, Basil Blackwell, Oxford.

Fabozzi, F.J. and Fabozzi, T.D. (1989), *Bond Markets, Analysis and Strategies,* Prentice-Hall, Englewood Cliffs, NJ.

Hull, J. (1993), *Options, Futures and other Derivative Securities* (2nd edn), Prentice-Hall, Englewood Cliffs, NJ.

Urry, M. (1991), The hidden timebomb in the convertible passage, *The Financial Times*, 14 May.

8 Managing interest rate and currency risk

8.1 One period forwards and futures

In Chapter 3 the *raison d'être* of forward and futures contracts was discussed at length. The advantages and disadvantages of both types of contract were listed, the underlying formulae used for calculating forward rates (FORWARDS.WK3) were developed, and a specimen contract specification for the LIFFE LTOM three month sterling futures contract was presented. Chapter 4 took the discussion a step further by introducing options. This chapter will now examine several cases of where, and how, futures and options contracts may be used to hedge short-term interest rate and currency exposure emanating from several sources. To start this process reconsider the interest rate problem of Case 1.1 which appeared in Chapter 1.

> **Case 1.1** revisited
> A company has a £1,000,000 bank loan to finance a development project. The rate of interest it pays on this loan is reset every three months. The corporate treasurer feels that government action will be needed soon to counteract steadily rising inflation. This could mean that interest rates will be raised as part of government policy.

Figure 1.1 identified the exposure faced by the company in this example, and Chapter 3 showed how an offsetting position could be taken in the futures market. Having established the background to the instruments involved, attention can now be turned to the numerical results that might ensue from the use of futures contracts. A spreadsheet entitled INT_1.WK3 has been designed to help analyse the problem and calculate the rate of interest achieved by using a futures contract to hedge the identified exposure. To set the scene assume that the date is 10 March and that the rate to be paid for the next three months has just been fixed and will hold until 17 June; further assume that the rate paid by the company is always 200 bps (2 per cent) above LIBOR and that currently LIBOR stands at $5^{15}\!/\!_{16}$ per cent. This means that the company will be paying $7^{15}\!/\!_{16}$ per cent for the next three months.

Table 8.1 shows the input frame for the INT_1.WK3 spreadsheet. The futures prices are close of business prices on 9 March 1993. Note that the spot rate is

Table 8.1.   Input frame for spreadsheet INT_1.WK3

Today	10-Mar-93			
Future Date of interest	17-Jun-93			
Contract Prices	MARCH	JUNE	SEPT	DEC
Future	94.03	94.49	94.69	94.64
Spot	94.01			
Implied Int. Rate	5.97	5.51	5.31	5.36
Current Portfolio Value (£s)	£1,000,000	Value of one Exchange Contract:	£500,000	
Value of One tick:	£12.50			
Projected Future Level of Index: 93.5		on	17-Jun-93	

indexed off 100 to match the way in which the future is reported, the 94.01 implies a spot LIBOR rate of 5.99 per cent. The £500,000 and £12.50 are contract and tick values, respectively, as defined in the LIFFE LTOM contract specification (refer to Chapter 3). The corporate treasurer's projection is that LIBOR will be at 6½ per cent when the time arrives for the next rate reset   (93.50) on 17 June. The appropriate contract to hedge this position is the June contract, of which two should be shorted. On the spreadsheet a short period is indicated by typing a *minus sign* before the number of contracts. To clarify this see the graphs in Fig. 8.1.

The company is at risk if interest rates rise and this can be seen from Fig. 8.1(a). However, presenting the figure in this way means that as the variable on the horizontal axis increases the value of the position declines, which is at odds with the normal way of interpreting the types of position that have been looked at in this text. For example a rising stock index for the holder of an index tracking portfolio is beneficial, rising interest rates are beneficial to depositors but not to borrowers.

To put the interest rate management problem into the same framework as that developed for the other instruments the interest rate can be subtracted from an index of 100. This simple arithmetical manipulation will permit analysis of positions to proceed in the usual way.

Figure 8.1(b) shows the same underlying position as that identified in Fig. 8.1(a) but now with the futures prices as the variable on the horizontal axis. The interpretation of this diagram is that a rise in the futures price is linked to a fall in interest rates and as such will benefit a borrower. A fall in the futures price is linked to a rise in interest rates which, of course, is not so palatable from the

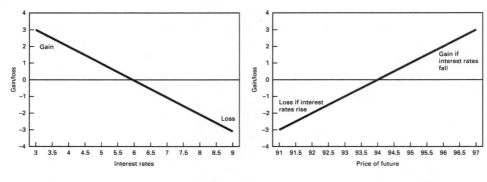

Fig. 8.1.(a).   Interest rate risk liability   **Fig. 8.1.(b).**   Interest rate risk liability

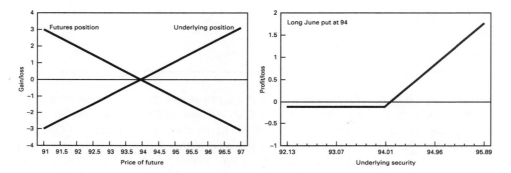

Fig. 8.1.(c).   Interest rate risk liability   **Fig. 8.1.(d).**   Profit profile of
                                                                              combined options
                                                                              and long underlying
                                                                              position

borrower's point of view. From the liability aspect an underlying exposure to increases in interest rates can be offset by a short futures position, this is demonstrated in Fig. 8.1(c). Logically the loss on the underlying position following a rise in interest rates can be counteracted by selling the future now and buying back once the price has fallen. Conversely, should interest rates fall, any gain to the underlying position will be offset by a rise in the price of the future which, if it has been sold at today's quote, will have to be bought at a higher price. The numerical outcome of this hedge, undertaken in the context of Case 1.1 and subject to the assumptions imposed above, is outlined below.

Example 8.1   Case 1.1

The amount of the loan is £1,000,000, a single contract is valued at £500,000 so that the short position in two June futures contracts will hedge the position. The operation of the hedge is as follows (see Table 8.2):

17 March 93	Sell, to open, two June futures contracts on margin for 94.49
17 June 93	Buy, to close, two June futures contracts for 93.5
	Profit/Loss: (94.49 − 93.50) × 100 = 99 ticks per contract
	2 × 99 × £12.50 = £2475

This profit can be used to offset the increase in interest rates that has occurred sometime during the period 10 March–16 June. The rate of interest faced by the company in the next period will be the LIBOR rate of (100 − 93.50) = 6.50 per cent + 200 bps = 8.50 per cent but less the 99 bps implied by the profit obtained from the entry into the futures market hence 7.51 per cent. Another way of calculating the achieved rate is:

− [(Profit/Loss)/Underlying exposure × Days in year/Contract period] + LIBOR + bp risk premium
= [£2475/£1,000,000 × 360/90} + 0.065 + bp risk premium
= 0.0551 + 200 bp risk premium
= 5.51 per cent + 2.00 per cent = 7.51 per cent

One question, of course, is what would have happened if interest rates had fallen rather than risen. Intuitively the achieved rate under each scenario should be identical.

From Fig. 8.1(c) a gain on the futures transaction will be offset by a loss on the underlying transaction. To illustrate this refer to Tables 8.3 and 8.4 where the falling interest rate scenario has been calculated. As expected, when the 200 bp risk premium is taken into account the achieved rate is 7.51 per cent + (LIBOR-LIBID spread) the rate was locked into by using the futures contract. Figure 8.1 (d) demonstrates how the position could have been managed using a long June put option in conjunction with the underlying position. If interest rates rise (lower futures price) the put option gains intrinsic value which can be used to offset the higher interest rate. If interest rates fall the option will expire worthless but the holder will still benefit from the lower interest rate charge on the underlying liability; more will be said about the use of options in this context in Sec. 8.2.

Table 8.2.   Future hedge result

Futures Hedge Result			JUNE	CONTRACT	
Dates	Cash Market		Futures Market		
10-Mar-93	Portfolio Value	£1,000,000	Sell (−) Buy (+) Futures contracts on margin		−2
17-Jun-93	Portfolio Value	£1,000,000	Sell (−) Buy (+) Futures contracts		2
			£2,475.00		
			5.51% ACHIEVED RATE		

Table 8.3.   Falling interest rate scenario

Today	10-Mar-93			
Future Date of interest	17-Jun-93			
Contract Prices	MARCH	JUNE	SEPT	DEC
Future	94.03	94.49	94.69	94.64
Spot	94.01			
Implied Int. Rate	5.97	5.51	5.31	5.36
Current Portfolio Value (£s)	£1,000,000	Value of one Exchange Contract:	£500,000	
Value of One tick:	£12.50			
Projected Future Level of Index:95.5		on	17-Jun-93	

Table 8.4.   Futures hedge result

Futures Hedge Result			JUNE	CONTRACT
Dates	Cash Market		Futures Market	
10-Mar-93	Portfolio Value	£1,000,000	Sell (−) Buy (+) Futures contracts on margin	−2
17-Jun-93	Portfolio Value	£1,000,000	Sell (−) Buy (+) Futures contracts (£2,525.00)	2
			5.51% ACHIEVED RATE	

Of course, higher interest rates will benefit those institutions or individuals who hold an underlying asset position as described in Case 1.2. In that situation the underlying exposure will appear as the mirror image of Fig. 8.1(b). As the price of the future rises, interest rates will be falling and interest income from deposits will be falling. By going long in the futures market (buying) a rate can be locked into in exactly the same way as the short futures transaction revealed above. Table 8.5 uses the same data as the previous examples in this section but suggests a scenario where interest rates fall to 3.5 per cent (projected futures price 96.5 on 17 June). When the June contract is used to hedge this asset position the rate locked into will be 5.51 per cent (LIBOR), but had interest rates risen the 5.51 per cent would still have been the achieved interest rate figure.

Table 8.5.   Interest rates fall to 3.5 per cent

Today	10-Mar-93			
Future Date				
of interest	17-Jun-93			
Contract	MARCH	JUNE	SEPT	DEC
Prices				
Future	94.03	94.49	94.69	94.64
Spot	94.01			
Implied Int. Rate	5.97	5.51	5.31	5.36
Current		Value of		
Portfolio		one Exchange		
Value (£s)	£1,000,000	Contract:	£500,000	
Value of				
One tick:	£12.50			
Projected Future Level of Index:96.5			on	17-Jun-93

Example 8.2

Again using the spreadsheet INT_1.WK3 but entering 96.5 as the projected futures price on maturity of the contract and 2 to indicate a long position for the June contract the achieved rate will be 5.51 per cent as shown in Table 8.6. In this example

17 March 93	Buy, to open, two June futures contracts on margin for 94.49
17 June 93	Sell, to close, two June futures contracts for 96.5
	Profit/Loss: $(96.50 - 94.49) \times 100 = 201$ ticks per contract
	$2 \times 201 \times £12.50 = £5025$

The achieved rate can then be calculated as:

$(£5025/£1,000,000) \times 360/90 + (100 - 96.50)/100$
$= 0.0201 + 0.0350$
$= 0.0551$ or 5.51 per cent.

Unfortunately not all transactions coincide with the maturity date of the futures contract. If such is the case for a particular identified exposure then estimating the likely basis and perhaps using contracts with different maturities will enable the position to be hedged. The idea of an interpolative hedge was discussed in Chapter 6 in the context of equity portfolios. The concept can also be applied in the interest rate and currency arenas.

Example 8.3

To illustrate this type of problem consider the situation where an institution has entered an FRA (forward rate agreement) with a client in which a future lending rate has been agreed—this is known as *selling an FRA*. The

Table 8.6.   Interest rate 5.51 per cent

Futures Hedge Result		JUNE	CONTRACT	
Dates	Cash		Futures	
	Market		Market	
10-Mar-93	Portfolio Value £1,000,000	Sell (-) Buy (+) Futures contracts on margin		2
17-Jun-93	Portfolio Value £1,000,000	Sell(-) Buy (+) Futures contracts £5,025.00)		-2
		5.51% ACHIEVED RATE		

institution's exposure is to rising interest rates. This is analogous to Case 1.1, discussed above, so that an appropriate strategy would be to sell the future thereby setting up a counter position with locked in rates. If, however, the date today is 31 March and the FRA is to come into effect on, say, 29 June and hold for three months after that date, clearly the available maturity dates do not match exactly the liability position that the institution has entered into. There are several futures contracts that could be brought into play to assist in the hedging of this position: the March, June and September contracts. One question to raise is how many contracts of each maturity should be bought?

Assuming an exposure of £10,000,000 in short-term sterling interest rates one approach would be to short 20 June contracts. From INT_1.WK3 this would lock in a rate of 5.85 per cent but would leave a gap between 17 June and 29 June when the FRA comes into effect. Another possibility would be to short 20 September contracts and lock into a rate of 5.71 per cent. However, in this case there is a basis risk involved. The 5.71 per cent is locked into a September maturity but the position needs to be tied in with the 29 June FRA date. Yet another approach would be to take out a number of futures contracts for different maturities weighted to reflect the day count between now and the maturity of the nearby contract (June in this example) and the number of days from the expiry of a nearby contract to the horizon of the following contract out (September).

31 March—Interpolative hedge
Number of days from 31 March to 17 June = 78
Number of days from 17 June to 29 June = 12

suggesting weights of 78/90 for the nearby contract and 12/90 for the next contract out. (These day counts can be obtained on Lotus using the @DATEVALUE (CELL) function where the 'CELL' has been date formatted. Thus @DATEVALUE (CELL.1)-@NOW would provide a figure for the number of days between now and some future date.) Twenty contracts are required to hedge the position: approximately 86 per cent (sell 17) should come from the June contract and 14 per cent (sell 3) from the September contract (refer to

Table 8.7.   Futures contracts to reflect the day count

	RECOMMENDED	Matching Dates	Non-Matching Dates
JUNE 16-Sep-93 CONTRACT	No. of Futures contracts to buy/sell:	20	17
SEPT 16-Dec-93 CONTRACT	No. of Futures contracts to buy/sell:	20	3
DEC 17-Mar-94 CONTRACT	No. of Futures contracts to buy/sell:	20	

Table 8.7)

(*Note:* selecting 'Contracts' on the `INT_1.WK3` worksheet will suggest the appropriate contract split for non-matching contract dates.)

17 June—Spot edge
Buy 17 June contracts to close the first leg of the transaction and roll over that position by selling 17 September contracts. The holding of September contracts now equals 20.

17 June—Basis risk hedge
Since there are still 12 days until the start of the FRA transaction the basis risk can, in part, be hedged by selling further 17 September contracts and simultaneously buying 17 December contracts. The rationale behind this transaction is that part of any change in the basis that occurs between the 17 June and 29 June will be counteracted by an opposite change in the September–December spread.

26 June—Closing transactions
The total position held comprises:

37 September contracts sold.
17 December contracts bought.

To close the position:

Buy 37 September contracts.
Sell 17 December contracts.

To calculate the outcome of this type of scenario the following information would need to be known or assumed:

1   The EDSP on 17 June.
2   The relevant futures prices on 26 June.
3   The rate agreed in the FRA to calculate any overall bp gain or loss.

Although Example 8.3 looked at the case of an FRA which had been sold, a similar approach could be adopted with respect to an FRA which had been bought. Under such a scenario each sell transaction would become a buy transaction and each buy transaction would become a sell transaction. The methodology described in this section is applicable to several other exchange-based contracts in addition to the short sterling contract used here. Other possibilities on LIFFE LTOM would be:

1 3 month ECU
2 3 month Eurodollar
3 3 month Euromark
4 3 month Euro Swiss Franc
5 3 month Eurolira.

The user of spreadsheet INT_1.WK3 is, however, advised to check on the contract value, tick value, and contract maturity dates when working with the spreadsheet, and to make any appropriate adjustments before using it.

Lotus demo   INT_1.WK3
This spreadsheet has been constructed to perform calculations to find the number of contracts required to hedge a date matching asset/liability position as well as the number of contracts to start up an interpolative hedge. The results of short or long hedges for three contracts can be viewed by accessing the special menu which can be activated by pressing the Alt + A keys simultaneously. The special menu for the spreadsheet is illustrated in Table 8.8.

  Selecting I (i) allows the user to enter current operational data in the following sequence:

● Future data of interest: input the horizon data, e.g. the control data in

Table 8.8.   Special menu for spreadsheet INT_1.WK3

Input_Data	Input operational data
Contracts	Suggested number of contracts
MARCH	Table of outcomes for this contract
JUNE	Table of outcomes for this contract
SEPT	Table of outcomes for this contract
DEC	Table of outcomes for this contract
Quit	Exit special menu

Table 8.1 shows `17-Jun-93`. Press [ENTER]. *Note that the entry must be prefixed by an apostrophe (') to indicate that the input is a label and not a number.*

- Future: input four sequential futures quotes, pressing [ENTER] after each input. Table 8.1 shows the quotes as: 94.03, 94.49, 94.64.
- Spot: input the current cash market quote. Press [ENTER]. The control data shows 94.01 in Table 8.1.
- Current portfolio value: type in the value of the portfolio under consideration. Press [ENTER]. Control data shows £1,000,000. *Note that the cell is formatted to display the number in currency (£).*
- Value of one exchange contract: input the nominal value of the contract. If no change is required press [ENTER] and the control value will be taken as the input. The control data uses the £500,000 short sterling contract nominal value.
- Value of one tick: input the exchange's valuation of one tick. If no change is required press [ENTER] and the control value will be taken as the input. The control data uses the short sterling contract which has a tick value of £12.50.
- Projected future level of index: type in your forecast of where the future will be at the horizon specified and press [ENTER]. The control input in Table 8.1 shows 93.5.
- Selecting C (c) advises the user about the number of contracts to use in the hedge for both matching and non-matching dates. *Note that the user should use these values to see the effectiveness of the hedge on the contract date frames in the special menu.* Press [ENTER] to continue.
- Selecting M (m), J (j), S (s), or D (d) moves the user to the section of the spreadsheet where the hedge results are displayed. *Note it is advisable to run C (c) before the date frames in order to see how many contracts should be used.* Press [ENTER] to continue.
- Selecting Q (q) exits the special menu and returns the user to normal Lotus operating mode.

8.1.1 Currency forwards, futures and options

In many respects the analysis applied above to the use of interest rate futures carries over directly to the use of currency futures with, as demonstrated in the FORWARDS.WK3 spreadsheet, the underlying determinant of forward exchange rates being the domestic rates of interest in the two countries concerned. *The Financial Times* and *Wall Street Journal Europe* provide forward currency quotes but presented in slightly different ways. *The Financial Times* reports one and three month forward exchange rates for all the major currencies, and the *Wall Street Journal* reports 30, 90 and 180 day forward rates for sterling, Canadian dollars, french francs, yen and Swiss francs.

In the case of futures contracts, while many exchanges throughout the world boast a wide variety of interest rate instruments, only a handful offer currency contracts and almost without exception they are for conversion to or from the US dollar. Moreover the contracts that are on offer are only for those currencies most in demand and frequently the type of exposure to risk identified in Case 1.3, the sterling/yen exchange rate problem, can only be hedged by using a tailor-made contract from the less liquid OTC market.

The Chicago Mercantile Exchange (CME) is one body which offers currency futures and options. These contracts are available for sterling, the Australian dollar, the Canadian dollar, the Deutschmark (DM), Japanese yen, Swiss francs and, in addition, there is a futures cross-rate contract in DM/yen. A typical contract will specify the size of the contract (the CME's British pound contract is for £62,500): the expiry months of the contract; delivery day; minimum price movement; value of one point (the CME's contract allows a minimum price movement of 2 points (0.0002)); maximum price movements allowed (if any); and trading hours.

The MidAmerican Commodity Exchange (MCE) which is an affiliate of the Chicago Board of Trade offers futures in sterling, Canadian dollars, Deutschmarks, Japanese yen and Swiss francs. On the currency option front a very large provider is the Philadelphia Stock Exchange which offers options contracts in the same currencies as the CME but also in French francs and the ECU. A (supposedly) useful feature of having more than one provider of such regulated contracts is that the contract specifications may vary between exchanges as a stimulus to competition. This is not the case, unfortunately: the contract values of the MCE are half those of the CME; the yen contract on the CME has a contract value of ¥12,500,000 million and MCE ¥6,250,000 but whereas the CME contracts are options on futures, the MCE contracts are options on the future spot rate and therefore require delivery of the currency. In the currency domain the only common contract features are that the CME and Philadelphia DM contracts are both for DM125,000 and that all the contracts have March, June, September, December maturity cycles. It must be stressed that, although there is a possibility of finding a contract with appropriate dates and matching value requirements, only the most popular, and perhaps well-known, currencies receive exchange-based attention and, given their tight specifications, the actual scope for their use as hedge instruments is limited. This argument goes some way towards explaining why many OTC products have led to the development of their own large-scale markets.

8.2 Interest rate options

In addition to the availability of futures contracts for short-term interest rates and currency, hedgers also have a variety of options contracts available. These operate in the same way as options on individual shares and stock indexes and some of the spreadsheets described earlier in this text can be used to evaluate pay-offs and premiums. For example, OPT_STR1.WK3 can be used to view option strategies on a stand-alone basis, or together with a short underlying position or with a long underlying position; B&S.WK3 can be used to calculate options premiums as well as delta and gamma hedge parameters for interest rate and currency instruments.

Perhaps the three most popular strategies encountered in connection with options in the interest rate and currency arenas are those described as the Cap, the Floor and the Collar. These strategies refer to the type of protection they afford to the user in conjunction with an underlying position that has been identified. Once again take Case 1.1, where the position is one which is vulnerable to increases in interest rates. The use of futures contracts, as demonstrated earlier, allowed the company treasurer to lock into a known future rate, but in doing so the potential benefit deriving from a fall in interest rates was forgone. Options allow a great deal more flexibility, offering as they do different strike prices over different periods of time and the ability to enjoy some of the benefit that would accrue should interest rates move in a direction opposite to that expected.

8.2.1 The Cap

In Case 1.1 the company treasurer could have bought a put option at some selected strike price that would have effectively created a ceiling beyond which the interest rates faced by his or her company would not rise. This situation is illustrated in Fig. 8.2(a) (see page 251) (obtained using OPT_STR1.WK3) where a June put option with a strike of 93.75 has been purchased to hedge against increases in interest rates. If the price of the future falls below 93.75 the put option starts to pick up intrinsic value which can be used to offset any rise in interest rates (Table 8.9).[1] Example 8.4 demonstrates how this works in practice.

Example 8.4

The strike of 93.75 appears to imply a maximum interest rate of 6.25 per cent, however, in order to enter into the option contract the option's premium has to be paid. This premium is calculated and quoted in terms of basis points. Table 8.10 shows quotes for call and put options with different expiration dates and several strikes.

From Table 8.10, for a June 93.75 strike Put, the option premium is 8 bps (0.0008) which will have to be added to the 6.25 per cent to arrive at an *achieved* rate of 6.33 per cent. (Premiums can be obtained from the financial

Table 8.9. Illustration of the cap strategy

EDSP	93.25	93.50	93.75	94.00	94.25	94.50
Strike	93.75	93.75	93.75	93.75	93.75	93.75
Intrinsic value	0.50	0.25	0	0	0	0

Table 8.10.   Sterling options LIFFE short

£500,000 points of 100%				
Strike price	Calls		Puts	
	March	June	March	June
93.50	0.53	1.04	0	0.05
93.75	0.30	**0.82**	0.02	**0.08**
94.00	0.11	0.61	0.08	0.12
94.25	0.06	0.44	0.28	0.20
94.50	0.03	**0.30**	0.50	0.31
94.75	0.01	0.20	0.73	0.46

Source: The Financial Times, 10 March 1993.

press or approximated using the B&S.WK3 spreadsheet.) If the EDSP is 93.75 or higher on expiration the intrinsic value of the option is zero but the achieved rate will be given by:

(100 − EDSP) + Option premium = Achieved rate
(100 − 94) + 0.08 = 6.08 per cent
(100 − 94.25) + 0.08 = 5.83 per cent, etc.

For futures prices with EDSPs less than 93.75 the intrinsic value will also play a role:

(100 − EDSP) + Option premium − Intrinsic value = achieved rate
(100 − 93.50) + 0.08 − 0.25 = 6.33 per cent
(100 − 93.25) + 0.08 − 0.50 = 6.33 per cent

In other words the maximum rate faced by the borrower will be 6.33 per cent wherever the futures price closes.

8.2.2 The Floor

From the opposite standpoint in Case 1.2 the company treasurer could have bought a call option at some strike which would have created a floor beyond which the interest rates faced by his or her company would not fall. This situation is illustrated in Fig. 8.2(b) (obtained using OPT_STR1.WK3) where a June call option with a strike of 93.75 has been purchased to hedge against sinking interest rates. If the price of the future rises beyond 93.75 the call option starts to pick up intrinsic value which can be used to set against any fall in interest rates (Table 8.11). Example 8.5, which again draws on the data reported in Table 8.10, demonstrates how this works in practice.

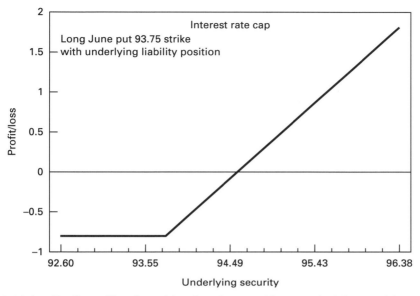

Fig. 8.2(a).   Profit profile of combined options and long underlying position

Example 8.5

The strike of 93.75 appears to imply a minimum interest rate of 6.25 per cent, however, in order to enter into the option contract the option's premium has to be paid. This premium is calculated and quoted in terms of basis points. For a June call 93.75 strike the option premium is 82 bps (0.0082) which will have

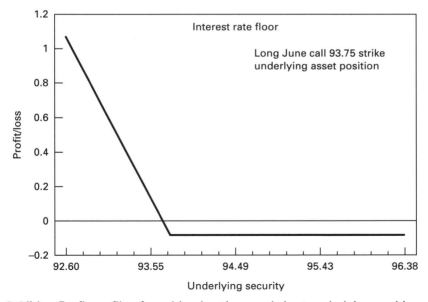

Fig. 8.2(b).   Profit profile of combined options and short underlying position

Table 8.11.   Illustration of the floor strategy

EDSP	93.25	93.50	93.75	94.00	94.25	94.50
Strike	93.75	93.75	93.75	93.75	93.75	93.75
Intrinsic value	0	0	0	0.25	0.50	0.75

to be subtracted from the 6.25 per cent to arrive at an achieved rate of 5.43 per cent. If the EDSP is 93.75 or higher on expiration the intrinsic value of the option is zero but the achieved rate will be given by:

$(100 - \text{EDSP}) - \text{Option premium} = \text{Achieved rate}$
$(100 - 93.50) - 0.82 = 5.68 \text{ per cent}$
$(100 - 93.25) - 0.82 = 5.93 \text{ per cent}$

For futures prices with EDSPs greater than 93.75 the intrinsic value will also play a role:

$(100 - \text{EDSP}) - \text{Option premium} + \text{Intrinsic value} = \text{Achieved rate}$
$(100 - 94.00) - 0.82 + 0.25 = 5.43 \text{ per cent}$
$(100 - 94.50) - 0.82 + 0.75 = 5.43 \text{ per cent}$

In other words the minimum rate that the lender would face would be 5.43 per cent wherever the futures price closes.

8.2.3 The Collar

Returning to Case 1.1, Sec. 8.2.1 demonstrated how the company treasurer could use a put option that would have created a ceiling beyond which the interest rates faced by his or her company would not rise. The use of a put option is, of course, linked to a cost—the basis point premium paid for the option. Should the company treasurer feel that the price of the cap is too high there is a way to reduce it; namely to write an option and receive a premium. The funds received can then be used to offset the purchased put's cost. The appropriate course of action is to write a call option at an appropriate strike price. The outcome of such a strategy—a written call and a long put to protect an underlying liability—is illustrated in Fig. 8.3(a) and 8.3(b) (obtained using OPT_STR1.WK3). In the example a June put option with a strike 93.75 has been purchased at a premium of 8 basis points to hedge against increases in interest rates and a June 94.50 call option has been written at a premium of 30 basis points apparently to more than offset the cost of the put. (The reader is reminded that no bid–offer spread is being assumed in the analysis and that other costs likely to be incurred in the transaction have also been ignored. If these were taken into account, although the position may be costless to put in place, a profit is unlikely to ensue.) Figure 8.3(a) demonstrates the profile of the options-only position; Fig. 8.3(b) illustrates the overall position. The actual ceiling rate and floor rate will be derived for this strategy below.

When considering a set of possible outcomes for this strategy it now becomes

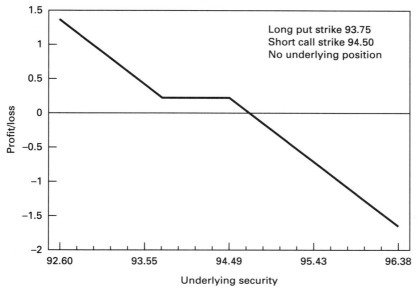

Fig. 8.3(a).   Profit profile of options only position

necessary to calculate the intrinsic value for the put and the call under the assumed EDSP scenarios. The case of the cap only was discussed above. But now it must be remembered that the benefits that would accrue to the overall position, if interest rates fall, have been sold. In effect this is the price of the collar. If interest rates fall below the rate implied by a strike of 94.50 the call option will start to pick up

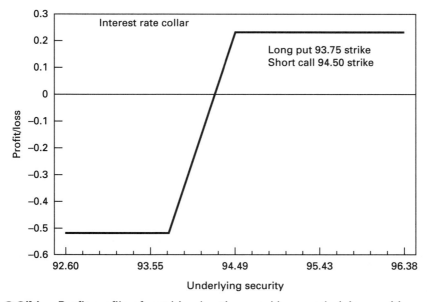

Fig. 8.3(b).   Profit profile of combined options and long underlying position

intrinsic value but this value will represent a cost to the writer of the option and will offset the gains that would otherwise have been enjoyed from falling rates.

Example 8.6

The strike of 93.75 appears to imply a maximum interest rate of 6.25 per cent, however, in order to enter into the option contract the option's premium has to be paid. This premium is calculated and quoted in terms of basis points. For a June put 93.75 strike the option premium is 8 bps (0.0008) which will have to be added to the 6.25 per cent to arrive at the achieved rate of 6.33 per cent. If the EDSP is 93.75 or higher on expiration the intrinsic value of the option is zero but the achieved rate will be given by:

(100 − EDSP) + Option premium = Achieved rate
(100 − 94.00) + 0.08 = 6.08 per cent
(100 − 94.25) + 0.08 = 5.83 per cent, etc.

For futures prices with EDSPs less than 93.75 the intrinsic value will also play a role:

(100 − EDSP) + Option premium − Intrinsic value = Achieved rate
(100 − 93.50) + 0.08 − 0.25 = 6.33 per cent
(100 − 93.25) + 0.08 − 0.50 = 6.33 per cent

These rates must be adjusted to give recognition to the fact that a call option has been written. All of the futures prices quoted have no intrinsic value when compared with the EDSPs so that the options will all expire worthless to the holder but will have generated 30 bps for the writer. This means that the maximum rate faced by the company will be reduced to 6.33 − 0.30 = 6.03 per cent. If, however, rates had fallen below 5.50 per cent the intrinsic value of the written call would have to be added to the capped rate—call premium. Thus a futures price of 94.75 (5.25 per cent) would generate a capped rate of:

5.33 + 0.25 − 0.30 = 5.28 per cent

The reader is encouraged to confirm that EDSPs above 94.75 will all result in a figure of 5.28 per cent. In other words the lowest interest rate the company will achieve under this strategy is 5.28 per cent.

Lotus demo   CAP_COL.WK3
In order to calculate the achievable rates for caps, collars and floors a spreadsheet entitled CAP_COL.WK3 has been designed. The input frame for this spreadsheet is shown in Table 8.12 and the achievable rates for a set of EDSPs are illustrated in Table 8.13. The spreadsheet, from which these results have been obtained, is menu driven and the special menu is activated using the Alt + A keys. The menu for the spreadsheet

Table 8.12.   Input frame for CAP_COL.WK3

```
INPUT
Long
PUT Strike            93.75 for CAP

PUT Premium           0.08

Short
CALL Strike           94.50 for COLLAR

CALL Premium          0.30

Long
CALL Strike           93.75 for FLOOR

CALL Premium          0.82
```

Table 8.13.   Achievable rates for a set of EDSPs

			CAP—achieved rates							
	STRIKE	EDSP	93.00	93.25	93.50	93.75	94.00	94.25	94.50	94.75
PUT	93.75		6.33	6.33	6.33	6.33	6.08	5.83	5.58	5.33
	STRIKE		COLLAR—achieved rates							
		STRIKE								
PUT	93.75	94.50 CALL	6.03	6.03	6.03	6.03	5.78	5.53	5.28	5.28
	STRIKE		FLOOR—achieved rates							
CALL	93.75		6.18	5.93	5.68	5.43	5.43	5.43	5.43	5.43

appears in Table 8.14.

- Selecting E (e) places the cursor on the first assumed exchange deliver settlement price. Type in a value and press [ENTER]. *Ensure that the price entered will match the strike prices and options premiums that are available from your data source, e.g. DATASTREAM, The Financial Times,* B&S.WK3, *etc.*
- Selecting D (d) allows the user to enter the required operational data in the following sequence:
  - Put strike: input an appropriate strike and press [ENTER]. The control data in Table 8.12 shows 93.75.
  - Put premium: type in a bp value and press [ENTER].
  - Call strike: this strike is associated with the setting up of a collar. The call will thus be written. Input a value and press [ENTER]. The control data shows 94.50.

– Call premium: type in a bp value and press [ENTER].
– Call strike: this input is required for the creation of a floor. Input a value press [ENTER]. The control data shows 0.30.
– Call premium: type in a bp value and press [ENTER].
The cursor will now return to the special menu.

- Type R (r) to view the table of achievable rates for the Cap, Collar, and Floor. *Note that no data input is required for this screen.*
- Select G (g) to view a graph of the strategy. The named graphs are Cap, Collar and Floor, highlight the desired graph using the arrow keys to guide the cursor and press [ENTER]. Pressing [ENTER] a second time will clear the graph from the screen and reactivate the special menu. *Note that the graphs displayed have achieved rates on the vertical axis and not pay-off.*
- Select Q (q) to exit the special menu and return Lotus to its normal operating mode.

Table 8.14.   Menu for spreadsheet CAP_COL.WK3

EDSP	Input expected EDSPs
DATA	Input strikes and Premiums
Rates	Achievable-rates
Graph	Graph of CAP or COLLAR or FLOOR
Quit	Exit Special Menu

8.3 Currency options

No special spreadsheet has been constructed to demonstrate achievable exchange rates as was the case with the CAP_COL.WK3 spreadsheet for interest rates. However, two spreadsheet are available and have been described and documented in depth elsewhere in this text; they are OPT_STR1.WK3 which will enable the user to construct caps, floors and collars from premiums either taken from sources such as DATASTREAM, BLOOMBERG, *The Financial Times*, the *Wall Street Journal Europe*, etc., or calculated from the B&S.WK3 spreadsheet.

A word of caution is in order when entering the data to put a strategy together or when interpreting the premium calculated using the B&S.WK3 spreadsheet. A typical quote from the pages of the financial press for the Philadelphia Stock Exchange $/£ option will show strike prices in $/£ but option premiums in cents/£.

In order to obtain a meaningful diagram of any option strategy using OPT_STR1.WK3 *a cent quote will have to be divided by 100 effectively converting it to a dollar quote which will then tie in with a strike price entered in dollars.*

The B&S.WK3 *calculates the European-style option premium and reports the value calculated in terms of dollars. In order to compare the option premium calculated from this spreadsheet with quotes in the financial press the* B&S.WK3 *calculated value will have to be multiplied by 100 to turn it into a cent per pound quote.* The reader should also bear in mind that there are many methods available for calculating option premiums, and that calculations will vary with the method and inputs used. It should not be expected that the calculated values obtained from B&S.WK3 will replicate exactly those quoted in the financial press.

In practice, when entering currency option contracts of an OTC nature the key volatility input will be agreed between the contracting parties at the start of the transaction. Apart from this there is essentially no difference between the basic operation of a currency option and any other type of option when hedging an underlying position. The differences that do exist lie in the interpretation of the cost of the contract and the potential pay-off to the user of the option. The following example illustrates how a currency option might function in practice.

Example 8.7

A US company has successfully completed a deal in the UK for which it will receive £625,000 in three months' time. With interest rates generally falling in Europe the company's treasurer reasons that UK rates may also be reduced leading to a further slide in the $/£ exchange rate. On the other hand the treasurer recognizes that the US economic recovery suggested by several indicators is on a flimsy footing and could collapse if a trade war follows from a breakdown in the current round of GATT talks. Under this scenario the treasurer feels that it could well be the US dollar that suffers in which case the incoming sterling would be worth more.

The treasurer decides to use options contracts to hedge the downside risk that would result from a depreciation of sterling but would still allow participation in an appreciation of sterling. The spot rate is now at $1.5420/£1. The three month forward rate is at $1.510. There are options available on the CME and one contract has a face value of £62,500. The appropriate expiration date is June and there is a strike of 1.525 with a put premium of 2.56 cents/£1. Dividing this premium by 100 and combining with the strike will yield the achieved exchange rate should the exchange rate decline enough to justify the exercise of the option.

If the put option is exercised:

Achieved exchange rate $/£ = Strike − Option premium

1.4994 = 1.5250 − 0.0256

If the put option is not exercised:

Achieved exchange rate $/£ = Current spot rate + Option premium paid

In order to put on a fixed hedge the treasurer will need to take out 10 contracts:

Value of exposure/Contract value = No. of contracts
£625,000/£62,500 = 10

The cost of each contract is given by the cent/£ premium multiplied by the value of the contract:

£62,500 × 2.56/100 = $1600

This, of course, means that for 10 contracts the total premium required will be $16,000.

If the premium for this position is felt to be too high, representing as it does a 2.76 per cent fall in income, then the treasurer might consider writing a call option and recouping some, if not all, than the premium paid for the put. This is the collar strategy discussed above in the section on interest rate option. In the currency arena the collar is often referred to as a *range forward contract*, the effect is the same as the collar. Should sterling depreciate the put option will click in providing a positive profit to offset the fall in sterling's value; if the US dollar depreciates the written call will be exercised against the treasurer reducing the gain from the long sterling position so that the exchange rate moves only within a range defined by the strikes and their associated premiums. However, the possibility of early assignment in respect of the written position must not be overlooked when using exchange-based instruments.

8.4 Hedging longer term interest rate and currency exposure

This section considers some ways in which a position with periodically arising liabilities can be hedged. The first example demonstrates how a one year, fixed interest liability covered by three month, floating interest receipts might be hedged by an institution; the second example looks at the use of options contracts, and finally interest rate and currency swaps are revisited.

8.4.1 Strips of futures

Example 8.8

A financial institution has issued a special bond on which it has been agreed to pay a fixed rate of interest of 5.25 per cent at the end of a one year period. The total amount received in deposits is £5,000,000. To simplify the illustration assume further that the maturity date of the bond coincides with the LIFFE LTOM short-term interest rate futures contract. The current LIBID spot rate is 5.8125 per cent and the bid rates implied by the strip of futures contracts; June, September, December are 5.51, 5.31 and 5.26 per cent, respectively.

    The identified exposure in this case is that of falling interest rates in which case the financial institution would be exposed to the risk of paying 5.25 per cent from receipts from loans, say, based on a lower interest rate.

If the institution goes long 10 contracts (£5,000,000/£500,000) for each of the June, September and December contracts the effective rate of interest it can lock into will be given by:

$$r = \left(1 + \frac{0.058125}{4}\right)\left(1 + \frac{0.0551}{4}\right)\left(1 + \frac{0.0531}{4}\right)\left(1 + \frac{0.0536}{4}\right) - 1 = 0.056125$$

where r represents the effective rate of 5.6125 per cent achieved using the strip of futures contracts to hedge the position.

8.4.2 Strips of options

Another way of hedging interest rate, or currency risk, is to use a strip of options which act as collars, range forwards, caps or floors for the holder, and which are operational over several time periods. For some time now financial institutions have been offering customers mortgages with rates that are guaranteed to vary within a defined band. Although not specifically advertised as such these deals are nevertheless *collars* which have been created from strips of OTC options issued by the institution concerned. The rates on offer will probably be based on some benchmark caps and floors such as those published periodically in *International Financing Review*. Basically all that happens is that as each of the options reaches its expiration date current interest rates are examined. If the call or put options have any intrinsic value that value will be used in conjunction with the current interest rate to calculate the effective rate of interest either to hold for the next period, or to calculate retrospectively what rate was relevant for the time period just ended, depending on the wording of the original contract.

8.4.3 Interest rate swaps

As discussed in Chapter 3 interest rate swaps provide an enormous potential for managing interest rate exposure over a long period of time. However, when considering the use of swaps there are many aspects which need to be fully considered:

1 All yields must be put on the same basis.

Example 8.9
In a swap contract that has just been signed a company has agreed to pay fixed and has issued debt in the bank market on which it will pay one month LIBOR. In the swap it will receive six month LIBOR with which to fund the debt. If currently six month LIBOR stands at 6.125 per cent while one month LIBOR stands at 6.0625 per cent there appears to be a benefit accruing to the fixed payer amounting to 6.25 bps. Is this really the case?

The effective six month cost will be given by:

$[(1 = 0.060625/12)^6 - 1] \times 100 \times 2 = 6.1396$ per cent which is now clearly greater than the amount of 6.125 per cent that will be received under six month LIBOR. An advantage of 6.25 bps has been converted into a cost of 1.46 bps on an annualized basis.

If both rates are put on an AIBD footing and compounding is taken into account the outcomes would be:

One month LIBOR (annual effective yield)

$[(1 + 0.060625/12)^{12} - 1] \times 100 = 6.2338$ per cent

Six-month LIBOR (annual effective yield)

$\{(1 + 0.06125/2)^2 - 1] \times 100 = 6.2188$ per cent

The difference between the rates is 1.5 bps and is a method of funding that is disadvantageous to the fixed rate payer.

2   Basis risk must be taken into account.

Example 8.10

The illustration in aspect 1 above provides a vehicle for demonstrating this idea; one month LIBOR and six month LIBOR are at different points on the yield curve (however defined), therefore any changes in rates could affect these two LIBOR rates in different ways. There is no guarantee that a ¹⁄₁₆th change in one month rates will be matched exactly by a ¹⁄₁₆th change in six month rates or vice versa. This type of risk must be recognized when the swap is entered into. The case discussed in 1 is by no means unique. Money market swaps, for example, are sometimes referred to as basis swaps and it could well be that the basis risk identified in 1 could be hedged in the money market by entering a second swap in which the company pays six month LIBOR one month LIBOR.

3   The risk that a counterparty may fail to meet one or more of the interest payments is essentially a problem that needs to be addressed by the financial intermediary arranging the swap. A larger risk premium might be charged at the outset of the transaction as one way of gaining some cover. The amount of this charge will, however, be restricted by market forces; too high a risk premium could well result in the counterparty concerned looking for another intermediary or adopting some alternative hedge instrument. Alternatively, the intermediary could insist on more frequent settlements of the periodic payments in order to monitor a counterparty's ability to perform in the contract and, should the fixed–floating interest rate gap widen sufficiently, take out exchange-based products to help minimize the impact of a failure to perform.

4   Default risk is also a danger which must be recognized. If a situation arises where a counterparty defaults completely on the swap the financial intermediary will be placed in the position of having to find a new counterparty to cover the remaining life of the swap. It is worth mentioning

that this situation may not always result in a loss to the intermediary. Any loss or gain will be dependent on the way that interest rates have changes since the swap was originally set up and which of the counterparties has defaulted.

Example 8.11

A default has just occurred on a swap which still has three years to run. The defaulting counterparty is the fixed rate payer. When the original deal was arranged the fixed rate received semi-annually by the intermediary was 11.55 per cent, rates have since fallen and, for a company similar in profile to the defaulter, are presently at 8.55 per cent. In effect the intermediary will probably be paying 11.45 per cent, allowing for its charge, but will only be receiving 8.55 per cent for the remaining lifetime of the swap. The cost of this in terms of a percentage of notional principal can be found by calculating the present value of the difference between the old rate and the new rate adjusted to take account of the number of times that payment will be made each year and discounting the remaining payments to be made using the appropriate point on the par yield curve (here assumed to be 8.5 per cent for the remaining life of the swap. This can be achieved on Lotus with the @PV function:

```
@PV(periodic payment:pmt, Interest rate: int. length of
the swap:term).
```

Calculating the revised position from the fixed interest receipts the entry on Lotus would simply be @PV((11.55-8.55)/2, 0.085/2, 6) where division by 2 indicates the semi-annual nature of the payments. In present value terms the cost to the intermediary, using this data, will be approximately 7.80 per cent of notional principal.

Had the position with respect to the interest rates been reversed the intermediary would have enjoyed a gain. Using the Lotus @PV function in the same way as above the present value of the benefit would be 7.80 per cent of notional principal.

When analysing interest rate swaps the concept of duration, discussed in the previous chapter can provide a useful risk measure. Recall that the change in the price of a bond brought about by a change in yield can be approximated using duration (see Chapter 7); an extension to swaps can follow quite straightforwardly since interest rate swaps represent a series of cash flows at intervals over time very much like a bond. The formula for approximating the change in the price of a bond, as derived in Chapter 7, is given by:

$$dP = (-1) \times \text{Mod}_D P_0 \times dr$$

Adopting the same methodology with swaps the formula can be expressed as:

$$dMV_{\text{fixed}} = (-1) \times \text{Mod}_{D \text{ fixed}} \times MV_{\text{fixed at start}} \times dr$$

for the fixed side of the swap;
where:

MV represents the market value of the swap at the start of the contract;

dMV represents a change in market value brought about by changes in interest rates;

$\text{Mod}_{\text{D fixed}}$ represents modified duration of the fixed side of the swap;

dr represents the change in interest rates that has occurred.

Similarly for the floating side of the transaction the change in market value can be approximated using the formula:

$$dMV_{\text{floating}} = (-1) \times MOD_{\text{D floating}} \times MV_{\text{floating at start}} \times dr$$

where:

MV represents the market value of the swap at the start of the contract;

dMV represents a change in market value brought about by changes in interest rates;

$\text{Mod}_{\text{D floating}}$ represents modified duration of the floating side of the swap;

dr represents the change in interest rates that has occurred.

At the outset of a swap transaction the market value of the deal is zero (see Chapter 3, in particular the last two columns of Table 3.14(b) reproduced again here and obtained from SPOT_PAR.WK3). This can be expressed algebraically as:

$$MV_{\text{swap}} = MV_{\text{fixed}} - MV_{\text{floating}}$$

Any change in value brought about by changes in interest rates can be expressed as:

$$dMV_{\text{swap}} = (-1) \times \text{Mod}_{\text{D swap}} \times MV_{\text{swap at start}} \times dr$$

where:

$$\text{Mod}_{\text{D swap}} = \frac{D_{\text{floating}} \times MV_{\text{floating}} - D_{\text{fixed}} \times MV_{\text{fixed}}}{MV_{\text{floating}} - MV_{\text{fixed}}}$$

Table 3.14(b).   Interest rate swaps

Monthly periods	Spot rate labels	Current spot rates %	Forward rate labels	Forward rates %	Swap floating rate	Swap fixed rate
6	O.R. 6	7.450			3.529	3.710
12	O.R.12	7.680	6.R.12	7.910	3.603	3.572
18	O.R.18	7.690	12.R.18	7.710	3.385	3.441
24	O.R.24	7.750	18.R.24	7.930	3.350	3.313
30	O.R.30	7.780	24.R.30	7.900	3.213	3.189
36	O.R.36	7.810	30.R.36	7.960	3.115	3.069
42	O.R.42	7.820	36.R.42	7.880	2.970	2.955
48	O.R.48	7.835	42.R.48	7.940	2.880	2.844
54	O.R.54	7.840	48.R.54	7.880	2.752	2.738
60	O.R.60	7.850	54.R.60	7.940	2.669	2.636
				PV:	31.467	31.467

measures the duration gap (see Strauss and Herman, 1988, for discussion of duration as an analytical tool).

Calculation of the fixed interest duration input required for computation of swap examples can be achieved using spreadsheet DURA.WK3 described in Chapter 7. The floating values can also be found using Lotus by calculating the forward rates from the spot-zero yield curve on SPOT_PAR.WK3 and using the forward rates to discount the stream of cash flows on the floating side.

A variation on the swap theme discussed so far is the forward swap. This instrument would be a useful hedge in the case where a company has a definite contract to undertake a large-scale project but is not planning to start work on that project until some months in the future, and does not require finance until the project commences. If the canopy treasurer suspects that interest rates are likely to move adversely in the coming months then forward finance can be arranged today at a locked-in, more favourable rate by entering a forward swap and becoming the fixed rate payer.

Of course, there is always the possibility that a company arranging finance for a long-term, future project may only require that finance should the bid it is submitting for the project be successful. In such a situation the company may well decide to take out an option on a swap at the time the bid is submitted. Once confirmation has been received of a successful bid—and if market movements in interest rates so warrant—the necessary finance, which has been fixed in advance by means of the option, can be taken with settlement taking the form of a physical swap or a cash settlement.

8.4.4 Currency hybrids

Recent years have seen the introduction of many innovative currency derivatives on the OTC market which can be adopted by end-users and market professionals as hedge instruments. Bankers Trust with its introduction of index currency option notes (ICONs) in 1985 probably acted as a catalyst. ICONs are bonds whose value at maturity is adjusted to take account of exchange rates at maturity.

Since that time currency protected swaps, also known as Diff swaps or cross-currency swaps have been introduced. These instruments are interest rate basis swaps in which one of the parties will pay domestic currency LIBOR against receipt of foreign currency LIBOR plus or minus a spread based on the current quote. There is no exchange of currency either at the commencement or on termination of the swap. In a sense these swaps can be regarded as being speculative instruments rather than hedge instruments. One of the prime motivations in using them comes from the end-users whose domestic LIBOR spot rates are high (low) and forward rates suggest they will rise even higher (lower). If the end-user feels that the forward rates are over-exaggerating the possible track of future rates, in either of the LIBOR rates, then he or she can swap paying an upfront cost or receiving an upfront payment in the form of a spread and enjoy interest savings at some point over the lifetime of the swap.

Cross-currency swaptions are instruments which give the holder the right but not the obligation to enter into a currency swap on a specified date in the future and like interest rate swaptions allow the user to delay the decision about entering into an agreement until it is definitely known that a swap is required for hedging purposes. An example of this would be a simple extension of that used for forward swaps in the interest rate swap section. In the case where negotiations are underway for a contract to undertake a large-scale project requiring long-term finance in the currency of a foreign country, until it is known with certainty that funding is required, it would be inadvisable to enter directly into a swap or a forward swap agreement. A currency swaption would be a more suitable instrument.

8.5 Spreadsheets

There are two demonstration spreadsheets used in this chapter:

1   `INT_1.WK3` which is described in Section. 8.1 and whose special menu is illustrated in Table 8.8;
2   `CAP_COL.WK3` which is discussed in Sec. 8.2.3 and whose special menu appears as Table 8.14.

8.5.1 `INT_1.WK3`

The special menu, which appears as Table 8.8, provides users with an opportunity of inputting the future date of interest, up-to-date futures quotes, the current spot quote, a portfolio valuation, the face value of the exchange's contract, the value of one tick, and a projected future level of the contract:

`(Input_Data);`

it provides a suggested number of contracts to use to hedge the position:

`(Contracts);`

and tables of hedge outcomes at the specified horizon for the:

`(Month_1), (Month_2), (Month_3) and (Month_4);`[2]

a final macro exits the special menu returning the spreadsheet back to normal Lotus operating mode:

`(Quit).`

8.5.2 `CAP_COL.WK3`

The special menu, which appears as Table 8.14, provides users with an opportunity of inputting a sequence of exchange delivery settlement prices in order to see the effectiveness of the strategy employed:

```
(EDSP);
```

of inputting the option strike prices and premiums:

```
(DATA);
```

it provides output in the form of achievable rates:

```
(Rates);
```

and output in the form of graphs:

```
(Graph);
```

and a final macro which exits the special menu returning the spreadsheet back to normal Lotus operating mode:

```
(Quit).
```

Questions

8.1   The IMM three month Eurodollar futures contract for March 1994 is quoted as 95.24.
Explain what this figure means.

8.2   The IMM's British pound futures ($s per £) contract for June 1993 is quoted as 1.5356.
Explain what this figure means.

8.3   Explain how short-term interest rate futures contracts might be employed to hedge a liability position in the case of:
(a)   matching dates;
(b)   non-matching dates.

8.4   Extract the current quotes for the LIFFE LTOM short sterling futures contract from the financial pages of one of today's newspapers and, using INT_1.WK3, hedge a £20,000,000 cash deposit portfolio against a projected 1 per cent fall in interest rates.
State clearly any assumptions that you need to make in setting up the hedge.

8.5   The Philadelphia SE's (cents per £) dollar/sterling June 1993 option contract for a 1.550 strike is quoted as 4.36.
(a)   Explain what this figure means.
(b)   If the Exchange specified value of one contract is £31.250, what would be the cost of a 1.550 contract given the 4.36 quote?

8.6   Explain what is meant by an interest rate cap. How might an interest rate cap work in practice?

8.7   In an environment of generally falling interest rates what simple strategies could an investor adopt if seeking to maintain the current deposit rate?

8.8   The LIFFE LTOM Euromark option contract offers the following strikes:

Strike price	Calls		Puts	
	March	*June*	*March*	*June*
91.50	0.53	1.28	0.03	0.03
92.00	0.17	0.83	0.17	0.08
92.50	0.05	0.45	0.55	0.20
93.00	0.02	0.20	1.02	0.45

(a)   Using a 92.00 March strike show how a 'cap' can be set up.

(b)   With the aid of the spreadsheet CAP_COL.WK3 demonstrate the effectiveness of the cap you have constructed.

(c)   Using a 92.50 June strike demonstrate how a 'floor' can be put into place.

(d)   With the aid of the spreadsheet CAP_COL.WK3 demonstrate the effectiveness of the floor you have constructed.

(e)   Demonstrate how an interest rate collar can be constructed.

State clearly throughout any assumptions that you have made.

8.9   Extract the current quotes for an exchange rate contract from the financial pages of one of today's newspapers and, using CAP_COL.WK3, show how a range forward strategy can be constructed.

Notes

1 Recall the decision rule for exercise encountered in Chapter 4: max{Strike–Share Price, 0}. In the interest rate example Share Price will be replaced by the Exchange Delivery Settlement Price (EDSP).

2 Note that the spreadsheet automatically updates the contract maturity months. In the display they will appear as MARCH, JUNE, SEPT, DEC, etc.

References and further reading

Blake, D. (1990), *Financial Market Analysis*, McGraw-Hill, London.

Dubofsky, D. (1992), *Options and Financial Futures: Valuation and Use,* McGraw-Hill, New York.

Eckl, S., Robinson, J.N. and Thomas, D.C. (1991), *Financial Engineering: A Handbook of Derivative Products*, Basil Blackwell, Oxford.

Hull, J. (1993), *Options, Futures and other Derivative Securities* (2nd edn), Prentice-Hall, Englewood Cliffs, NJ.

Strauss, M. and Herman, B. (1988), Why swappers need duration, *Risk Magazine*, 1(3), February.

9 Conclusions

9.1 Who needs to hedge?

On a fundamental level two categories of market players can be identified:

1   Market professionals acting in the capacity of an intermediary and/or helping to ensure the efficiency of the market in which they operate: by quoting binding prices and trading in individual shares, bonds, interest rate instruments, exchange rates, swaps, etc.
2   Banks, building societies, institutional fund managers, large companies and individuals.

One distinguishing feature of participants in the first group is the time scale to which they work. Typically they will have a very short time perspective. They will be driven by instantaneous impact factors, responding positively or negatively to news as it enters the market. The news to which they react can be practically anything: domestic, foreign, political, economic, social. The level of reaction can, and does, vary from the opposite to that expected—*the initial FT-SE 100 Index reaction to a rise in German interest rates in July 1992 measured on a closing price basis*—to extreme —*the recent stock market crashes.* Chapter 2 looked at some of the technical, statistical and scenario-writing methods that these players may use as a way of forecasting market direction. For this group exchange-based instruments provide excellent, liquid and cheap instruments with which they are able to hedge their net, identified exposures.

In the second category the time framework will normally be much longer. All participants in categories 1 and 2 will be watching the economic and political indicators but those in category 2 will be particularly concerned about the lasting effect of reported events. They are likely to be concerned about cash flows at some future date, or set of future dates, and the possible need to insure the value of those flows. For those participants falling into category 2 forecasting market direction could bring into play more advanced model building methods based on time-series analysis and/or econometrics but will often rely soley on descriptive scenarios or simple 'gut-feeling'. This group has available to it a vast array of hedge instruments. The traditional exchange-based instruments offer a supply of easy access hedge instruments, but for those with requirements which do not match those offered by an exchange the OTC market can step in to create exactly that instrument necessary to hedge the identified exposure.

9.1.1 Hedging equity risk

In chapter 6 attention was focused on the use of exchange-based instruments to hedge portfolios of shares. Basically the use of futures enables the investor to lock into a future value of an equity index, of which there are many throughout the world. Options, on the other hand, provide much more flexibility. Positions can be engineered which: (i) protect against a fall in the price of the underlying security be it an individual share or portfolio shares; (ii) enhance the returns due to holding the share; (iii) enable delayed purchase of a share at a known price, etc.

When options are being used as hedge instruments it is important to understand what is being insured. In the case of a put option on an individual share both the diversifiable and the market risk are being insured. If the price of the particular share falls enough to warrant the exercise of a put option on that share then 1000 of the shares will be delivered into the contract and will no longer be components of the portfolio. If the holder wishes to retain the portfolio intact, which would almost certainly be the case with an index-tracking portfolio that has been painstakingly put together, but still wishes to insure against a feared market downturn then put options on the index would be an appropriate instrument to use. If the market falls by enough to warrant the exercise of the option, settlement is in cash and does not require delivery of the underlying security. This, of course, means that no dismantling of the portfolio is necessary. Table 9.1 indicates the extent of insurance cover provided by both types of option.

When using exchange-based, American-style options as hedge instruments it must be remembered that if options are written there is a possibility that early assignment may occur. If early assignment does occur this can disrupt any strategy that has been put in place (for example setting up a collar requires the writing of a call option). Recent developments have seen the introduction of OTC collars for use with equity. Since OTCs are tailor-made to suit requirements of the investor, there is no danger of early assignment—in effect the options are European-style, exercisable only on a certain date—and the investor is assured of an underlying pay-off lying within the construction bounds. In fact very recently a UK building society offered investors the opportunity of buying a bond whose pay-off on a defined date in the future would be linked to the performance of the FT-SE 100

Table 9.1.   Hedged equity risk

	Index options	Individual options
Non-systematic risk	No	Yes
Systematic risk	Yes	Yes

Share Index. If the index performed positively the investor would receive a proportion of the growth in the index but if the index performed negatively investors would receive a nominal interest rate payment on the funds they had invested over 'x' years. Investors buying the bond would be participating in the growth in the index but would be cushioned, to an extent, from falls in the index.

Another recent innovation in the equity market is the use of equity swaps. These swaps, like interest swaps, do not involve an exchange of principal only an exchange of cash flows over an agreed period of time. In this type of OTC transaction one counterparty will pay an amount equal to the return of the notional amount of principal invested in the index and will receive in exchange the return on some other asset or a fixed or floating interest rate plus or minus a spread.

Example 9.1

In 1990 a UK-based equity fund manager constructed a portfolio of German blue chip shares which tracks the Deutsche Aktien Index (DAX). In 1991 and 1992 the returns from the index were poorer than expected and although the long-term prospects for growth, and a large pay-off are felt to be good, the short- to medium-term prospects are not. The fund manager could decide on an appropriate time horizon and arrange, through an intermediary, to swap the returns on the DAX tracking portfolio for the returns on some other index virtually anywhere in the world, in virtually any currency or, if the fund manager's outlook for equity growth is negative, to receive a regular interest payment. Since the customer decides what to swap, what to swap into, and for how long to swap, such transactions are likely to become important instruments in the future.

9.1.2 Hedging interest rate risk

The number and type of interest rates that can be hedged is enormous. Chapters 7 and 8 examined in depth the types of exposures that might exist and how those risks might be hedged; Table 9.2 summarizes some of the major instruments that are available and what basic action should be taken when interest rates are expected to rise or fall. One omission from the table is options: this omission is deliberate. From the discussions and illustrations included in this text the reader will be aware of the vast flexibility provided by options. Hedging a particular position is no longer simply a question of buying or selling an instrument, many different types of strategies can be set up which make combined use of the underlying position and long and/or short positions in options on the underlying position directly or options on futures contract on the underlying position. The OPT_STR1.WK3 spreadsheet enables the user to consider many types of vertical strategies, and some of the better known of these received attention in Chapters 4 and 8.

Table 9.2.   The management of interest rate risk

Underlying interest rate	At risk if:	Hedge In:			
		Cash market	Swaps	FRA	Futures
Asset floating	Interest rates fall	Extend duration	Receive fixed pay floating	Sell FRA	Buy future
Asset fixed	Interest rates rise	Decrease duration	Receive floating pay fixed	Buy FRA	Sell future
Liability floating	Interest rates rise	Re-finance	Receive floating pay fixed	Buy FRA	Sell future
Liability fixed	Interest rates fall	Re-finance	Receive fixed pay floating	Sell FRA	Buy future

9.1.3 Hedging currency risk

Fundamentally hedging currency risk involves the use of the same types of instruments as adopted for the hedging of interest rates. Since interest rate differentials are the driving force behind currency movements and the calculation of forward rates this is not surprising. In addition, though, currency has provided financial institutions with a proving ground for many innovative products some of which received a mention in Chapter 8.

To close, it is worth giving an example of a hybrid instrument—an instrument which has two or more underlying references (these transactions are often linked to commodity prices). In the future, as market professionals and end-users of their products become wiser and more demanding, it is likely that the adoption of such instruments will be widespread and their availability taken for granted.

Example 9.2
A UK company wishes to raise finance to fund the exploration for a scarce natural resource, traded in US dollars, in a foreign country. The company decides to raise the necessary finance by issuing a fixed interest rate bond directly in the foreign country. To achieve a favourable rate of interest the company issues the bond with call options giving the holder of the option the right to buy the resource at a fixed price in sterling on a fixed date in the future, but only if the exploration proves successful and certain production targets have been met. The value of the option in this case depends on the

success of the exploration, the price of scarce resources and the $/£ exchange rate at expiration.

As long as a transaction can be broken down into its constituent parts, institutions will be able to construct instruments which match their client's needs exactly while at the same time hedging their own individual components of the transaction, or a net position, as necessary. The only limit to the types of hedge instruments that can be constructed, given the array of basic instruments that are available, is *imagination*.

Glossary

Arbitrage: undertake a trade that enables a risk-free profit to be made.

At-the-money option: an option with a strike price equal to, or very close to, the current market price of the underlying security.

Back-to-back: a series, or strip, of sequential contracts. As one contract expires the next comes into effect.

Basis risk: the risk that price differences between two instruments does not behave as expected.

Benchmark: a yardstick against which the performance of a portfolio may be measured.

Breakout: is what happens when the price of a security departs from a current behaviour pattern defined by resistance and support levels. When a breakout occurs a new behaviour pattern is likely to develop bringing with it a new trend (see *Resistance level* and *Support level*).

Call option: a derivative security giving the holder the right to buy an underlying security on a specified date (European) or on or before a specified date (American), at a fixed price.

Cap: an option strategy that enables the construction of the upper limit or ceiling on the price taken by the underlying security. For example, the holder of an interest rate cap possesses an instrument that limits the extent to which interest rates may rise.

Cash market: the market that determines the current trading price of a security.

Clean risk: the risk that agreed interest payments into a swap will not be made when they fall due.

Close a position: to clear a portfolio of its all contents. For example, if a portfolio contains one long March futures contract the position can be closed by shorting (selling) a March futures contract.

Collar: an extension of the cap described above. It is an option strategy that creates both an upper and lower limit on the price taken by an underlying security. For example, the holder of an interest rate collar possesses an instrument that restricts the movement of interest rates to between defined bands. This strategy is also referred to as a *cylinder* or *range forward*.

Convexity: a term which describes the curvilinear nature of a bond's price/yield relationship. It is used along with duration to adjust the price of bond following large changes in yields.

Coupon: the regular interest payment associated with fixed income securities. Coupon is usually quoted as a percentage of a bond's par value.

Covariance: a statistical measure of the way in which two variables vary together.

Covered position: the position where an option is held in a portfolio which also contains the underlying security. For example, a put option is written on shares in a company of which the option writer holds a sufficient quantity of deliverable shares.

Default risk: the risk that one counterparty will fail to honour its part or the remaining part of an agreed transaction.

Delta hedge: to create a hedged position which takes into account the sensitivity of an option's premium to changes in the price of the security on which the option is based.

272

Derivative security: a security whose existence is dependent, or contingent, upon the existence of another security.

Duration: the average time over which the stream of cash flows from a fixed income security are to be received. There are several types of duration measures. The most frequently referred to are: Macaulay duration, modified duration, and dollar duration.

EDSP (Exchange Delivery Settlement Price): the price calculated by an exchange at the maturity of a contract and is the price from which gains and losses accruing to parties with open positions will be calculated.

Equity: the share capital in a company. In the United States this is known as *stock*.

Eurocurrency: deposits denominated in a currency other than that of the domestic banking system. For example, Euro-Deutschmark deposits could be deposits held in London by German banks or held in Germany by foreign banks. Such deposits would not be subject to German domestic banking regulations.

Exercise price: the price specified in an option contract — also known as the *strike price*.

Expiration: the maturity date of an option contract.

FIBOR: (Frankfurt Interbank Offer Rate): the interest rate on short-term loans between large banks (see also *LIBOR*).

Fixed income security: a security which offers a stream of fixed, nominal cash flows over its life span.

Floor: an option strategy that enables the construction of a lower limit on the price taken by an underlying security. For example, the holder of an interest rate floor possesses an instrument that limits the extent to which interest rates may fall.

Forward contract: a contract in which the parties involved agree to undertake a trade at a pre-determined price on a pre-determined date in the future.

FRA (forward rate agreement): an interest rate agreement where the parties involved agree to pay the difference between the current market rate of interest and the rate of interest agreed in the contract. FRAs are generally used to hedge short-term interest rate exposure.

FRNs (floating rate notes): an interest-bearing security with the facility to alter the coupon it pays at specified future dates.

Front-end payment: a once off payment made at the commencement of an agreement to trade or contract.

Futures contract: a tightly specified exchange-based contract to undertake a trade at a fixed nominal value on a specified date in the future.

Gilts: UK government bonds issued with titles such as Treasury, Exchequer, and Conversion stock. Also known as *UK Government Stock*.

Holder: the title given to the purchase of a call or put option. The position is synonymous with a long position.

In-the-money option: an option with a positive intrinsic value.

Instrument: an umbrella term used to cover all types of securities. For example, a futures contract can be regarded as an instrument for hedging risk.

Intrinsic value: an option with an intrinsic value. For example, a call option with a strike price lower than the current market price of the underlying instrument, or a put option with a strike price above the current market price of the underlying security. In either case, at expiration, exercise of the option is the rational course of action on the part of the investor.

LIBOR (Loans Interbank Offer Rate): an interest rate quote on short-term loans between large banks. LIBOR and dollar are used as benchmarks when arranging swaps.

Lock-in: enter a position which guarantees a particular return.

Long position: a portfolio which contains an instrument which has been purchased.

Margin: a cash payment or securities deposit made into an account as a means of establishing, or maintaining, a position in a derivative security. The payment made will normally be substantially less than the actual market value of the derivative concerned.

Market risk: the risk associated with a particular market.

Money market: the market for paper with less than one year to maturity.

Naked position: describes the position where an option is held in a portfolio which does not contain the underlying security. For example, a put option is written on the shares in a particular company without the writer of the option possessing the deliverable shares. A naked, written position can be a very risky strategy.

Open interest: a statistic which reports the number of matched, live, long and short positions in an exchange-based contract.

Option premium: the price to be paid for the option to buy or sell an instrument.

OTC (over the counter): a transaction tailored by a financial institution to meet the exact requirements of a customer.

Out-of-the-money: an option with, theoretically, a negative intrinsic value.

Paper: a term used to describe financial instruments which have been issued to raise finance.

P/E ratio (price/earning ratio): A company's current share price divided by its earnings per share. This measure is often used to compare companies on an intra-sector basis.

Plain vanilla swap: a term which describes a basic fixed–floating interest rate swap.

Portfolio: a point of reference for one or many financial instruments combined and used for investment or for analytical purposes.

Position-delta: the sum of all the deltas associated with derivative securities multiplied by their respective holding in the portfolio. A position-delta of, say, $-10,000$ in a portfolio would require a 10,000 long position in the underlying security to achieve a delta-neutral portfolio—a position delta of zero. A delta-neutral portfolio is protected against small price movements in the underlying security.

Position-gamma: a delta-neutral portfolio can only be made gamma-neutral by taking out an additional position in an option. This requires that the quantity of the underlying security held in the portfolio, to achieve delta-neutrality, initially will have to be adjusted to reattain a delta-neutral position. A gamma-neutral portfolio protects the portfolio, to an extent, against larger price movements.

Put option: a derivative security giving the holder the right to sell an underlying security on a specified date (European) or, on or before specified date (American), at a fixed price.

Resistance level: A barrier beyond which the price of a security may have difficulty passing (see *Breakout*).

Risk premium: an interest rate add-on, imposed by a financial institution advancing funds. The level is set to reflect the anticipated ability of the receiver of the funds to repay the loan on maturity and service intermediate interest payments. The higher the risk premium the greater the doubt that the receiver of the funds will be able to meet the contracted, financial obligation. A number of companies offer commercial credit ratings as a guide to the potential riskiness of corporate borrowers; Moody's Investor Service and Standard & Poor's Corporation are among the best known of these.

ROCE (return-on-capital-employed): An accounting measure used to judge the health of a company when considering the purchase or sale of the company's shares.

RSI (Relative Strength Indicator): A technical analytic measure used to assess an instrument's overbought/oversold position on the market.

Sector risk: the risk associated with a group of instruments possessing common features/profiles. For example, a group of companies all engaged in the manufacture of machine tools would be subject to the risk associated specifically with that sector.

Settlement date: the date on which the ownership of an instrument passes from one party in the transaction to the other.

SPAN: A method widely used by clearing houses worldwide to determine the amount of margin required to cover open positions in futures/options accounts.

Specific risk: the risk associated with a particular instrument.

Spot market: the market which determines the current trading price of an instrument for almost immediate delivery (see also *Cash market*).

Spot zero rates: rates of interest payable on maturity of the instrument and with no intermediate payments. For example $a_0 r_6$ rate of interest would indicate the return on an investment now payable at the end of a six month period.

Strip of: a sequential series of contracts, as one contract expires the next commences.

Support level: A price level at which buyers might be attracted into a market to purchase a security (see *Breakout*).

Swap: an agreement between two parties to exchange each other's commitments at intervals over a period of time. There are many types of swap contracts but the two most well known are interest rate and currency swaps. Some swaps have extremely long maturity horizons, for example 20 years.

Time value: the portion of an option premium linked to time remaining until expiration; the shorter the time period to expiration the smaller the time value of the option.

Underlying position: the fundamental portfolio position whose risk needs to be managed.

Up-front payment: a payment made at the commencement of a contract.

Vega (also known as lambda, kappa and sigma): a measure of the sensitivity of the call/put premium to incorrect estimation of volatility. In mathematical notation vega $= \partial C / \partial \sigma = \partial P / \partial \sigma$.

Warehouse: denotes the situation where a financial institution carries a position on its books until a suitable long-term counterparty can be found. The identified short-term risk associated with this position can usually be managed using forward, futures or option contracts.

Writer: the seller of an option contract. The writer of a call or put option has short position.

Index